Counseling
for Family
Violence and Abuse

RESOURCES FOR
CHRISTIAN COUNSELING

RESOURCES FOR CHRISTIAN COUNSELING

(Other volumes forthcoming)

Counseling for Family Violence and Abuse

GRANT L. MARTIN, Ph.D.

RESOURCES FOR CHRISTIAN COUNSELING

—— General Editor ——

Gary R. Collins, Ph.D.

WORD PUBLISHING
Dallas · London · Sydney · Singapore

Unless otherwise indicated, all Scripture quotations in this publication are from the New International Version of the Bible, copyright © 1983 by the New York International Bible Society. Used by permission of Zondervan Bible Publishers. Scripture quotations identified AMPLIFIED are from The Amplified Bible, copyright © 1962, 1964 by Zondervan Publishing House. Used by permission. Those identified NASB are from the New American Standard Bible, copyright © 1977 by the Lockman Foundation. Used by permission. Those identified KJV are from the King James Version.

Permission to quote from the following sources is gratefully acknowledged:

"CSR Abuse Index" in *The Family Secret* by William Stacey and Anson Shupe. Copyright © 1983, published by Beacon Press.

STRESSMAP: Finding Your Pressure Points, copyright © 1982 by C. Michele Haney and Edmond W. Boenisch, Jr. Reproduced by permission of Impact Publishers, Inc., P.O. Box 1094, San Luis Obispo, CA 93406. Further reproduction prohibited.

The Ferguson-Beck H.A.L.F. Assessment Tool for Elder Abuse.

15 Steps in the Relaxation Process, on pp. 112–113, from *Stress and the Art of Biofeedback* by Barbara B. Brown. Copyright © 1977 by Barbara B. Brown, published by Bantam Books, Inc. All rights reserved.

Library of Congress Cataloging-in-Publication Data

Martin, Grant.
    Counseling for family violence and abuse.

    (Resources for Christian counseling, v. 6)
    Bibliography: p.
    Includes index.
    1. Church work with problem families. 2. Family violence—Religious aspects—Christianity. 3. Pastoral counseling. 4. Problem families—Counseling of.
I. Title. II. Series.
BV4438.5.M37 1987   261.8'3587   86-32457
ISBN 0-8499-0587-7

89801239 AGF 987654321

Printed in the United States of America

This book is dedicated to my grandfather
Bruce Tharrington
whose early encouragement gave me the vision of writing.
"Papa" influenced me by his life as well as his words.

CONTENTS

EDITOR'S PREFACE

LESS THAN TEN YEARS AGO, I wrote a textbook that attempted to deal with the major issues facing Christian counselors. Whole chapters were devoted to depression, grief, marriage problems, homosexuality, and a number of other issues. In contrast, only two of the 477 pages dealt with rape. I discussed physical violence in two pages more, and considered mate beating on one page.

How things have changed in less than a decade. Family violence has become a major issue of concern for journalists, police departments, community leaders, and counselors. Sobering statistics, many cited in the following pages, have demonstrated repeatedly that the physical abuse of spouses, children, and the elderly has reached almost epidemic proportions.

Was it there all the time, but either ignored or hidden from view until recently? Maybe family violence has become worse during the stressful times in which we live. More likely, we finally are allowing ourselves to admit the existence of a problem that for many years has created terrible suffering in thousands of human lives.

The problem would be serious enough if it was limited to non-Christians or to people in economically deprived communities. But we now know that incest, beatings, sexual abuse, and other forms of violence are common in Christian homes and among families at all levels of society. Some professional person in your community, a deacon or Sunday school teacher in your church, or perhaps even a pastor, may be guilty of involvement in abusive or sexually exploitive acts that are well hidden from unsuspecting neighbors or even from close relatives.

How do you counsel with abusive family members and their victims? When the facts become known, it is easy for a counselor to be repulsed and angry—rejecting people who have a desperate need for understanding, forgiveness, and competent help. In the pages that follow, Grant Martin gives insights that will help you deal with your own feelings and will guide your counseling with abusers and those who are abused.

We live in a time when counseling is popular. Many people have sophisticated knowledge about psychological problems and there is an abundance of counseling books, seminars, training programs, and tape presentations. Counseling centers are popping up around the country and numerous counselors have appeared, some with good training and great competence, but others with little sensitivity and not much awareness of what they are trying to accomplish.

The counseling field is confusing to many people, threatening to some, and often criticized both within the church and without. Nevertheless, people still struggle with personal problems and many look for counselors who can give guidance, relief, and help.

And how does the counselor keep abreast of latest developments? Many turn to books but it is difficult to know which of the numerous volumes on the market are of good quality and which are not. Emerging topics, like counseling and family violence, often are discussed in technical journal articles, and there are few, if any, books written specifically for the pastor or other Christian counselor.

The Resources for Christian Counseling series is an attempt to provide books that give clearly written, practical, up-to-date overviews of the issues faced by contemporary Christian counselors. Written by counseling experts, each of whom has a strong Christian commitment, the books are intended to be examples of accurate psychology and careful use of Scripture. Each is intended to have a clear evangelical perspective, careful documentation, a strong practical orientation, and freedom from the sweeping statements and undocumented rhetoric that sometimes characterize books in the counseling field. All of the Resources for Christian Counseling books have similar bindings and after all have been published the volumes will comprise a complete encyclopedia of Christian counseling.

I am especially pleased that Dr. Grant Martin has accepted the invitation to write such an important book in this series. The following pages deal with one of the most important, relevant, and neglected topics in Christian counseling. It won't take long for you to discover the author's in-depth knowledge of his subject, impressive command of the recent professional literature on family violence, deep spiritual commitment, understanding of scripture, and skillful ability to counsel with abusers and their victims.

Dr. Martin summarizes what currently is known about family violence. His book gives practical counseling guidelines, and his clearly written manuscript is interspersed with case histories and illustrations that add interest and will increase your understanding of this difficult problem area.

I know of no other book on this subject that is written specifically for Christian counselors. I hope it will increase your understanding of abuse, and better equip all of us to help those who know about family violence from painful personal experience.

Gary R. Collins, Ph.D.
Kildeer, Illinois

INTRODUCTION

WHEN PAM WAS FIFTEEN, she ran away with her boyfriend. There was a rumor that she was pregnant. Her friends thought leaving home was a dumb thing to do, but none of them knew about the secret trauma Pam had left behind.

Pam's mom always sat in the back row at church. She usually seemed to have a sad expression on her face and a tenseness about her whole body. She seldom mixed with other women in the church even though her husband was a deacon. Her two daughters didn't go to any of the youth group activities, but were good students.

After Pam left, her younger sister, Connie, confided in a friend, "We're Daddy's girls. He doesn't like us having any boyfriends." Later, after seeing a movie at school, Connie told a school counselor about her sexual abuse. She said it hadn't been so bad when Pam was at home, but that it was getting worse. Connie suspected her father had been having sexual relations with Pam before she left home, but the two sisters had never talked about it.

One out of every five girls may have experienced unwanted sexual intimacy with a close relative or neighbor before reaching adulthood. Three-fourths of those relatives are fathers or stepfathers. Pam's father was one of them.

Two years after Pam had left and Connie had confided in the counselor, the man was still a church deacon. The church leaders refused to believe the daughter's accusations. Pam became a mother at sixteen and never went home again. Connie later recanted her story and remained with her parents.

Our picture of the storybook family, with the warm, nurturing, and safe home, has been shattered by stories of victims such as Pam and Connie. Additional reports stream in describing husbands beating their wives or children assaulting their parents. And it doesn't stop there. Husbands are assaulted by wives, sisters by brothers, and brothers by sisters. Even the aged and elderly are reported to be abused. Violence is more prevalent in the home, perhaps, than it is on the streets.

While numbers can be reported, we must remember real people are involved here. People who go to church with us, bowl with us, and borrow our lawnmowers. The statistics are more than numbers. They represent broken bones, hearts, and lives. As will be described in more detail, violence does not occur in all families, but it does occur in all types of homes. It occurs regardless of the checkbook balance, church denomination, or geographic region. Violence is wreaking havoc throughout our country and something must be done to stem the tidal wave. The outrage of counselors and pastors must be channeled into constructive action that brings about healing and prevention.

Violence within the family is disastrous in all respects. It may be life-threatening. Some 65 percent of all couples engage in some form of physical abuse during marriage. Serious beatings take place in about 25 percent of these cases. FBI figures show that 3,312 people were murdered by relatives in 1982.[1] A spouse killing a spouse accounts for 15–25 percent of all homicides committed in the United States each year.

Estimates suggest that more than two thousand children may die each year from abuse.

Even if abuse is not fatal, it's an affront to human dignity. It denies the integrity and value of the person who is harmed, even if the offender doesn't seem to care. Whether within the home or on the streets, violence is in total contradiction to the Christian message of love and respect for one another. If the home is not safe, society will only pay a higher price. For example, one out of five police officers killed each year is fatally wounded while intervening in family disputes.

Family violence is like cancer. It's part of an organism, but at the same time corrupts and destroys its host. Family violence is a growing threat to the future of society. It can even be passed on from parents to children, making many families a breeding ground for future generations of violent adults.

The family is intended to be the basic unit for learning about relationships, developing trust, and building self-esteem. But if this foundation block is not functioning as it should, the rest of our social structure is likely to deteriorate.

Family violence can probably be found in every church and among every counselor's clientele. Through the material presented in the following chapters, it is hoped the pastor or counselor will become better equipped to deal with this tragic, yet common, problem.

Sexual abuse of the kind that affected Pam and Connie is just part of a much larger family violence problem. Over a million (1,007,658) reports of child maltreatment were documented nationwide in 1983 by the American Association for Protecting Children.[2] Experts say that as many as six million children suffer from physical, sexual, and emotional abuse or neglect.

To put family violence in a different perspective, Kentucky's Senator Wendell H. Ford stated in *The Congressional Record* on March 16, 1978 that while 39,000 Americans died in the Vietnam conflict (between 1967 and 1973) 17,570 Americans were dying from family violence. FBI statistics estimate that a wife is beaten every thirty seconds in this country. This adds up to 2,880 women who are beaten every day, or 1,051,200 beatings every year.[3]

Even abuse of the elderly has begun to receive attention. The most frequently cited statistics suggest that cases of elder abuse range from .5 to 2.5 million a year.[4] Another estimate is that one in ten elderly persons, living with a family member, is abused each year.[5] From the cradle to the rocking chair, it seems abuse exists in some fashion.

The reader, if coming from a Christian perspective, may respond with concern about these national statistics but then breathe a sigh of relief: "Thank God these things don't happen in Christian homes."

The evidence suggests that the incidence of abuse, particularly sexual abuse, is every bit as high in some types of Christian homes as in the general public. Admittedly, formal data is limited; but informal evidence of the extent of abuse within the church is significant. Maxine Hoffman, in an article in a Christian periodical, interprets statistics to say that one out of two women, Christian or otherwise, is battered at some time in her life.[6]

In a national sample conducted in Seattle, Washington, by the Center for the Prevention of Sexual and Domestic Violence, it was determined that the typical parish minister or pastor sees almost fourteen persons every year with problems involving family violence.[7]

The United Methodist Church surveyed a portion of its membership and found that 68 percent of those questioned had personally experienced family violence. Examples of violence in this case included physical and verbal abuse of a spouse, abuse of a child by the respondent, and physical and sexual abuse experienced by the respondent as a child.[8]

A national survey of pastors completed by the Task Force on the Family for the National Association of Evangelicals in 1984 suggested that the "problems of today's Christian families, compared with those of non-Christian families, are more similar than different." The report went on to conclude that pastors are lonely persons in matters of competence and security in assisting family development in their churches. Almost half of those surveyed have never, or only once, attended any sort of workshop or program of assistance relating to his or her skills in dealing with family matters.[9] This study highlights two things. Christian homes apparently experience the same kinds of problems as non-Christian homes, and many pastors have not had any training in dealing with violence and abuse. The need for education in this area is widespread and urgent.

Victims and abusers are the new lepers among us and we can no longer remain silent and indifferent to their needs. Often in my counseling victims of abuse, I have heard testimonies of those who had gone to their pastor or board of elders with a plea for help, only to be met with rejection and disbelief. Many times an abused wife has been told to "suffer for righteousness' sake," and returned home to endure more abuse. This kind of advice usually increases emotional turmoil and can sometimes end in death or permanent injury. It's no wonder the church has a bad reputation among some community agencies and mental health workers.

Yet pastors and Christian counselors can be a source of safety, hope, and healing. To be a place of refuge, we must know our enemy. The balance of this book intends to present the basic components of family violence. We will look at the definition and history for each type of abuse, along with instructions for giving help to both victim and abuser. The material will be divided into three major sections: Spousal abuse, child abuse, and elder abuse. Each section will include more details about the frequency and nature of abuse, and then move to methods of recognizing, treating, and preventing the problem.

PART ONE

SPOUSAL ABUSE

CHAPTER ONE

THE FREQUENCY AND HISTORY
OF SPOUSAL ABUSE

A LOADED SHOTGUN was pointed toward her head. She quivered in fear, but her pleading eyes were of no avail as the blast of the gun filled the air. Moments later the family dog lay in a pool of blood, the victim of a senseless killing at the hands of a violent husband. No explanation was ever given for Tom's action. At the time, his wife, Linda, was in the hospital for major surgery. The dog had been a gift to the wife. Later while relating the incident to her counselor, Linda said she was lucky to have been away or else her life might have been sacrificed during Tom's fit of rage.

Linda described Tom as active in his church, very friendly with the pastor to his face, but quite critical in conversations at home. Although Tom had no real close friends, he was an adequate provider. Yet the man who could be quite charming in public was the same person who had threatened his wife with guns, knives, and axes. In spite of the years of constant fear, it was the death of her dog and concern for her children that finally brought Linda to action.

Love, affection, understanding, kindness, and consideration are qualities usually associated with marriage. The idea that individuals would use physical violence against those they are supposed to love seems both contradictory and unlikely. Yet it is becoming increasingly clear that individuals do use violence within their intimate relationships. In addition, the number of families and couples affected by violence is far more extensive than we ever imagined.

Although accurate data are difficult to obtain, it is estimated that almost two to three million spouses have experienced abuse at the hands of a mate. It's estimated that at least one-sixth of all American couples experience at least one violent incident each year. One-fourth of all couples have at least one such violent episode sometime during their marriage.[1]

Data in *The Battered Woman Syndrome* by Lenore Walker compared the religious affiliation of four hundred women who were battered by their husbands. The chart below shows a summary of the data.

Reported Religion	Batterer		Nonbatterer	
	Number	Percent	Number	Percent
None	114	29	71	37
Agnostic/atheist	16	4	6	3
Protestant	147	37	64	32
Catholic	110	28	42	21
Jewish	4	1	3	2
Other	9	2	10	5

Sociodemographic Data for Batterers and Nonbatterers at Time of Relationship as Reported by Women.[2]

The distribution of religious affiliation for both batterer and nonbatterer is very similar. Thirty-seven percent of the women came from homes where the husband was alleged to be Protestant, while 32 percent of the nonbatterers were also

Protestant. It might be assumed that nonbattering mates would be more likely to claim a religious affiliation, but it appears that husbands who batter more often claim to be Protestant or Catholic. While only suggestive, this type of data adds to the opinion that coming from a religious home is certainly no guarantee of freedom from abuse.

In an attempt to identify how evangelical pastors deal with wife abuse, a questionnaire was sent to several thousand pastors of conservative Protestant churches. Although the response was very low (7 percent), the results confirm the widespread presence of battering. Seventy percent of the pastors indicated wife abuse occurs "sometimes" to "often" in Christian marriages. Eighty-four percent of the pastors had counseled at least one battered wife. Thirty-five percent of those who reported seeing abused wives had counseled six or more victims of battering. Wife abuse is more prevalent in Christian homes than most people believe, but, as one minister observed, "Guilt within the church keeps it repressed."[3]

Data and clinical experience suggest that the incidence of abuse is all too common within the church. Almost all pastors and counselors, at one time or another, will deal with someone who parallels the experience of David in Psalm 55:

> My heart is in anguish within me; the terrors of death assail me. Fear and trembling have beset me; horror has overwhelmed me. I said, "Oh, that I had the wings of a dove! I would fly away and be at rest—I would flee far away and stay in the desert; I would hurry to my place of shelter, far from the tempest and storm." . . . If an enemy were insulting me, I could endure it; if a foe were raising himself against me, I could hide from him. But it is you, a man like myself, my companion, my close friend, with whom I once enjoyed sweet fellowship as we walked with the throng at the house of God. . . . My companion attacks his friends; he violates his covenant. His speech is smooth as butter, yet war is in his heart; his words are more soothing than oil, yet they are drawn swords (Ps. 55: 4–8, 12–14, 20–21).

WIFE BEATING: A PERSISTENT FACT OF HISTORY

The statistics suggesting nearly six million wives will be abused by their husbands in any one year probably do not represent an increase in domestic violence, but rather a more accurate picture of what has been happening all along. For centuries wife beating has been accepted as a natural, although unfortunate, consequence of a woman's status as her husband's property. The high levels of reporting tell us wife beating in the U.S. is no longer accepted as an inevitable and private matter.

Throughout much of history, male violence toward women and children has been socially, legally, and religiously endorsed. For countless generations the man was not just the head of the household, he *was* the household.

In Roman legal precedent, the *Law of the Twelve Tables* granted the father the absolute right to sell his children, as well as the power of life and death over the child. From this ultimate position of power came lifelong authority over all members of the father's household. That authority, known in Roman jurisprudence as *patria potestas,* is one of the most far-reaching legacies of the private law of Rome.[4]

In ancient Greece, the wife and children were also the man's absolute property. The order of priority was: father, cattle, mother, children. It's easy to see how custom could dictate violence toward wives if they had less status than a Hereford steer.

Although Christ came to teach total equality, the Jewish tradition was blatantly biased as can be seen from a line in the prayer of a Jewish man spoken daily: "I thank God that He did not make me a Gentile, a slave, or a woman." This makes Paul's statement in Galatians 3:28 so very relevant to the culture in which he lived: "There is neither Jew nor Greek, slave nor free, male nor female, for you are all one in Christ Jesus."

Paul's message was delivered to a society with a history of female subjection. The prevalent view permeating all of Jewish law was that a woman was not a person. She was chattel. The wife had practically no legal rights. She was her husband's possession, and he was free to do anything he pleased.

Jewish divorce laws reflected this inequality. The wife had no rights of divorce unless her husband became a leper, an apostate, or engaged in a "disgusting trade."[5]

A man, on the other hand, could divorce his wife for almost any cause. If he wished a divorce, all he had to do was hand his wife a bill of divorcement in the presence of two witnesses; the marriage was ended.

The idea of a man managing and controlling his family with absolute authority made its way into European society and law. For many centuries, including the Dark and Middle Ages, as well as the Renaissance, women were routinely subjugated. The physical punishment that accompanied their inferior status was justified by so-called "laws of chastisement." Although today we would label this behavior abusive, history questioned it very little. Such violence was simply taken for granted as part of the divinely ordained order of things.

The medieval church included a majority of clergy who taught that a husband had the right, and sometimes even the obligation, to beat his wife. An example is found in Friar Cherubino's "Rules of Marriage." He stated that if a husband's verbal correction of his wife was not effective, then he was to ". . . take up a stick and beat her, not in rage, but out of charity and concern for her soul, so that the beating will rebound to your merit and her good."[6]

The use of physical punishment was also sanctioned by secular institutions during the Middle Ages. One thirteenth-century French law code stated that, "In a number of cases men may be excused for the injuries they inflict on their wives, nor should the law intervene. Provided he neither kills nor maims her, it is legal for a man to beat his wife if she wrongs him."[7]

For the most part, medieval society viewed women as needing strict control. Here is an excerpt from one of the "marriage enrichment" manuals of that time. "The female is an empty thing, easily swayed: she runs great risks when she is away from her husband. Therefore, keep females in the house, keep them as close to you as you can, and come home often to keep an eye on your affairs and to keep them in fear and trembling. . . . If you have a female child, set her to sewing and not to reading, for it is not suitable for a female to know how to read unless she is going to be a nun. . . ."[8]

Although medieval society was slowly beginning to grant the woman some rights and privileges, she was still provided little protection from a violent spouse.

Throughout history there have been those who have tried to call attention to the abuse of women. For example, a Jewish rabbi made the following comments in the thirteenth century: "The cry of the daughters of our people has been heard concerning the sons of Israel who raise their hands to strike their wives. Yet who has given a husband the authority to beat his wife? Is he not rather forbidden to strike any person in Israel? Nevertheless have we heard of cases where Jewish women complained regarding their treatment before the Communities, and no action was taken on their behalf."[9]

Rabbi Perez then goes on to outline a process whereby the wife was able to get a type of restraining order against the abusive husband. If that did not stop the beatings, the wife or her relatives could bring forth a complaint and receive a financial settlement, much like a maintenance or alimony agreement.

The Renaissance and Reformation brought significant social, political, and religious change. But there was still a consistent perspective on the proper role for a woman. The Elizabethan wife was a curious mixture of slave and companion, a necessary evil, and a valued lieutenant. According to custom, a wife's primary duty was to be subject to her husband. She was always to acknowledge herself as an inferior being, and be ready at the beck and call of her spouse.[10]

The sixteenth-century Protestant Reformation did very little to improve the social position of women in Christian Europe. Early church leaders such as Martin Luther, John Knox, and John Calvin were as stern as their Roman Catholic contemporaries on the issue of physical discipline of wives. A statement is attributed to Martin Luther who, in boasting about his successful marriage, noted that when his wife occasionally became "saucy" all she received was a "box on the ear."[11]

During the 1800s, legal changes occurred which actually left women with fewer protections under the law than they had during the Middle Ages. Due to the legal theory known as "couverture" it was held that, in marriage, a husband and wife are one person under the law. The legal existence of the woman is suspended during marriage and incorporated into that of her husband. The net effect of couverture was that a married woman could not own property, have money in her name, make contracts, and sue or be sued in court. This latter restriction had particular application to violence. A woman could not prosecute her husband for beating her, since, in the eyes of the law of the land, she did not exist.[12]

The attitude of permissiveness toward striking women became part of the American tradition since the colonies borrowed much from English law. In fact, the common colloquial expression "rule of thumb" originally came from British Common Law and a section regulating wife beating. The intent of the law was to help the plight of abused women by modifying the weapons a husband could legally use when chastising his wife. The old law had authorized a husband to chastise his wife with any "reasonable" instrument. The new law stipulated the reasonable instrument be only "a rod not thicker than his thumb."[13]

During the late 1860s influential persons such as John Stuart Mill did speak out against the abusive treatment of women. His book, *The Subjection of Women*, contained the following admonition: "The sufferings, immoralities, evils of all sorts, produced in innumerable cases by the subjection of individual women to individual men are far too terrible to be overlooked. . . . The law of servitude in marriage is a monstrous contradiction to all the principles of the modern world. . . . Marriage is the only actual bondage known to our law. There remains no legal slaves except the mistress of every house."[14]

For a long time an attitude of permissiveness toward striking women was a part of the American tradition. For many years the battering of women was assumed and accepted as a male's right in American society. There were some exceptions, however. In the Massachusetts Bay Colony as early as 1655, men who beat their wives were fined a maximum of ten pounds and/or given corporal punishment.[15]

By the 1870s states such as Massachusetts and Alabama began to reject the legal justification for wife beating. In Maryland, by 1882 a wife beater could receive forty lashes or one year in prison. In Delaware wife beating was punishable with five to thirty lashes at the whipping post. And in New Mexico the crime carried a fine of $225 to $1000, or one to five years in prison.[16]

By 1910 only eleven states still did not permit divorce by reason of cruelty by one spouse to the other.

This brief review of history serves to highlight the centuries of social, political, and religious tradition that has perpetuated the existence of violence toward women. Again, the more recent accumulation of statistics only serves to give current documentation to a phenomenon that has been present for centuries.

SINS OF THE FATHERS: PERPETUATING THE CYCLE

Scripture makes very clear the generational influence of wrongdoing (Exod. 34:7; Lev. 26:39). Spousal abuse is not only a violation of a person's right to safety and security; it contaminates the lives of children who live with violence. Research shows there is a real danger that children will learn aggressive behavior patterns if exposed to them in their homes. Violent patterns of behavior are transmitted from generation to generation. Abused children often become abusive parents and spouses.

A person who has experienced violence as a child will have strong negative feelings against that abuse. But they will also have ambivalent feelings of love and identification with their parents. Those early parental examples will influence the child to take on the role of an abuser or victim. The child learns ways to avoid being victimized often by becoming the abuser. All he or she has to do is find a partner who will tolerate the abuse.

The male child who lives with violence will usually identify with his mother and have strong negative feelings about his father's abusive behavior. He may even attempt to intervene in the violent episodes. The older son in the family will tend to move toward meeting some of his mother's needs and end up taking on some of the father's role as confidant and nurturer to his mother. The relationship between mother and son will become very close, while the distance between father and son becomes wider.

Problems are likely to emerge later in adolescence as the son becomes violent and rebellious. As he attempts to break out of the close relationship to his mother, he may start being abusive to her and begin to identify with his father. His abuse may spread to younger siblings or girlfriends. The mother then finds herself trying to cope with a carbon copy of her husband, and another power struggle develops.

Girls who have experienced violence between their parents may take either the victim or abuser role. Girls who see their mother responding only as a victim will tend to model that role. They will tend to assume child-rearing responsibilities for the younger siblings because the mother is so overwhelmed. These girls tend to be quiet, shy, and withdrawn. The daughter may resent her task, but will rarely express her anger. The daughter's roles as surrogate mother and mediator often make her a potential victim of incest. Without some outside intervention, these children will become victims.

Another possibility for females who have lived with violence is that they will have acting-out, behavioral problems. As they become teenagers, many of these girls run away from home, abuse drugs, perform poorly in school, and become promiscuous. Often they marry early to escape the unhappy home life. Their dream is to have a better marriage than their parents'. But because they have the same style of coping as their mother and father, their marriages turn out to be repeat performances. They, in turn, transmit to their children the same unhealthy behavior patterns, and the cycle is continued.[17]

This cycle can and must be broken! While sinful human nature will always be with us, we, as Christian counselors and pastors, are to be used by God wherever we can to spread the good news and help restore the brokenhearted. In the next chapter we shall examine the current definitions and nature of spousal abuse to help better understand the beast we battle.

CHAPTER TWO

THE NATURE OF SPOUSAL ABUSE

CAROL'S LEFT EYE was swollen shut. There was a two-inch scratch on her right cheek. A formerly dazzling smile was now marred by the absence of a lower front tooth. Although Carol was obviously bruised and beaten, the feature that made the pastor catch his breath was the horrible look of fear in her eyes. Pastor John had served as a chaplain in Vietnam, and he recalled that same look in the eyes of young servicemen returning from the combat zone. The eyes looked straight ahead, unmoving, but the impression of stark terror was unmistakable.

Sarah, a young mother who appeared at Pastor Tom's door, was seeking refuge and protection. It was clear she had either been beaten or had lost out in a game of chicken with a Mack truck. The pastor invited her in, called his wife to join them, and asked Sarah what had happened. What unfolded was another of the thirteen or fourteen cases of domestic violence the average pastor sees each year. In Sarah's case, the occurrence of wife battering was apparent. She was severely injured and it wouldn't take a Philadelphia lawyer to determine that the injuries were serious enough to consider filing charges against her husband.

DEFINITIONS OF ABUSE

There seems to be no single, generally accepted definition of spousal abuse. But there are some consistent components. Most current studies include both partners and spouses in their descriptions, whether married or involved in any other type of intimate relationship. While most Christian counselors and pastors will have moral questions about unmarried couples living together, some abused persons coming for help will not be married. It is more important to first deal with the emergency and safety needs and reserve moral or commitment issues for a later counseling session. The balance of this discussion will use the terms *husband, wife,* or *spouse,* but will be referring to any intimate relationship where a man and woman live together.

Spousal abuse generally refers to brutal rather than accidental or insubstantial physical contact. Physical violence includes any act or behavior that inflicts bodily harm or that is intended to inflict physical harm. Physical violence may consist of kicking, hitting, shoving, choking, throwing objects, or use of a weapon. The severity of physical assaults may range from a slap across the face to homicide.

Emotional abuse may include ridiculing or demeaning another person, withholding affection or privileges, and blaming him or her for family or interpersonal problems. Emotional abuse often occurs in conjunction with physical violence, but it may occur in isolation. While physical abuse may leave broken bones or bruises as evidence, the consequence of emotional abuse is lowered self-esteem or a feeling of helplessness.

Threatened violence is a particular form of emotional abuse. It can include verbal expressions of intent to inflict bodily harm, wielding of weapons, threatening gestures, injury or killing of family pets, destruction of property, or any other intimidating verbal or nonverbal behavior.

Whether or not the threatened violent acts are carried out, the resulting apprehension and uncertainty regarding potential physical assaults may be more damaging than the violent act itself.

Marital rape is a form of sexual abuse where an unwilling partner is forced to participate in intercourse or other sexual acts against one's will; this force is often accompanied by physical abuse or the threat of physical harm.

In the vast majority of cases the woman is the victim of abuse. There are statistics that indicate men are sometimes victims. The difficulty is in differentiating when the woman is the pure aggressor and when it is a simultaneous violent interchange, retaliation, or self-defense by the woman. In one study it was estimated that approximately 3.5 million women and 250,000 men in the United States are battered by their spouse or intimate partner.[1]

Although men may infrequently be the victims of battering, the relatively minor nature of injuries men receive pales when compared to the more frequent and severe type of harm inflicted on women. Because of the heavy imbalance toward the battering of women and the lack of reliable descriptions of victimized men, this discussion will concentrate on the violence directed toward women.

CONTEXT OF MARITAL VIOLENCE

Social scientists have collected a good deal of statistical knowledge about the places or times of marital violence. For example:

The typical location of marital violence is in the home. The living room or bedroom is the most likely scene of violence.

The bedroom is the most likely place for a female to be killed. The conflict often occurs at night, when there is no place to go.

The bathroom is the most frequently occupied room during domestic violence. The bathroom is the demilitarized zone of the home and typically is the one room in the house that always has a lock. Often this room is used as a refuge for family members to avoid violence.

Marital couples most often engage in physical conflict between 6:00 P.M. and midnight.

Marital violence is more frequent when neither spouse works or when spouses work on alternating shifts.

The evening meal is a particularly dangerous time due to the accumulation of daily frustrations. The frustrations build to a crescendo during dinner time as the wife complains about the children, the husband complains about his work, and the children yell, cry, fight, or spill their milk.

The conflict is most likely to begin over management of the children, with disagreements over money as the second most frequently cited cause.

Weekends are more conducive to domestic violence than weekdays.

Holidays such as Christmas or New Year's Eve are notable trouble times.

There is a slight tendency for more violence to occur during the warm summer months.

Violence is more likely to occur when the wife is pregnant.

As the frequency of battering episodes increases, the more severe they become.[2]

CHARACTERISTICS OF MEN WHO BATTER

Abusive men are found among all races, socioeconomic classes, and occupations. Only in the past few years have sufficient descriptions been gathered to allow some tentative listing of both the personality and environmental factors that an abuser brings into a relationship. The combination of the personality of the abuser and social influences can go a long way in predicting the likelihood of marital violence.

Personality Characteristics[3]

Inability to manage anger. Individuals who have experienced violent and abusive childhoods are more likely to grow up and become child and/or spouse abusers.[4] Individuals who either observed their parents abusing each other or who were abused as children are more likely to engage in or have a tolerant attitude toward the use of violence. For example, researchers have found that adults who, as teenagers, were frequently punished physically have a spouse-beating rate four times greater than those who were not struck as teens.

Not only does research show that violence begets violence, but the evidence strongly suggests that the greater the frequency of violence, the greater the chance the victim will grow up to be a violent partner or parent.[5]

The family acts as a powerful socializing agent. An abusive family provides not only the initial setting for exposing its members to physical violence, but also provides the example that gives permission for the use of violence to resolve conflict. A person who sees violence as the primary method for settling differences as a child is not going to have available, as an adult, very many alternate ways to channel anger. At best, abusers come from dysfunctional family environments where appropriate problem-solving was never observed. Either way, the end result is an inability to manage one's own anger or to deal with the angry feelings or behavior of the spouse.

Inexpressiveness. Maybe it's due to the later development of the language areas of the left hemisphere of the brain, cultural conditioning, or something else. But most men in American society are less capable than women in expressing their feelings with words. Abusive males have an especially hard time in expressing their emotions, as well as identifying and handling those feelings when they occur. This type of man is rarely capable of true intimacy and may feel very threatened by the prospect of being open and vulnerable.

Because of a likely background of violence, abusive men tend to have difficulty in identifying and being able to express emotions other than anger. Anxiety, fear, frustration, and sometimes even affection are expressed in one way only—violent anger. Although many of these men have sufficient verbal skills to function in day-to-day living, they do not have the verbal ability to express what they think or feel. Particularly when frustrated, the abusive male expects instant gratification from his wife, who is expected to read his mind and "know" what her mate wants. When she is unable to do so, the husband may interpret this as meaning she does not really love him, and he may react to this "rejection" with violence.

It has even been suggested that men use their inexpressiveness as a power strategy to maintain a position of dominance within the family. Silence gives the father power, because the family never knows exactly what he is thinking. They will tend to comply with his wishes rather than risk disturbing the peace. If this inexpressiveness proves to be ineffective in maintaining their authority, some men resort to physical violence as the only way they know how to get what they want.[6]

Emotional dependence. Men who abuse their spouses are usually very emotionally dependent on their wives or intimate partners. Their extreme dependency is expressed through their need for nurturance, comfort, and constant reassurance. Because they harbor a continual underlying fear that they will lose their wives, self-doubt is reinforced. As a result of their inner rage at being so dependent, abusive men act in controlling ways to exert power and to deny their own weakness.

A major symptom is strong jealousy and possessive actions toward a partner. The jealousy is usually sexual in nature. The man will often accuse the woman of sexual relations with others. Often the jealousy is extended to family and friends.[7] The husband is likely to spend lots of energy in monitoring his spouse's activities and making accusations. An example might be timing how long it takes to go from the apartment to the laundry room, and then calling the wife to make sure she didn't meet her "boyfriend" on the way.

An abusive man lacks other supportive relationships and tends to maintain only superficial contact with persons outside his own family. Although he may identify a number of people as friends, the typical batterer tends to view these relationships as nongratifying.[8] Because of his fear of losing his spouse and his distrust of family and friends, it's possible the abusive male may perceive physical violence as his only recourse.

Another sign of dependency is what happens when an abused wife leaves her husband. It is common for the husband to make extraordinary attempts to persuade the wife to return. The wife may find herself besieged with phone calls, letters, unwanted gifts, or middle-of-the-night visits from her husband. He may claim that he cannot live without her, and will promise to make any changes necessary to get her back. Some will even threaten suicide, although very few actually carry out this threat.

Low self-esteem and lack of assertiveness. Studies indicate abusive men are generally nonassertive outside of the home, possess a low self-esteem, and are depressed.[9] The jealousy, depression, and sensitivity to criticism often seen in these men can be a result of low self-esteem. Since many abusive men come from violent backgrounds, it's easy to understand how hard it would be for one to reach adulthood with his self-image intact. The lack of self-esteem, combined with a history of hurt and fear, are quickly converted to anger and then aggression. The cultural emphases on male productivity, on being a high achiever, emotionally tough, and dominant over women, add to the feelings of failure. While these influences impact all men, abusers or not, the personal resources are not present in sufficient degree to prevent men who batter from overstepping their bounds. It can easily be said that men who batter are like all other men, only more so.

Depression can result from internalized anger, so it is very possible for some abusive men to ricochet between depressed nonassertiveness and aggression. Sometimes the aggression will spread outside the home and abusive men will lose their friends and jobs because of aggressiveness, in addition to harming their families. Many times the depression will be hidden under a macho exterior.

As I've pointed out, it has been suggested that the more a husband lacks verbal skills, the more likely he will be to resort to physical violence in order to win domestic disputes.[10] In general, poor communication skills are characteristic of violent households.[11] Further illustration of this characteristic is the finding that abusive males are less assertive with their partners than nonabusive males.[12] Lack of assertiveness means the inability to take initiative to openly express one's needs without coercion. This lack of assertiveness may result from the cultural stereotypes of masculinity which reinforce aggressive behavior. As a result, abusive males may resort to violence rather than verbal communication as a means to build their own masculine self-image. Because the aggressive behavior is periodically rewarded, the use of violence is perpetuated and the appropriate verbal skills are never learned. Abusive men may not assert themselves because they have not developed the skills to do so.

Rigid and domineering application of traditional sex role attitudes. Violent men tend to have more inflexible beliefs about the roles and functions of their spouses. Many batterers are very dominating and demand control of almost every aspect of their families. They expect to make all major decisions, and they tend to become angry if their wives disagree or act independently. Often the abusive husband tries to monitor his wife's activities outside the home, such as refusing to let her go to college or church. The net effect is that the wife usually becomes socially isolated and is dependent on her husband for emotional support.

Using his religious beliefs for support, the man who beats his wife tends to adhere to a male dominant role which requires that he: 1. never appear weak; 2. can solve his problems without asking for help; 3. make all important family decisions; 4. receive deferential treatment from his wife and children; and 5. be in control of his emotions, particularly in public.[13]

Whether "Christian" or not, the abusive husband expects his wife to fulfill a traditional sex role. He wants her to be responsible for all household and mothering chores and to be submissive and subservient. Because he is already insecure, the most innocuous of actions may be seen as a threat to his status as head of the family. He might hit his wife because she served the children's dinner plates before his, for example.

For the Christian reader, this characteristic of violent men is not to be taken as a rejection of the biblical concept of headship and subjection. Those ideas will be discussed later in more detail. The problem is not with God's order for the family, but with man's inflexible, overdomineering misuse of headship beyond the requisites of love, mutual subjection, and understanding.

Alcohol and drug dependency. Men who abuse their partners have often been found to have a problem with substance abuse. Walker's most recent study indicated there was more alcohol abuse than drug abuse. It was reported that 67 percent of the batterers frequently abused alcohol.[14] It was also found that the abuse of alcohol is likely to result in more serious injuries to women.

Although some form of substance abuse is usually present in abusive relationships, this does not mean that drug or alcohol abuse is necessarily causing the violence.[15] The use of alcohol and drugs may often allow the abuser to avoid responsibility for his behavior. His excuse is, "I was drunk out of my mind and didn't know what I was doing."

It is likely substance abuse and marital violence are related, in that both problems represent an inappropriate response to stress. This is important to remember for treatment purposes, since merely treating the substance abuse will not remedy the entire problem of coping styles.

Social Factors

In addition to the personality characteristics of the male batterer, some environmental factors can influence the likelihood he will resort to violence. To some degree, these can be viewed as social stressors that interact with the vulnerable personality qualities previously described and produce the probability of violence toward wives.

Economic problems. Economic stressors such as unemployment, underemployment, or high levels of job dissatisfaction have been found to be related to marital violence.[16] A recent study, however, reported only 15 percent of the batterers were actually unemployed at the time of the abuse.[17] Perhaps, like alcohol, stress from unemployment has been used as an excuse for the man to hit, rather than its being a cause-and-effect relationship.

Whether unemployed or underemployed, the abuser may have doubts regarding his self-worth which leads to arguments over the bills. This can be especially difficult if the husband perceives he is unable to live up to his own or his spouse's expectations. Establishing himself as economically successful is an important goal in fulfilling the role of father and husband. Any financial instability may erode a man's confidence in his ability to be the primary breadwinner.

The power of the husband is often related to the amount of resources he acquires through his work. Consequently, when abusive males feel threatened in their role as provider and feel they are losing their power, they may resort to violence as an alternative means for expressing their authority in the family.[18] Also, as seen earlier, the abusive male does not have adequate ways to channel his anger, express his feelings, or resolve conflict. So financial pressures can easily trigger violent responses that are directed to the mate rather than to the frustrating situation.

Financial problems are not the only stressors related to family violence. Any major event that would serve to upset the individual or family equilibrium, such as medical problems, discipline concerns, or pregnancy can lead to violence.

Social isolation. Another major finding of spousal abuse is that social isolation raises the risk that there will be severe violence between spouses. Physical isolation can also contribute, since access to social service agencies, medical or educational help, and family or friends may be limited. Families experiencing violence have been found to be unable to utilize the resources necessary to cope with their particular problems.[19] Most people who undergo stress are able to turn to other family members, friends, neighbors, or their church for financial and emotional support. Many abusive couples lack such a network. This isolation may be the result of frequent moves that were made to search for work, escape creditors, or to avoid social service intervention. Isolation can also be self-induced because either the abused woman or her partner may feel embarrassed or fearful that the problem would become known by others. Abuse leads to isolation and this, in turn, leads to more abuse.

Cultural norms. Family violence would not be as common if our society did not condone violence. The media inundates families with the message that violence is an appropriate means to solve problems. We saw earlier the historical tradition that viewed women as subservient to men. The history of accepted violence toward women and the view of women as property of the husband has been described as utilizing the marriage license as a "hitting license."[20]

The reluctance of police to intervene in cases of domestic violence, clergy who encourage the abused woman to be more submissive to her husband, and mental health workers who blame women for the violence all contribute to the perpetuation of violent relationships.

At the bottom of all of society's norms and expectations is the very nature of human beings. The violent nature of our culture simply reflects the violent nature of mankind. The words of Jeremiah seem so very appropriate, "The heart is deceitful above all things and beyond cure. Who can understand it?" (Jer. 17:9). Jesus pointed to the same root problem. "For from within, out of men's hearts, come evil thoughts, sexual immorality, theft, murder, adultery, greed, malice, deceit, lewdness, envy, slander, arrogance and folly. All these evils come from inside and make a man 'unclean'" (Mark 7:21, 22).

While definite changes need to be made in our society, it is only when the heart of each person is touched by the love of Jesus Christ that permanent improvements will be made. William Golding, author of *Lord of the Flies*, worded the solution this way: "The basic problem of modern humanity is that of learning to live fearlessly with the natural chaos of existence. For too long we have never looked further than the rash appearing on the skin. It is time we began to look for the root of the disease instead of describing the symptoms."[21]

CHARACTERISTICS OF BATTERED WOMEN

One in ten women will be seriously assaulted by her husband sometime during the course of her marriage. It will happen again and again to at least one in twenty wives. Those who finally press charges will have been attacked an average of thirty-five times.[22]

Why is it that these women stay in such painful situations? There are many different answers to that question. The following descriptions attempt to sketch a composite picture of the battered wife.

Battered women enter marriage with the same desires and goals as other women. They may tend to be somewhat more tolerant of physical aggression because they are likely to have come from homes with a history of violence.

The initial episodes of violence typically begin during the first year of marriage. In the beginning, the woman tends to blame herself, thinking that if she had acted differently her spouse might not have resorted to physical violence. The first several assaults are infrequent. Because the husband is usually remorseful, the wife may try to excuse his behavior. Her belief in the excuses dissolves, however, as the assaults occur more often and become more severe. Quite often, by the time the wife realizes the beatings are a dangerous and continual part of her marriage, she feels paralyzed to take action.[23]

Low self-esteem. A battered woman is likely to have grown up with a low self-esteem. In addition, this lack of self-worth makes her vulnerable to her husband's verbal and physical abuse. These women are ridiculed, threatened, told they are stupid, worthless, incompetent, bad wives, and poor mothers. Often the emotional abuse is more damaging than the physical abuse because it tends to be self-fulfilling and self-perpetuating. As the emotional abuse increases, it's hard for the woman not to believe her husband. Eventually she may conclude that she does not deserve anything better, and may give up any attempts to improve the situation. Her husband may tell her, "You ought to be thankful I keep you around, because no one else would have you." She is likely to believe what he says, partly because there is no one else around to contradict his statements.

The battered wife tends to put everybody else's needs before her own. She will make many personal and emotional sacrifices to meet the needs of her husband and children. She will virtually burn herself out trying to please her family. The battered wife will tend to take on the guilt for her husband's abusive behavior. Her focus will be on what *she* can do to make

39

the violence stop, without major consideration of what her husband's responsibility should be. In counseling, it may take a long time to get the battered wife to be able to verbalize *her* needs, feelings, and expectations. She will tend to focus on the needs and behaviors of the husband and children exclusively.

Unrealistic hope. Most abused women value their marriages and are intensely involved with their husbands. In spite of the pain they suffer, they still love and feel loyal to their mates. Others feel responsible for their husbands and believe the husbands need them. Many battered wives are rescuers. They believe if they hang in there long enough, eventually their husbands will change for the better. That may have even been one of the reasons such a woman married the fellow with problems in the first place. Many wives of abusive or addictive husbands are first drawn to such men because of the need to be responsible for and nurture someone who has problems coping with life.

Time and time again the husband will promise to change. The wife clings to this eternal hope because she wants to believe it is true. Also, the wife often enjoys the relationship when abuse is not occurring. During those periods the man may be a good father and an affectionate husband.

Another aspect that draws an abused woman back to the vicious cycle is a process of traumatic bonding. After a beating, the woman is hurt and exhausted. She feels both vulnerable and dependent. Her husband is likely to feel guilty and tries to make things better by being especially loving and kind. The wife accepts his comfort because she has no other options. At this point the battered woman bonds to the warmer side of her husband because he still meets some of her needs to be loved.[24]

Isolation. Martha used to be active in many women's activities in the church. She had been in a Bible study group, substituted as a Sunday school teacher, and regularly attended most of the worship services. But in the past few months her pastor noticed she wasn't attending very often. The pastor learned from the Sunday school coordinator that Martha had said she couldn't substitute teach any more.

When the pastor called Martha, she seemed reluctant to talk and made numerous excuses about how her husband needed her at home, and that she and the children had been fighting a cold for weeks. The pastor was puzzled by her change in attitude. But it finally made sense one night when Martha showed up on his doorstep with bruises and cuts all over her face and two frightened children clinging to her skirt.

Another characteristic of battered women is gradual social isolation. Often, by the time a battered wife comes for help, she has cut off most of her family, friends, and social networks, such as the church. Often she is denied access to family and friends because her husband prefers she stay at home. Sometimes her isolation is self-imposed because she fears her family and friends will find out about the abuse. Sometimes fear is a part of the picture because the wife doesn't want any retaliation against anyone who might find out about the situation and incur the wrath of her husband.

Isolation tends to perpetuate ignorance of resources. So the battered wife becomes even more bonded into the abusive relationship, because she believes she has no alternatives for help or protection.

Emotional and economic dependency. The battered wife is very dependent on her husband. She may not have the skills, education, or experience to obtain help for her situation. Abused wives are usually financially dependent on their husbands for support and cannot see the possibility of any other alternatives. Even if the battered wife is working, there is a strong chance the husband still controls the expenditure of the money.

Also, many abused women have very little self-confidence after years of abuse. They are apt to show a sense of helplessness far below their potential for coping. They find security in the familiar. The prospect of making a change involves too much risk. They don't want to be alone outside the confines of the destructive relationship, even though their marriage is lonely and isolated.

This dependency can also show itself in a gradual loss of the sense of a woman's own personal boundaries. She may become unable to accurately tell when she is in danger. In spite of numerous beatings, she is not able to read the signs, in terms of her husband's behavior, and she is not able to acknowledge to herself that she is living in a lethal situation.

Abused women often will come for help only when they believe their children are in danger. Hospital emergency room personnel report that abused individuals only show up for treatment when there is blood. The sight of blood seems to trigger a realization there is personal danger involved. Even if there are internal injuries or broken bones, many abused wives will not go to the hospital. They have lost touch with their physical boundaries, including the awareness of pain.[25] For most victims abuse has become familiar and common. So it usually takes something significant to break the thinking pattern that abuse is a way of life the battered wife must accept. Unfortunately the only thing that sometimes gets through to a victimized wife is the broken arm of her daughter.

Strong traditional view of marriage. Most battered women, whether Christian or not, try to fulfill a traditional role in marriage. They see themselves primarily as wives and mothers who should be nurturing, submissive, and forgiving of their spouses' failures. If the marriage is not satisfying, then the major responsibility to make it better lies with the wife. Also the wife tends to view the relative success of her marriage as a reflection of her own worth. Therefore, if the marriage is not successful, she is failing as a person—and as a wife and mother.

Many abused wives seek help from their pastors or Christian counselors only to be told they should be more submissive and/ or sexually available to their husbands—the implication being that the wife is not an obedient Christian woman, and that it is her fault her husband gets angry. This kind of counsel only serves to increase the guilt level and keeps the husband from taking responsibility for his actions.

The abused wife will have a high commitment to the sanctity of the relationship. This commitment can be motivated by her faith, as well as other factors. If raised in a broken home, the abused wife may not want to "fail" as her parents did. Cultural or religious constraints regarding separation or divorce may deter the wife from seeking help. Fears—of physical retaliation, economic loss, and losing custody of children—create a paralysis and keep the wife locked into a vicious cycle.

Of course, the Christian wife has a high level of commitment to keep the marriage together. But she often cannot distinguish between the steps needed to get help for herself and her husband, and the actual eventuality of divorce. Something significant has to happen in the life of the husband in order to get him to recognize his needs and responsibility. Divorce need not be the only solution. But the battered wife tends to view the situation as all or nothing. She must either stay and be abused or leave and risk divorce. Neither extreme seems palatable, so she will take no action at all.

PHASES IN MARITAL VIOLENCE

Spouse abuse is cyclic in nature. A complete understanding of violence not only includes the characteristics of both spouses, but also the progression of events that seem to repeat themselves again and again in an abusive relationship. Lenore Walker has identified a three-phase violence cycle. Her research suggests there are three distinct recurring battering phases: 1. The tension-building phase; 2. The explosion or acute violent episode; 3. The loving contrition or remorse phase.

Phase One: Tension Building

This is a period of mounting stressors and tension. There is a gradual escalation of incidents of irritation over such things as finances or children. Some expression of dissatisfaction is present, but often the frustrations are not dealt with directly. The feelings are held inside where they become more intense. Communication and cooperation diminish as the husband and wife tend to withdraw from each other. The batterer may express dissatisfaction and hostility, but not in an extreme form. The wife may attempt to placate her husband, trying to please him, calm him down, and avoid further confrontations. The wife, at this point, tries not to respond to his hostile actions. She will tend to use some type of anger-reduction technique which often works for a little while. This temporary reduction of hostility reinforces her belief that she can control her husband or prevent things from getting worse.

The tension continues to increase and the wife finds she is unable to control her husband's angry responses. At this point the wife usually withdraws from her husband, not wanting to do anything to make things worse. The husband sees her withdrawal and reacts with more intense anger. The second phase becomes inevitable unless there is some type of intervention. Sometimes the wife will precipitate the inevitable explosion so she can at least control where and when it occurs. This allows her to take better precautions to minimize her injuries and pain. The husband may also get drunk, anticipating a violent confrontation. This phase may last anywhere from an hour to several months.[26]

Phase Two: The Acute Violent Episode

This phase is characterized by the uncontrollable discharge of the tensions that have built up during the initial phase. Prior to this episode of violence there is often the feeling that an outburst is inevitable. Both parties may feel the situation is out of their control. This is when the batterer unleashes his aggressive behavior toward his wife. If injuries occur, this is when they are inflicted. It is also the time police become involved, if at all. This phase is ended when the battering stops. With it comes a reduction in the amount of tension. The temporary elimination of tension and apprehension has a reinforcing effect. The violent behavior is reinforced, and likely to be used in the future, because it worked.

Sometimes, just before the violence occurs, the husband may withdraw and refuse to communicate. The man often does this because he can't compete with the verbal, argumentative skills of his wife. His retreat is motivated by frustration. He may then signal to her he is about to "lose it" and demand his wife "back off." She may then try to increase her efforts to get through to him by talking louder, moving closer, or preventing him from leaving. This makes things worse and the violence erupts. In this case, both husband and wife feel victimized. The husband believes he was provoked into retaliation in the only way he knew how to respond. The wife ends up being the obvious victim of physical and/or verbal attack. There are many occasions where the battering is unprovoked in the eyes of an objective third party, but in the eyes of the husband, "she brought it all on herself."[27]

Phase Three: Remorse

After the explosive release of violence comes a period of relative calm. The tension has been dissipated, at least until it happens again. The abusive spouse may apologize profusely, try to help his wife, show kindness and remorse, and shower her with gifts and promises that it will never happen again. This behavior often comes out of a genuine sense of guilt over the harm inflicted, as well as fear of losing his spouse. The husband, at this point, may really believe he will never allow himself to be violent again. The wife wants very much to believe her husband, and for a time may renew her hope in his ability to change.

The remorse phase provides the reinforcement for remaining in the relationship. Interviews with battered women indicate that even if the abusive husband did not engage in observable loving-contrition behavior following the violent episode, the reduction of tension alone was sufficient reinforcement for the wife.[28]

The level of intimacy during this "make up" phase may be better than any other period in the lives of the couple. They may communicate feelings in the context of guilt and vulnerability that usually aren't revealed. There may be a shift in power during this phase. The wife may now feel protective of her repentant husband and that she is the stronger of the two. She now has gone from being comparatively powerless to powerful. If she were to make any statements or efforts to leave, the balance of power is even more evident. The wife may try to punish her husband or obtain concessions and privileges. This may be satisfying for a while. But once the husband feels more secure about his wife staying with him, or after stressors build up again, he will resent his loss of power, and the cycle will start all over again.

If the police, family, pastor, or mental health worker makes contact with the family during the early part of Phase Three, they will likely meet with resistance. While the couple are sharing their mutual feelings of closeness and protectiveness, they tend to believe everything is okay. The problem has been solved and the violence will not occur again. This ray-of-hope phenomenon and the belief that "love is enough" contribute to a couple believing it doesn't need any outside help.[29]

The pastor or counselor should be aware of this potential response from a violence-prone couple. While the two may refuse help initially, an opportunity to intervene may open up within a few days or weeks after the remorse and guilt have dissipated.

In this chapter I've presented the definition of spousal abuse, along with descriptions of the context of violent acts. I've described the major characteristics of both the abusive male and victim. Finally, I've presented the cyclic nature of domestic violence. Although many additional features of spousal abuse could be given, this section provides an adequate overview. The interested reader can consult some of the references for more detail.

Let's now turn our attention to how the counselor or pastor can effectively intervene on both a crisis and long-term basis.

CHAPTER THREE

CRISIS COUNSELING IN SPOUSAL ABUSE

CANDICE HAD BEEN BATTERED by her husband for many years. She was a Christian and very much wanted to keep her marriage together. After years of silence she sought out a Christian counselor. Candice told the counselor she didn't want a divorce but felt both she and her children were in danger; she asked the counselor to help her explore her options.

The counselor took the position that Candice had married for better or for worse. Implying there must be something she was doing to aggravate her husband, the counselor went on to suggest she might have a persecution complex and somehow need to be victimized. The counselor told Candice she should go back to her husband, pray, and try not to upset him.

Candice asked about the possibility of getting a restraining order, or having her husband arrested so that he might be forced to get help. The counselor said such options were wrong for the Christian. He added that no matter how serious the abuse, her responsibility was to endure the suffering and hold the marriage together.

Too many Christian counselors or pastors seem to get caught up in the issues of divorce or submission and lose sight of the woman suffering from abuse. Those of us in the helping professions must make sure the abused and battered Candices of our communities do not fear entering the doors of our churches or counseling offices. We must be equipped to give them new hope and safety, and not doom them to return to their torturous cycle of violence.

Based on detailed histories of 542 battered women and 2,096 telephone interviews with persons who called a telephone hotline in Dallas, Texas, William Stacey and Anson Shupe made the following comments about the effectiveness of clergy in helping victims of domestic violence. "The sad fact is that ministers and priests are currently much better at marrying men and women than they are at dealing with spouse abuse and domestic conflict. . . . We have yet to talk to a woman who felt she received much aid from a clergyman."[1]

Recognition of the seriousness and prevalence of family violence has been slow in coming to all sections of American society, and the church is no exception. Courses in pastoral counseling do not normally deal with assault, incest, and rape. On the other hand, many professional counselors have not had formal training in dealing with violence either.

Clergy are often the first people families in trouble will contact. Pastors are one of the largest groups of professionals who could have an impact on domestic violence. But they need to know how to help, rather than make things worse. The following chapters will try to set forth procedures which are sensitive to the emotional, physical, as well as spiritual needs of violent families.

The direction and content of counseling will depend on the circumstances under which the situation comes to the attention of the counselor or pastor. A crisis situation calls for a different strategy than does a couple that comes in together requesting help.

There are four possible outcomes following the violent episode. Three of these result in restoration of calmness for a time, and one leads to further crisis.

1. The first possible outcome is for the abuser to become very remorseful, guilty, and ask his spouse for forgiveness in either verbal or nonverbal ways. This is the typical sequence of events as described earlier. If the victim forgives, excuses, or avoids making an issue of the event, calmness is restored. Tension has been reduced, but the behaviors of both victim and offender that led to that reduction have been reinforced.

2. The abuser may not feel remorseful at all. He may believe that his violence was justified and necessary to establish control. If the victim accepts that state of affairs, and acquiesces to the authority of her husband, whether out of fear or belief in her own wrongdoing, calmness is restored. The wife has yielded to the threats of her husband and his behavior has been rewarded.

3. If the victim takes assertive action to either get help, threatens to leave, or establishes conditions for continuing the relationship, the couple may move toward improvements in the situation. If so, calmness is restored. This would probably be the ideal outcome, if it resulted in changes that stop the violence and improve the marriage relationship.

4. In contrast, if the victim takes assertive action to change the occurrence of violence, the abuser may reject the proposed changes. The result in this case will be a crisis. The wife is no longer willing to subject herself to the threat of violence, but the husband will not go along with her proposals. If the wife decides to leave and the husband is made more angry by that decision, he may try to stop her. Many times wives have been seriously harmed by a distraught husband who couldn't handle his wife's departure.

If the wife demands that they get counseling, that he join Alcoholics Anonymous or get other treatment, and the husband rejects such an option, the situation continues in crisis. Often, at this point of crisis, the outside world becomes involved. The husband may call the pastor because his wife has left. The wife may contact the pastor because she fears for her safety or needs a place to stay. The balance of this chapter will focus on ways to intervene when the situation is in crisis. More long-term treatment will be discussed in the next chapter.

CRISIS INTERVENTION[2]

A pastor or counselor may come across a crisis situation in one of several ways. The victimized spouse may request help during or right after an act of violence. A victim may come to the counselor with another related concern, such as discipline problems, and careful questioning may reveal a need for immediate intervention because of a crisis. A referral may come from a community agency such as an emergency shelter. The victim may have sought refuge at a shelter but wants her pastor to be involved. A member of the family may contact the pastor or counselor out of concern for the abused victim.

It's important to remember that if a battered wife has been pushed by others into bringing the violence out into the open, she may be very ambivalent about taking action. Sometimes it is only when the violence is directed toward the children that the mother will take drastic action. It is important to be as accepting and comforting as possible. The abused wife has already been physically and emotionally traumatized; she doesn't need to be put on the defensive by questions, such as "What did you do to set him off?"

The first step in the intervention process is to determine what has motivated a family member to seek help. Very often the first person to contact a pastor or counselor will be the wife or an adolescent child. There will be times when an abusive husband will initiate the contact, usually during the remorseful phase, or after the wife has taken drastic action. It's important to take the situation seriously. Whatever your relationship to the person who seeks your help, listen to him or her carefully. Violence should not be minimized. But both victims and abusers will tend to understate the extent of the abuse. Above all, believe the woman has been abused!

Sometimes a person will contact a pastor or counselor with a secondary type of crisis. You should always be alert for signs that could be indirect symptoms of spousal abuse. Some of these indicators are:

- history of miscarriages
- history of or recent increase in prescriptions for tranquilizers
- history of or recent increase in excessive use of alcohol
- repeated visits to emergency room for medical treatment of injuries or illnesses
- signs of ongoing stress, such as headaches, gastrointestinal ailments, or vague "not feeling well" complaints
- contacts with community mental health agencies or other psychiatric facilities
- suicide attempts
- nonprescription drug abuse
- isolation from friends and family
- reports of police intervention
- reports of conflict with others outside the home
- description of spouse as being moody or unpredictable
- reference to abusive or violent history

When several of these symptoms are present, the counselor should question further about the possibility of spousal abuse. Their presence does not mean abuse is certain, only that you should investigate further. Ask questions. If a woman comes to you and says "things are pretty tense at our house. My husband really lost his cool the other day," explore the details of the encounter—even if there are not any bruises. Ask if she has ever been hit, and how often the outbursts occur. By asking questions, you show you're taking the situation seriously.

Intervention is more likely to be effective when the family perceives the situation as a crisis. It's the counselor's role at this time to use the crisis to maximize the opportunity for positive changes. Remember that any crisis has both potential for danger and for opportunity.[3]

The initial role of the counselor is to:

1. Determine the nature of the crisis.
2. Assess the potential for harm or danger.

3. Offer support and provide calming influence.

4. Facilitate the exploration of options and help direct family to appropriate resources.

DETERMINE NATURE OF CRISIS

The goal here is to assess what has happened. When intervening in family violence it is important to listen to each person's perception of the problem. The counselor wants to understand what the client/victim sees as the most important problem now. The victim may be sitting in your office or on your doorstep at midnight because she has been threatened with a gun and is afraid to go home. But on the other hand, her highest priority may be not to disturb the plans for her son's birthday party scheduled for the next day.

The counselor needs to solicit enough information so that an adequate assessment and appropriate plans can be established. Empathy and concern are important ingredients of this step.

Whenever possible, it is helpful to obtain a history of previous violent episodes, along with a description of the stressors that have impacted the family. This will help the counselor assess the potential for future violent episodes. A crisis situation may not allow for a detailed history, of course. The wife and children may be so frightened and distraught as to not be reliable sources of information anyway. But at some early point in the process, you do need to get the necessary background.

When interviewing the family, it is important to be frank and honest with them. Ask specific questions about the violent incidents. Learn what happened before, during, and after the episode. Unless a referral is made to another agency or counselor, it is advisable to interview each family member, including the children. If possible, talk with each one privately, as well as together, to get an idea of their interaction patterns.

Try to learn about the family background. Ask about each partner's personal and social history; the composition of the nuclear and extended family; any incident of violence that occurred in either partner's family of origin; any incidents of the partners' being abused or neglected as children.

The information gathered will assist in assessing the family's strengths and weaknesses. It should provide the counselor with an indication of how the extended family will respond to remedial actions such as separation. It will also help to identify stress points for the spouse to use in coping with future situations.

One of the first priorities is to determine if medical attention is needed. If the injuries are severe and visible the need is obvious. Often, battering does not leave highly visible evidence. Question the victim carefully, and get her to a doctor if there is any possibility of injury.

Victims of family violence are often reluctant to use medical services for fear that this action will result in further violence. They worry about running up more financial obligations, causing their insurance coverage to stop, or that the abuse will become public. A mother may agree to medical assistance for the children but not for herself. Encourage a complete examination as soon as possible. Old injuries may never have been treated, and may be in need of medical attention.

Another important consideration in working with any kind of abuse is to file a police report. More and more states are establishing Victim Compensation Programs for victims of violence and crime. These programs can provide financial support for living, medical, and counseling expenses incurred as a result of being a victim of crime. To get compensation, victims or their representatives must report the crime to law enforcement officials within seventy-two hours, or as soon as reasonably possible (check the availability and specific requirements for your locality). After that, victims must apply within a specific period of time, usually one year, to the Victims Compensation Program to obtain benefits.

The crucial action at this stage of intervention is to report the incident to the police. If the woman waits too long, she may not be eligible for this source of help. Only recently have some states included victims of domestic violence among those eligible for benefits. Find out what is available in your state.

ASSESS POTENTIAL FOR HARM AND ENSURE SAFETY

When a pastor or counselor deals with family violence, he or she must be able to assess whether or not there is imminent danger. The following list of factors would indicate a high level of risk to the family.

Abuser Profile

- Presence of weapons
  - —Are there weapons available to the abuser?
  - —Has the abuser used weapons in previous episodes?
  - —Has the abuser made previous threats with a weapon?
  - —Is the abuser threatening to use a weapon?

- Presence of alcohol or drugs
  - —Is the abuser intoxicated when threatening his or her spouse?
  - —Has the abuser been violent during "high states" in the past?
  - —Do family members fear that they will be harmed when the assailant returns home intoxicated?

- Presence of suicide threats
  - —Is there a past history of psychiatric hospitalization or treatment resulting from episodes of violent behavior?
  - —Has the abuser threatened to kill himself and family members?

- Presence of violence outside of the immediate family
  - —Has the abuser assaulted extended family members?
  - —Has the abuser assaulted friends?
  - —Has the abuser assaulted strangers?
  - —How many times has the abuser assaulted others and how serious were the injuries?

- Presence of previous court involvement
  - —Does the abuser have a court or prison record?
  - —Does the abuser have previous assault records or charges?
  - —Is the abuser on probation?

- Presence of sophisticated knowledge of the legal system
  - —Has the abuser manipulated the legal system previously?
  - —Does the abuser know the terms and degrees of court

sanction, and for which behaviors court action can be initiated?

—Does the abuser respect the law?

- Presence of intimidating behavior
  —Does the abuser follow his spouse?
  —Does the abuser threaten family members and friends?
  —Does the abuser make threatening phone calls?
  —Does the abuser threaten to assault or kill his spouse?
  —Has the abuser attempted to kill any member of his family previously?
  —Has the abuser killed or injured a family pet or damaged property?

- Presence of previous violent episodes
  —When did the last incident occur?
  —What was the severity of the last incident? What was the outcome?
  —Was legal action undertaken? What was the effect?

If several of these factors are present, the situation should be interpreted as dangerous and appropriate precautions taken. When assessing the level of risk to the victim, the following factors may also indicate the abused spouse is in imminent danger.

Victim Profile

- Presence of previous abuse
  —Has the victim been abused previously?
  —Has the victim been abused by her current partner?
  —How severe were previous injuries? Was hospitalization required?
  —Is the victim in jeopardy by seeing you?

- Presence of previous legal action
  —Has the victim called the police before?
  —Has the victim initiated court action before? Has she followed through with court action?

- Presence of previous separations
  —Has the victim separated from her spouse before? How many times? What was the outcome?

- Presence of limited ability to make decisions or function effectively
  —Does the victim seem to be able to develop a workable plan to avoid future violence or is she immobilized?
  —Are there barriers that prevent the victim from developing a plan?
  —Does she have a place to go in emergencies?
  —Does she have a network of support? Who and where?

- Presence of suicidal thought and behaviors
  —Does the victim have self-destructive thoughts?
  —Has the victim ever attempted suicide? If so, what was the plan and method?
  —Does she experience depressions? How does she behave when she is depressed?
  —Does the victim have access to weapons or drugs?
  —Is she currently receiving any mental health treatment or prescribed medication?

- Threats to children
  —Have the children suffered abuse in the past?
  —Does the victim plan to take the children if she separates? Has she made an appropriate plan?

- Potential for violence by the victim
  —Does the victim have access to weapons for use against the abuser?
  —Does the victim believe that she could harm the abuser when angry? If so, how?
  —Does the victim plan to fight back? If so, how?

Stacey and Shupe have developed an index of abuse that can be used to gauge the degree of violence and danger of a domestic relationship. The CSR Abuse Index (Center For Social Research, see pages 58–59) allows a victim, or even a friend or relative of the victim, to estimate the level of danger. It can help provide concrete data to the victim about her situation, and can give additional incentive to take action.

According to Stacey and Shupe, a woman with a score of

0–14 lives in a nonabusive relationship. A woman with a score in the 15–36 range lives in a home where she has experienced some violence at least once in a while. The thing to watch out for here is the possibility of escalation.

Women with scores in the 37–93 range are in a seriously abusive situation that can become most dangerous if outside pressures impact the family. There is the likelihood the woman has experienced injury already, and the prospect of serious injury is high. The woman needs to enter into counseling and try to involve her husband in counseling. Perhaps she should leave the home for a while and work through her options. She needs help.

Women with scores in the top range of 94–120 are in serious jeopardy. They need to consider carefully at least temporary separation or other outside interventions. The violence will not miraculously disappear. The chances are that the woman's life is very much at risk and perhaps the lives of her children as well.

Developing a composite assessment based on both abuser and victim situational factors will help to determine whether any or all family members are in imminent danger. It is also important to find out if there are any mitigating conditions, such as the presence of a third party in the home, which could prevent violent behavior.

If there are a number of risk indicators present in a particular family, some type of intervention is usually required. The type of intervention will depend on the level of risk and the cooperation of the family member(s).

The level of risk to children in situations of family violence must also be assessed immediately. In homes where violent episodes are recurrent and attempts to remedy the situation are not successful, the children are more likely to be at risk.

A threat or attempt made by the wife to separate from the abuser presents the greatest risk of harm to the children. If there are any concerns, a Child Protective Service worker or law enforcement officer should be involved and take any steps necessary to protect the child or children from harm.

CSR ABUSE INDEX [4]
Are You In An Abusive Situation?

This questionnaire is designed to help you decide if you are living in an abusive situation. There are different forms of abuse, and not every woman experiences all of them. Below are various questions about your relationship with a man. As you can see, each possible answer has points assigned to it. By answering each question and then totaling these points as directed, you can compare your score with our Abuse Index. You will know if you are living in a potentially violent situation. And if you are abused, you will have some estimate of how really dangerous that abuse is.

Directions: Circle the response to each question that best describes your relationship.

	Frequently	Sometimes	Rarely	Never
1. Does he continually monitor your time and make you account for every minute (when you run errands, visit friends, commute to work, etc.)?	3	2	1	0
2. Does he ever accuse you of having affairs with other men or act suspicious that you are?	3	2	1	0
3. Is he ever rude to your friends?	3	2	1	0
4. Does he ever discourage you from starting friendships with other women?	3	2	1	0
5. Do you ever feel isolated and alone, as if there was nobody close to you to confide in?	3	2	1	0
6. Is he overly critical of daily things, such as your cooking, your clothes, or your appearance?	3	2	1	0
7. Does he demand a strict account of how you spend money?	3	2	1	0
8. Do his moods change radically, from very calm to very angry, or vice versa?	3	2	1	0
9. Is he disturbed by you working or by the thought of you working?	3	2	1	0
10. Does he become angry more easily if he drinks?	3	2	1	0
11. Does he pressure you for sex much more often than you'd like?	3	2	1	0

12. Does he become angry if you don't want to go along with his requests for sex?	3	2	1	0
13. Do you quarrel much over financial matters?	3	2	1	0
14. Do you quarrel much about having children or raising them?	3	2	1	0
15. Does he ever strike you with his hands or feet (slap, punch, kick)?	6	5	4	0
16. Does he ever strike you with an object?	6	5	4	0
17. Does he ever threaten you with an object or weapon?	6	5	4	0
18. Has he ever threatened to kill either himself or you?	6	5	4	0
19. Does he ever give you visible injuries (such as welts, bruises, cuts, lumps on head)?	6	5	4	0
20. Have you ever had to treat any injuries from his violence with first aid?	6	5	4	0
21. Have you ever had to seek professional aid for an injury at a medical clinic, doctor's office or hospital emergency room?	6	5	4	0
22. Does he ever hurt you sexually or make you have intercourse against your will?	6	5	4	0
23. Is he ever violent toward children?	6	5	4	0
24. Is he ever violent toward other people outside your home and family?	6	5	4	0
25. Does he ever throw objects or break things when he is angry?	6	5	4	0
26. Has he ever been in trouble with the police?	6	5	4	0
27. Have you ever called the police or tried to call them because you felt you or other members of your family were in danger?	6	5	4	0

To score your responses simply add up the points following each question. This sum is your Abuse Index Score. To get some idea of how abusive your relationship is, compare your Score with the following.

120-94	Dangerously abusive
93-37	Seriously abusive
36-15	Moderately abusive
14-0	Nonabusive

OFFER SUPPORT AND PROVIDE CALMING INFLUENCE

Since victims of abuse experience a great deal of frustration, confusion, and pain, they require both emotional and physical support in order to make needed decisions. The pastor or counselor can support family members by being empathic and sensitive to their needs. You should convey a willingness to stick by them throughout the crisis and should maintain a non-judgmental attitude. The goal at this time is to help facilitate decisions, and not make permanent decisions for them. Emphasize the woman's responsibility to make decisions and take action. The abused wife has learned to be helpless, and needs to gain confidence in her ability to take control of the situation.

Fear is an important ingredient at this time. The victim may fear the spouse will retaliate with further violence. She may also fear court action or separation will result in the loss of a job for the abuser, loss of income, or loss of custody of the children. On the other hand, the abusive spouse may fear the consequences of possible court action. This can become an opportunity for change in that the abuser may be amenable to outside help in order to avoid appearing in court and suffering the consequences of his actions. The children may fear separation from the family. It is important for the counselor to do as much as possible to alleviate the fear, but also be aware of its value in making changes.

As a facilitator, the counselor tries to assist the family members in making appropriate decisions and plans. An important part of this process is to help the family become aware of the pressure points in each of their lives that lead to violent episodes.

Another aspect of the facilitator role is to assist family members in setting priorities for action. Victims of abuse have many factors to consider and may be overwhelmed by the complexity of the situation. The pastor or counselor can be of significant help in determining what steps need to be taken to alleviate problems in the family.

Prayer should be a high priority component of the intervention process. First of all, prayer works to change things. All of the human interventions in the world may not change the mind of a battering husband, but God can. Use prayer. God asks us to pray, and it works (Matt. 21:22; John 15:7).

Prayer also has psychological value. Very likely the victim has been praying in some fashion for relief from her abuse. Up to this point, she may not believe her prayers have been answered. Praying with another person tends to give renewed hope.

Be sure you do not just pray and send the victim right back into the abusive situation. Pray with her, but move on to practical forms of intervention that can be God's tools to change things for the better. Affirm the fact that God loves her. Emphasize God does not want her to suffer abuse and she does not have to put up with it.

EXPLORE OPTIONS AND SELECT INTERVENTION

If there is a high degree of risk, based on the abuser or victim profile, one or a combination of the following intervention strategies may be appropriate:

- emergency shelter for the abused spouse and children
- law enforcement involvement
- court action
- commitment of abuser to a psychiatric hospital
- removal of children from home
- involvement of extended family, church, or community agencies in providing a place to stay and/or other necessities

Many pastors and counselors do not have training and experience in the case work aspect of crisis intervention. If this is true, you may need to know how to make an appropriate referral. You need to know about existing services, the appropriate use of those services, key contact persons, emergency and regular referral procedures, any limitations of the resources (for example, waiting lists, eligibility requirements, cultural or language barriers, etc.), and the law with regard to domestic violence.

In cases of family violence, the following services represent those that are most frequently needed. I suggest that you make up a list with phone numbers and contact persons for the services in your community. You can start by looking in the phone book, a directory for community services, or by talking with other counselors.

- Child Protective Services
- crisis intervention (twenty-four-hour availability on a telephone or walk-in basis)
- police intervention
- medical care (emergency and ongoing)
- emergency shelter for abused spouse and children
- child care (emergency, ongoing and respite)
- legal services for both spouses' protection
- Christian Conciliation and Mediation Services
- court services
- alcohol drug treatment (residential and outpatient)
- financial assistance, such as Aid to Families with Dependent Children
- Victim Compensation Program
- employment services (career counseling, job training, and placement)
- supportive counseling
- mental health services
- permanent housing
- family planning
- volunteer outreach
- transportation

Battered Women's Shelters

The concept of a shelter for victims of family violence is important because it deals with one of the most difficult problems for victims of violence—where to go. Family violence usually takes place on weekends, in the late evening, or early morning hours when everything is closed. Stories abound of battered wives spending hours on the street in their bathrobe, locking themselves in their cars, or fleeing into the night without enough money to make a phone call. Most of these victims had to return home and encounter more violence and torment.

One means of providing relief for battered women and their

children has been the shelter or safe-home concept. It began in Chiswick, England, when Erin Pizzey, author of the book *Scream Quietly or the Neighbors Will Hear,* opened the first refuge in 1972. While there have been a variety of shelter models proposed, all of them meet the primary purpose of protecting women and children from the abuser. Most shelters are located in a home-like building, the address of which is not widely known within the community. But neither is it completely hidden. The point is not to encourage a "hide and seek" type of game for batterers. Usually twenty women and children can be accommodated at any one time.[5]

There are a variety of philosophies represented in the operation of battered women's shelters. Some have a very strong feminist orientation, others have a family perspective. You would be wise to visit several shelters in your area so you can be comfortable making referrals to the resource that matches the needs of your client.

Why might it be better for a woman to stay at a shelter, rather than with family or friends? A shelter can take the pressure off of the family who might otherwise be responsible for keeping the abuser at bay. Furthermore, shelters are used to dealing with angry and upset husbands, and have been fairly effective at keeping wives and children safe. Shelters are only temporary solutions, but can be very helpful in giving victims a protected place to sort out their feelings and consider options. Victims can also get comfort and feedback from women in similar circumstances. The staff at the shelters can also provide direction and resources for the victim in deciding what action to take next.

There are disadvantages to going to a shelter. The communal or group living situation is an abrupt change from the privacy of family living. The woman will have to adapt to some rules, such as signing out, keeping curfews, and keeping the location confidential. There are likely to be a variety of social, ethnic, racial, and educational backgrounds represented, which can make adjustment more difficult for some. Usually the maintenance, cooking, and baby-sitting tasks must be shared by the women who live in the shelter. This may not be appreciated by some victims. Many shelters impose a rule that no physical form of punishment or discipline can be used with children. Some mothers find this very difficult, and may be asked to leave if they cannot honor it.

In spite of the problems in adjusting to a group living environment, most women report the experience as being positive. The Texas Department of Human Resources collected follow-up data from every funded shelter in the state. That study found that one-fifth of the women later returned to the shelter or moved in with friends or relatives. One-third of the women decided to live independently. Half of the women returned to live with their mates. And of the 50 percent that returned to their mates, two-thirds said violence had not reoccurred. If the violence had reoccurred, it was both less frequent and less severe than it had been before the women went to the shelters. Furthermore, 71 percent of the women said they felt they had more control over their lives since their stay at the shelter and 79 percent indicated that the batterer had been, or was then, in counseling.[6]

These data give some evidence of the positive effects of shelters. Divorce is by no means the most frequent decision made after staying in a shelter. Rather, it seems a shelter gives an abused woman some time and leverage to create change in a violent relationship. Shelters can offer battered women alternatives to enduring violence. Having such an option can help modify or eliminate violence in the home. From this perspective, shelters can assist both the victim and the abuser.[7]

Law Enforcement Intervention

There are two reasons why legal action might be helpful for a victim. First, if the victim is in danger, legal intervention may help keep the abuser from imposing further injury or trauma. Second, legal intervention may prove to be a way to get the family into long-term counseling and help. Although self-referred counseling is theoretically preferable, in reality, court-ordered treatment may be the only way some batterers will ever be helped.

When an assault has occurred, the first recourse is to call the police. A law enforcement agency is usually called to intervene in a domestic disturbance because of its authority and twenty-four-hour availability. Wife beating is a criminal offense in every legal jurisdiction of this country. Since spousal abuse is considered assault, it is against the law and the police could be called. But the counselor or pastor needs to know the limitations of law enforcement officers as well as their usefulness.

One study in Dallas, Texas, found that only 45 percent of the abused women had ever called police. Furthermore, only 69 percent of the time did the women report police actually responding to their calls. This means that in one out of three cases the police did not even show up.[8]

Other studies have shown only one out of five female victims ever calls the police. But, at the same time, virtually every police department in the country is swamped with domestic disturbance calls. Think what would happen if all of the abused women did call the police! One expert reported some time ago that the number of police responses to minor family conflict exceeds the total number of murders, aggravated batteries, and all other serious crimes.[9] In Chicago, for example, a legal expert found that family violence calls make up to 83 percent of all calls to police.[10]

Seldom do the police resolve the violence problem to everyone's satisfaction. Most localities classify assault and battery as a misdemeanor. This often requires that the law enforcement officer must be a witness to the assault before he or she can make an arrest. Often the violence has ceased before the law enforcement officer arrives. Also the abuser may deny any violence has occurred.

In a detailed study of 380 cases of wife abuse, only twenty arrests of the men were made.[11] Those arrests occurred only because the woman was visibly and seriously hurt, the man threatened the police, or the man became violent to the woman in front of the officers. There is a tendency not to believe the victim, and the bruises and accusations made by the victim are not usually sufficient to make an arrest.

But arrests do make a difference. There is some evidence supporting the results of arrests for wife abuse. Susan Jacoby, writing in the *New York Times* (May 5, 1983), cited a study in which Minneapolis police followed up on wife beaters for six months to determine the effects of different police intervention. When the man was simply ordered out of the house, 22 percent repeated the offense. Out of those who went through counseling, 16 percent repeated. But only 10 percent of those who were arrested beat their wives again.[12]

A California study showed the effects of arresting the abuser lowered the likelihood of his offending again by 31 percent.[13] Police intervention can make a difference.

For the abused woman or counselor wondering if the police can be of help, there are some general suggestions. Remember, the police don't want to get involved in domestic violence, and they are limited in what they can do when they arrive. Calling the police may not be a long-term solution unless it leads to the batterer getting help. If there is a high likelihood of danger, the police should definitely be called. They can provide temporary protection. Unless the woman is willing to press assault charges against the man, there is little the police can do unless you live in one of the few states with mandatory arrest laws. They cannot make the man leave because it's his home, too. If the abuser is arrested, he will often be out of jail within a few hours, angrier than before.

Mandatory arrest laws. Legislation in a few states has tried to deal with domestic violence by giving police mandatory arrest authority in domestic disputes. Overzealous or inconsistent application of this authority has resulted in both the abuser and victim being taken off to jail, thus subjecting the victim to double peril. Not only is she abused, but she is taken off to jail because her husband said she hit him during the dispute.

Clarification of the mandatory arrest legislation has now been implemented in states, such as Washington, to give law enforcement officers better guidelines for their handling of a complaint. If there is evidence of injury or the likelihood of injury, the officer will arrest the batterer. If the batterer has left the scene, the police are obligated to search for a specified period of time, such as four hours.

Under the mandatory arrest law in Washington State, a batterer who is arrested must post bail. Batterers cannot be released on their personal recognizance. They must also sign a no-contact order which requires that there be absolutely no contact with the victim for one year. This includes telephone, mail, third party, or direct contact with the spouse. There are perhaps only four to six states that have such legislation at the time of this writing, but the result is significantly more protection for the victims.

If the offender is very drunk and there is potential for injury, but no obvious injury to anyone on the premises, the officer may make the determination to take the person to a detoxification unit rather than make an arrest.

The officer will advise the victim of the right to file an assault warrant or to take other possible action, and the officer may attempt to mediate a cooling-off time. Sometimes the police are able to make referrals to community agencies and to offer transportation to the magistrate's office (to file a warrant) or to a safe place. In a situation where the victim has fled the home, the police may offer to notify the victim when the spouse will be arrested so that she can return home and safely pick up the children and/or belongings.

Temporary restraining orders. Only a few states have a mandatory arrest law, so in the remaining states the chances of the police taking action are better if the woman has obtained a peace bond or a temporary restraining order. A peace bond requires the man to put up a certain amount of money, which he forfeits if he breaks his peace with the person. Failure to post the bond can result in imprisonment. The peace bond may not be available in all states, so you should check with someone familiar with the law in your area.

A temporary restraining order is a legal document issued by a judge, and it can be obtained without the abuser's presence. It requires the husband to stay away from the wife or to refrain from offensive conduct for a specific period of time. A restraining order is usually good for ten days. After the initial ten-day period, the man has the right to contest the order. A hearing can be held to determine whether or not the order should be made permanent. If the restraining order is violated, the violator can be cited for contempt of court, which is a misdemeanor. Misdemeanor charges are generally resolved by fines, probation, or court-ordered counseling. Short jail sentences are sometimes available. Civil remedies may also be available if a person is found in contempt of court.

The consequences of violating a temporary restraining order are often very slight, and certainly do not give much protection if the abuser has little respect for the law. Another problem is that historically a restraining order could be issued only after a divorce suit has been filed; if a woman was not willing to file for divorce, that form of protection was not available. Recent domestic violence laws have been altered in some states so that a dissolution procedure does not have to be initiated in order to issue a temporary restraining order.

In Washington State, for example, a Temporary Protection Order is the civil action used in domestic violence situations. This order is in effect for fourteen days and does not require divorce action. At the end of the fourteen days a hearing is held to determine whether or not a permanent order should be granted.

Again, each state will be different, so you should check with a resource such as a domestic violence hotline and become aware of the procedures available in your region. Each state has its own definition and options for civil remedies, and you should become familiar with the regulations in your area of service.

Conciliation and Mediation Services

Another approach would be the use of Christian Conciliation Services. Sponsored in many areas by the Christian Legal Society, this process is intended to be an alternative to the adversarial procedure found in most civil remedies. A conciliation service can recommend action in a dispute which can be implemented independently. They can make referrals to counseling and legal resources. Either informal or formal mediation procedures can be completed to facilitate agreements emphasizing mutual consideration and biblical principles.

The key ingredient is the requirement that both parties agree to a binding form of mediation. At the point of crisis intervention, getting both parties to agree on such a procedure will be most unlikely. The balance of power in most violent relationships is heavily weighted toward the abuser. There is the possibility the mediation process will end up focusing on what the victim does that displeases her spouse, rather than giving attention to the fact the abuser is committing a crime and must stop. Most violent men need an authority figure, definite structure, and punitive consequences to direct them to change their behavior. Mediation may not be able to fulfill these functions, particularly during the crisis phase.

The counselor should have this information available, however, as it might be appropriate later in the process. Check your local area for the availability of conciliation or mediation services. The national office of the Christian Legal Society can be contacted for referral assistance.[14]

Commitment of Abuser to Psychiatric Hospital

Unless the abuser is willing to enter a hospital, this option has limited possibilities. The involuntary commitment laws vary from state to state, but do have some common procedures. The process begins when any concerned person initiates a call to the involuntary commitment team or the police. If the mental health unit is called, a "flying squadron" of mental health professionals may come to see the person in question. Their purpose is to make a determination of whether or not the abuser could be committed against his will. If there is a question of endangerment, the police may be involved and can take the person to a mental health facility where the evaluation is done.

The determination is based on whether or not the person is judged to be of high danger to himself or to others. The criteria is pretty stringent, and almost requires the person to have a gun to his head or pointed at his wife.

If the team believes a person to be at risk to himself or others, that person will be immediately taken to a mental health facility for observation. This period usually lasts for seventy-two hours. At the end of that time one of three things can happen: The person may be judged no longer at risk and released; the abuser may voluntarily agree to enter into treatment; a petition can be filed to commit the person for up to fourteen days. If the person still meets the criteria for commitment after the two-week period, the formal legal process continues, possibly involving a jury trial, which can result in commitment for three to six months.

Most involuntary commitments are terminated after the initial seventy-two hour period because most people cannot be shown, at that moment, to be dangerous to themselves or others. At any point they can voluntarily keep themselves in treatment, but it is difficult to maintain the criteria for involuntary procedures.

By the time most pastors or counselors become involved, the abuser is probably well into the remorse phase of the battering cycle. It would be unusual if the husband could not exert enough self-control to pass the inspection of the involuntary commitment team. However, you should know the procedures in your area—should the need present itself in a crisis situation.

Other Options

Violence-prone families may be receptive to services only during the crisis phase. The pastor or counselor should first focus on helping the family handle the immediate crisis. The pastor could have an advantage over secular professionals in helping bring about long-term effects. The violent family may have more of a commitment to a church relationship than to an outside community agency. Once the crisis is past, the church still has an opportunity to be a caring community.

If families are unwilling to work toward long-range treatment and goals once the crisis is alleviated, the counselor should not pressure them. Just make it clear that resources are available, should they want to use them. The counselor should always keep in mind the cyclic nature of family violence. It is probably going to happen again unless the basic methods of coping are changed. A pastor or church staff should contact the family on an ongoing basis as a natural part of the church's relationship with the family.

Be alert for potential harm to the children after the crisis has passed. Some type of monitoring of the family may need to be done, in spite of their resistance. Usually monitoring for the welfare of the children will be done by a community agency, such as Child Protective Services. It is wise for the pastor or counselor to establish a working relationship with several professionals in such agencies to ensure consistent and effective follow-up.

POTENTIAL RISK TO HELPING PROFESSIONALS

Since situations of family violence are potentially volatile, they can present a substantial risk to anyone who becomes involved with the family. A counselor or pastor may be especially at risk when the abusive husband sees intervention as a threat to the status quo. National statistics indicate there are more police injuries incurred in responding to domestic violence calls than any other category.

For this reason, the pastor or counselor should take precautions to minimize personal risk. Interview family members in a neutral, safe setting. Don't get caught talking to a victim on a park bench at midnight. When possible, have your spouse or a colleague present when interviewing an abuser. If an abused wife meets with you late at night, make sure your spouse, staff member, or other person is present. All you need is for an already jealous-prone husband to catch you comforting his wife late on a Saturday night on the sofa in the church office.

The basic principle here is: don't try to deal with family violence by yourself. A team approach is needed, not only for safety reasons, but because violent families have a multitude of needs and will need to draw on many resources to work for change.

Once the safety issues are resolved and a sense of direction is established for the family, attention can be given to the longer term treatment and prevention ideas. That will be the focus of the next chapter.

CHAPTER FOUR

TREATMENT OF BATTERED WOMEN

SHARON SAT NERVOUSLY in the waiting room, twisting the strap of her purse around and around her fingers. As the counselor came to greet her, she noticed the Ace bandage wrapped around Sharon's wrist and bruises on her arms and face. While walking into the counselor's office, Sharon favored the left side of her body and winced noticeably when she sat down. When asked why she came, Sharon relayed a string of horrible beatings and verbal abuse at the hands of her husband. Only after months of urging by one of her close friends had Sharon contacted a counselor. With great fear, Sharon scheduled the appointment with a counselor who had been recommended as a committed Christian who had helped many victims of violence.

Sharon expressed waves of emotion as she vacillated from anger to remorse. But she knew she was right when she forced her husband to leave the home after beating her and threatening to kidnap the children. Her immediate concern was the Order of Protection hearing coming up in four days. Sharon's attorney had told her she would have to testify in front of the judge and her husband about the details of her battering. She wasn't sure she could face it. Her mother-in-law had called several times pleading with Sharon to drop the proceedings. Sharon's current concern was whether or not she should go ahead and seek the permanent order to keep her husband from returning home.

Counselors may work with many similar cases of abuse. But most of us never cease to be amazed at the anguish caused when a victim of abuse makes the effort to extricate herself from an abusive situation.

COUNSELING PRIORITIES AND THERAPEUTIC ISSUES

When confronted with a case of spousal abuse, the counselor should follow this list of priorities. The highest priority is to protect the victim. Using any combination of legal and social services, the victim and her children should be relieved of the threat of violence and abuse. Often safety is possible only by separating the couple. If the wife has gone to a safe house or shelter, the staff of that facility will play an important part in ensuring her safety.

The counselor should also make sure the wife has a plan for escape to safety if her husband becomes violent again. The plan should be specific and detailed. It should include the manner of transportation, a place to stay, whom to call for help, financial arrangements, and both short- and long-range plans for work or school. Of course, the husband should not know the specifics of the plan.

If the wife has filed assault charges or for an Order of Protection or restraint, she will need a great deal of support. Many pressures can be applied to the victim that can leave her with strong ambivalent feelings about her decisions. The counselor can be instrumental in giving support and encouraging the victim to draw on her network of family and friends. Be alert to the possibility of the husband engaging in strong lobbying efforts through that same network to get the wife to change her mind. All sorts of guilt can be induced by family members who have been duped by a remorseful husband. The sympathetic relatives may well tell the wife her husband has changed his ways and that she should allow him to return home.

The next priority is to implement the combination of programs and resources that will lead to a termination of the violent behavior. Whether he acts voluntarily or by the order of a court, the abuser must get into a treatment program that will teach him nonviolent ways to deal with stress and conflict. Sometimes it takes a jail sentence to convince the batterer that his methods are not acceptable. Whatever the method, punitive or therapeutic, the goal is to stop the violence.

The final priority is restoration of the relationship. Many pastors and counselors tend to move prematurely to some form of marriage counseling in domestic violence situations. This places the wife back in a destructive relationship before the behavior has had a chance to change, and it increases the likelihood that the cycle of violence will be repeated. Only when the husband has made significant progress in controlling his violence should a focus on marriage counseling begin.

The preceding chapter dealt with initial intervention procedures that served to protect the victim of abuse. This chapter will focus on the major topics that must be included in the more lengthy process of helping the couple stop the violent behavior and restore the relationship when possible.

Assuming the first priority of safety from further abuse has been met, the counseling can move to other areas of concentration. The next phase is usually centered around whether or not to remain in the marriage. This decision is greatly influenced by the reaction of the husband and the degree of commitment to the relationship.

The woman, if married, has several options: She can return to the situation with no guarantee of changes, leave the relationship, return on the condition that the violence stops, or return only after being convinced the husband has learned alternative ways of behaving. Factors such as fear, economic dependency, and desire to save the marriage can weigh heavily in the woman's decision-making. The counselor has the tough job of helping the woman maintain a sense of responsibility for her decisions. This is difficult because many battered wives have trouble making decisions and taking appropriate action on their own behalf.[1]

Walker reports the most difficult aspect of counseling involves a battered woman's inclination to manipulate. The tendency to manipulate may subside when the stress level is low, but it is always there. The behavior was reinforced by its effectiveness in avoiding or slowing down the tension building in the first phase of the violence cycle. As a result, the manipulation can be almost automatic. The woman can become frightened of the counselor's offers of help. If still living with the batterer, she may be afraid that any changes in the relationship caused by the counseling could set off her husband's anger. The counselor may view this wariness or reluctance to trust as paranoia. But it should be accepted as a natural outgrowth of living a life of terror. In order to be successful at manipulation, the woman must always be on the alert for ways to keep from setting off her husband's anger. This can appear to be a frantic hysterical reaction, but makes sense when related to the wife's goal of establishing a stress-free environment for her husband.[2]

This distorted thinking—that she can always keep her husband from getting angry or violent—must become a vital focus of the therapy. The counselor must realize that the woman has a very real basis for her reluctance to make changes. The woman's fears must be taken seriously. This acceptance and understanding will help the woman relax and trust the counseling process. She may then be able to look at the reality of her beliefs, and eliminate some of her distorted assumptions. This will allow her to consider less emotionally and physically dangerous methods of achieving a balance in her family.

Even after repeated episodes of violence, the victim will often minimize the situation after an immediate crisis has passed. The beaten and bruised wife may have come to the pastor requesting a place to hide from her rampaging husband. Three days later, this same woman will turn around and intend to go home to an apparently remorseful husband. The counselor may need to repeat discussions of previous attacks, having the victim include some of the violent details, to help convince or remind both the victim and the counselor of the dangers.

With these general features in mind, the counselor should help the woman explore her options: if, when, and how should she go back to her husband? This discussion should include how she would carry out her plan by drawing on her personal, family, and community resources. When one has become very skilled at being helpless, deciding what to do and how to do it is not an easy task.

The following discussion parallels the characteristics of battered women presented in the earlier chapter. This time I will highlight ways to help alleviate each problem area.

Low Self-Esteem

The battered woman has probably grown up with a low opinion of herself. In addition, her husband has likely ridiculed and criticized her, leaving extreme doubts about her ability to function without him. One of the major goals of counseling the victimized woman is for her to grow to love herself in spite of her abusive history. This will occur slowly. Improved self-esteem results from many different activities. But the following ideas can serve as a basic springboard into application and exploration.

These concepts, summarized from *Transformed by Thorns*,[3] can be used with any client, including victims of abuse, who have a basic understanding of the Christian faith. Sensitivity should be used when determining the right time and manner for presenting this type of material in the counseling sequence.

For the Christian, self-esteem is comprised of three building blocks: A Sense of Being, a Sense of Purpose, and a Sense of Ministry.

Sense of Being

This first element in self-esteem requires us to come to an understanding of our fundamental nature. It asks the question, "Who am I?"

We need an accurate vision of our personal possibilities. In Christ, we are whole and complete (2 Cor. 5:17; Col. 3:10). If we can understand and accept ourselves, whether victims or not, we will grow toward that essential completeness.

Our Sense of Being can start with the admission of weakness. We may have to acknowledge the existence of personality defects, social inadequacies, or spiritual failures. It may not be pleasant. The victim of violence has endured injustice and made some poor decisions. But without this admission, growth cannot occur.

Self-love

Developing a Sense of Being doesn't stop with the recognition of weakness and inadequacies. The process must move on to an appropriate love of self.

The reason failure or trauma can be stepping stones to improved self-esteem resides in the fact of God's unconditional love for us (John 3:16; 16:27). It's a major step forward for a person to realize he or she is loved regardless of personal failures. We have done nothing to deserve God's love, yet it is freely given (Rom. 5:15–17).

The first time the Bible mentions self-love is in Leviticus 19:18: "Do not seek revenge or bear a grudge against one of your people, but love your neighbor as yourself. I am the LORD."

The great commandment given in Mark 12:29–31 summarizes the most important of all the commandments of God. To love God, to love our neighbor, and to love oneself—the rest of our Christian life hinges on our fulfillment of this commandment.

The statement to "love your neighbor" is repeated several times in Scripture, but never without the command to love yourself (Rom. 13:9; Gal. 5:14; James 2:8). God knows it's important for us to love ourselves, even though we don't naturally do a very good job of it.

It is a *fact* that God loves us unconditionally. We are fearfully and wonderfully made (Ps. 139:13–16). We are the product of God's workmanship (Eph. 2:10). We are created in the image of God. His likeness resides in each of us (Gen. 1:26). Furthermore, God likes what he sees in us (Gen. 1:31). He didn't take a look, see some imperfections, and say, "Oops, I'd better try again."

God values us enough that he seeks our worship (John 4:23). Christ, his Son, accepts us as we are with no strings attached (John 6:37). We are precious in God's eyes (Is. 43:4). We are important enough to God that he allowed the spilling of the blood of his Son, Jesus Christ, for our benefit (1 Pet. 1:18, 19).

Further, we have been adopted by God and made sons and daughters equal to Jesus Christ (Rom. 8:14–17)!

These are the facts of our value and importance to God. To assist in developing a Sense of Being we must help the victim of abuse *know* these facts.

The next crucial step is to help the client *accept* the love God has given to us. For many, it is difficult to simply receive his gift. The battered wife will need to learn to become aware of her own needs and expectations. This will be difficult. She has spent so much time making sacrifices, she will feel guilty doing something good for herself. She may need to learn how to receive, just as Jesus did in allowing the woman to wash his hair with expensive perfume (Mark 14:3–9).

Many try to earn God's love by being extra good. Others try to qualify by suffering pain. A few battered wives may have tried to justify their abuse as suffering for Christ's sake. This is faulty thinking. The truth is, all we have to do is accept what is freely given.

Other Components of Sense of Being

Learning to love ourselves and learning to accept God's love is the foundation of a complete Sense of Being. But once this is established, there are additional building blocks to add in response to the "Who am I?" question. These include interests, abilities, and spiritual gifts. All of these components will arise as the victim of battering learns to take control of her life, as she learns to make decisions based on an appropriate love for herself.

Psychological testing, for example, might reveal interests and abilities that would guide the counselee into the best kind of career or training opportunities. Often victims of abuse discover undeveloped talents and skills awaiting refinement.

These may not have been pursued earlier because they would have proved too threatening to insecure husbands.

Sense of Purpose

The next stepping stone in helping the battered woman develop a complete self-image is to address the issue of our purpose for living. The question is "Why am I here?" A Sense of Purpose gives direction to our lives. If we don't know where we are going, we may very well get lost. Knowing why God placed us here will give us a compass bearing so we can cooperate with his intention.

Genesis 1:26 tells of our assignment by God to have lordship over creation: "Let us make man in our image, in our likeness, and let them rule over the fish of the sea and the birds of the air, over the livestock, over all the earth, and over all the creatures that move along the ground."

From the beginning, God has given men and women the task of subduing and ruling over the earth as God's representatives (Gen. 9:2; Ps. 8:6). We are here to be of service to God. We are called to worship and honor our Creator (Deut. 26:10; Ps. 95:6; 96:9). We are asked to be wise and good stewards over creation, just as a loving and obedient son would respond to his father (Luke 19:13; 1 Cor. 4:2; 1 Pet. 4:10; Rom. 14:12).

As children of God, our destiny is to enjoy fellowship with our Father while standing in awe of him as our Creator and Maker (Gen. 28:15; Exod. 25:22; Ps. 34:18; Matt. 28:20; Acts 17:27).

Our calling is to be God's representatives on earth. As stewards of all that he created, we have the major purpose of bearing fruit. "You did not choose me, but I chose you to go and bear fruit—fruit that will last. Then the Father will give you whatever you ask in my name" (John 15:16).

This Scripture and others (Matt. 3:8; Rom. 7:4; Phil. 1:11; Col. 1:10) encourage us to use our abilities and our gifts in service for others. Then the fruit of love, joy, peace, patience, kindness, goodness, faithfulness, gentleness, and self-control will be planted, nourished, and multiplied (Gal. 5:22, 23).

This Sense of Purpose becomes our long-range goal. The nagging questions, "Why do we exist?" "What gives meaning to life?" "Where is this all heading?" and "Why am I here?" are answered by God's directive to bear fruit. We can know why God placed us here. In spite of an abusive history, a victim can find hope in her reason for existence.

A fully developed self-esteem that can stand up against the rigors of competition, changing values, family violence, and other frustrations, must include a solid Sense of Purpose. A person's Sense of Purpose is fulfilled by producing fruit. Focusing on the nature of a person's fruit and principles for increasing her productivity will give direction and meaning. A victim can know where she is going and how to get there. Self-esteem and self-confidence are enhanced as a result of this process.

Sense of Ministry

This component in self-awareness asks the question, "How am I to serve?" The battered woman has experienced significant isolation. This component speaks to that feeling of separation and abandonment and focuses on her place in the body of believers.

A Sense of Ministry provides focus on *how* Christians participate in the daily workings of the kingdom. Our ministry gives us a blueprint for carrying out our purpose. Our ministry can include our vocation, as well as our function within the family and the larger community of believers. While our Sense of Purpose tells us that we are to bear fruit, the Sense of Ministry gives us clarity as to *where* and *how* that fruit is to influence the rest of the Christian community.

This step in self-esteem is necessary because we are all called to be ministers of God (Isa. 61:6). Each Christian is part of the priesthood of believers (Exod. 19:6; 1 Pet. 2:5). This means there are no positions of a "higher calling." We are *all* called to glorify God and to serve. As believers we are all equally accountable for how well our responsibilities are carried out. A paid clergyman, who serves full time, is no more accountable (and has no higher calling within his or her Sense of Ministry) than is a Christian bookkeeper, firefighter or truck driver.

Each person has been given different talents and abilities.

Each is exposed to different opportunities. Our common task is to put to wise use what we've been given. Our Sense of Ministry is fulfilled when we apply our abilities and gifts to the purpose of reproducing fruit.

That sense of where and how we are to minister builds upon our knowledge of ourselves. Our Sense of Being tells us *what* we have to work with, and our Sense of Ministry tells us *where* and *how* to use it.

Once the client has internalized most of these components of self-esteem, the counselor may find it helpful to have the woman think about how she would alter some of the incidents in her abusive relationship. Her new identity and God-given power to take responsible action will help reverse the learned helplessness that was such a dominant part of her past. While the past is not changed, the ability to think about alternate forms of responding will help build her sense of control and self-esteem.

UNREALISTIC HOPE

Most abused women, particularly if they are Christians, want their marriage to succeed. In spite of the pain they have experienced, they have sincere love and loyalty for their husbands. Counselors must help these women distinguish between hope and the actions that help.

Hope has resulted from the cyclic nature of battering. The cycle has included periods of calm followed by escalating tension, which leads to violence. After the violent episode, the husband, much like many alcoholics, will promise to change. The wife clings to these promises of change. She wants things to be better. For a time, the husband may become loving and kind. This reinforces the wife's hopeful attitude. The honeymoon is temporary, however, because in most violent relationships, the tension begins to build again, leading to another episode of abuse.

There is nothing wrong with realistic hope, particularly hope built on God's promises. But the victim of violence needs encouragement and direction on how to avoid the trap of appeasement. Her hope is partially built on her belief that she can keep her husband from getting angry and violent. She cannot control her husband's feelings and methods of coping. But she will need help to learn to back off. Many abused wives are rescuers. They take responsibility for the problems of their husbands, and the husbands are perfectly content to let the wives take the blame. The end result is that the men are able to go about their lives without serious interruption. Neither do they have to experience many negative consequences for their behavior.

Realistic hope can result from the wives learning to enact a "love must be tough" response. This is the type of response suggested by Dr. James Dobson in response to a letter from a victim of battering.

> In essence, Laura is being emotionally blackmailed by her husband. He is saying by his behavior, "Do what I wish or I'll beat you." She must break out of that tyranny while she's still young enough to cope with the consequences. This might be accomplished by forcing the matter to a crisis. . . . I would suggest that Laura choose the most absurd demand her husband makes, and then refuse to consent to it. Let him rage if he must rage. . . . Separate living quarters may be necessary until her husband settles down. He should be made to think that he has lost his wife over this issue, and in fact, I would recommend that she not return until there is reason to believe that he is willing to change. If that takes a year, so be it. When (and if) her husband acknowledges that he has a severe problem and promises to deal with it if she'll come home, a period of negotiations should follow. . . . I don't believe anyone should be required to live in that kind of terror, and in fact, to do so is to tolerate a behavior which could eventually prove fatal to the marriage, anyway.[4]

The only things I might alter in Dr. Dobson's recommendation would be asking the husband to leave, rather than having the wife find other living arrangements, and suggesting that the wife not agree to let him come home until there has been evidence of change. Too often a husband will promise to make changes or will promise to seek counseling, but not follow through once his wife is again living with him. Once his comfort level is reestablished, his motivation declines dramatically.

The initial crisis of separation may have already taken place by this point in the counseling process, but this example illustrates the necessity of a woman taking action. The counselor must take every opportunity to instruct the victim about the necessity of taking action rather than lapsing into her passive learned helplessness.

ISOLATION

Battered women are often socially and emotionally isolated. The counselor or pastor should encourage efforts at reestablishing family and social connections. It is a process that should not be limited to individual counseling. The victim needs to be exposed to other women who have experienced similar traumas. These groups can be formed within a shelter or in conjunction with a counseling center or domestic violence agency.

If carefully formed and monitored, self-help groups might be established through the church. This could help meet the need for mutual support and sharing, but with an added spiritual foundation. The church-related groups should probably contain women who have had similar experiences. Do not place a battered woman in a Bible study group where pressure will be placed on the victim to return to her husband, forgive, or submit prematurely. Several churches might combine personnel and conduct groups if there are not enough women from any one congregation to form a support group.

It might be advisable to try to bring the extended family together for several counseling sessions. Issues, such as continued safety procedures, channels of communication, how members might support the relearning of habit patterns, and methods of support, could be discussed. The counselor should be alert to destructive qualities in the greater family. It is likely the wife learned some of her victim role from her parents.

If the wife is experiencing some pressure from her family or from her husband's family, it might be good to draw them into some of the counseling activity. The victim will need your support to stick by her decisions that prove unpopular with her family. Direct contact with them may help clarify the reasons for the wife's decisions.

Not all of the woman's social contacts should be heavy duty in nature. Encourage her to play and have some fun. Have her join a bowling league, coed softball team, or other such active groups. Exercise is good for coping with stress, and it gives a chance to make friends and find support.

Isolation, from the point of view of the victim, may be seen as abandonment. A victimized woman may have experienced abandonment by her friends, family, pastor, and attorney. Whether by her own seclusion or by the action of others, the woman may feel everyone has let her down. It may be very natural for her to believe God has also abandoned her. Give her reassurance. Point out that the apostle Paul experienced stonings, beatings, floggings, shipwrecks, and imprisonment, yet his God did not leave him (2 Cor. 11:23–28). Passages such as Romans 8:38, 39 are strong statements about God's promise not to leave us alone. "For I am convinced that neither death nor life, neither angels nor demons, neither the present nor the future, nor any powers, neither height nor depth, nor anything else in all creation, will be able to separate us from the love of God that is in Christ Jesus our Lord."

Another aspect of isolation is ignorance of community resources. This may have been covered during the crisis intervention phase of the process. But make sure the victim has phone numbers and descriptions of various social and legal agencies. Resources should include: shelters, counseling services, abused women's support groups, local sexual assault centers, adult protection services, legal services for abused women, sources for protection orders, crisis phone line, drug and alcohol treatment, sources for financial assistance such as Social Security, welfare, or Aid to Dependent Children, churches, day-care programs, career planning and placement centers, and other agencies or programs that may exist in your community.

Don't rush the socialization process. The victim will be battling a great deal of fear and hesitancy. She needs to be stretched in this area, but not overextended.

EMOTIONAL DEPENDENCY

The term *learned helplessness* has been used to explain why women find it difficult to escape a battering relationship. Early studies with laboratory animals demonstrated that if they were repeatedly and randomly shocked, they became unable to escape from painful situations. They were unable to escape even when a method of escape was available and easily understood. It has been assumed that if animals or humans experience continued pain and trauma over which they have no control, motivation decreases.[5]

Battered women have the same experience. Their attempts to control the violence do not work, so over time they respond with a type of depression or helplessness. The motivation to do something different is reduced to zero.

Therefore, if a woman is to escape violence in her marriage she must learn new methods of survival. Apathy, indifference, depression, and avoidance do not work. The woman must learn to activate healthy anger rather than getting depressed or blaming herself. Her thinking must change. Rather than continue the distortions that things will eventually get better or that nothing can be done to change things, she must learn healthier thoughts and actions.

The use of cognitive restructuring and appropriate ways to channel anger have been shown to be valuable with abused women. Books such as *Telling Yourself the Truth*, by William Backus and Marie Chapian, and *Feeling Good*, by David Burns, can be helpful in identifying destructive thought patterns and developing positive ones.

The following ideas based on a biblical approach to cognitive restructuring of worry and anxiety will illustrate how the pastor or other counselor can help the battered woman move from extreme dependence on another person to an appropriate dependence on God.

Changing Thoughts

God doesn't transform us by the elimination of our problems but by the renewing of our minds. The goal is to learn how our inner thoughts can be changed to produce a more productive mind. The key to eliminating worry is to place our trust in something solid, predictable, and helpful for growth.[6]

An excellent passage of Scripture dealing with anxiety is Philippians 4:6–9. It begins by admonishing us to "Do not be anxious about anything." Then we are told to tell God about our needs and to give thanks. And then comes the important concept for this discussion. We are to let our *minds dwell* only on those things that are true, honorable, pure, and lovely. Here we have it again. We are to *think* of good things. If we think on the negative, our mind will be filled with worry and anxiety, depression and grief.

For the battered wife, her experience is filled with legitimate fear and pain. Nothing in this discussion is intended to minimize the reality of her abuse. But the unhealthy overdependence on an abusive husband must be redirected. There are very appropriate reasons to love and cherish a spouse. But the first priority for the Christian is to place our allegiance on One who does not fail. The pathway to emotional freedom is correct thinking.

Listen to what God says in his Word about the importance of a sound and steadfast mind:

A heart at peace gives life to the body (Prov. 14:30).

You will keep in perfect peace him whose mind is steadfast, because he trusts in you (Isa. 26:3).

Do not conform any longer to the pattern of this world, but be transformed by the renewing of your mind. Then you will be able to test and approve what God's will is— his good, pleasing and perfect will (Rom. 12:2).

Therefore, prepare your minds for action; be self-controlled; set your hope fully on the grace to be given you when Jesus Christ is revealed (1 Pet. 1:13).

The major step in replacing our misbelief is to claim the facts of God's promises—to place our faith in his trustworthiness, instead of our own, or in the promises of an abusive spouse. Our prayer should be like that of the psalmist, "Create in me a pure heart, O God, and renew a steadfast spirit within me" (Ps. 51:10).

Our own faith will have its ups and downs, trials and tribulations. But we have a choice about what we learn from those experiences. The choice is to depend on our own understanding and resources for solving life's frustrations, or to trust in the Lord God of Abraham and all generations. "Trust in the LORD with all your heart and lean not on your own understanding; in all your ways acknowledge him, and he will make your paths straight" (Prov. 3:5, 6).

In order to change our thinking we must understand the nature of faith. Faith is knowledge acted upon. We must exercise our mind and choose to believe that God is who he says he is, that he can deliver what he promises.

Paul stated it this way, "For I know—I perceive, have knowledge of and am acquainted with Him—Whom I have believed (adhered to and trusted in and relied on), and I am [positively] persuaded that He is able to guard and keep that which has been entrusted to me and which I have committed [to Him], until that day" (2 Tim. 1:12 AMPLIFIED).

Our knowledge is based on these facts:

1. God cannot lie (Heb. 6:18); he has never failed to keep his promises (1 Kings 8:56); he has guaranteed to be faithful (Deut. 7:9; 1 Cor. 1:9).

2. The nature of his promises is that he knows our limits (Isa. 43:1–3; 1 Cor. 10:13; 2 Pet. 2:9); he will deliver us from afflictions (Ps. 30:5; 41:3); he will comfort us in hard times (Isa. 43:2); his Grace is sufficient for our weakness (2 Cor. 12:9); he will take care of our bodily needs (Ps. 37:3); he will answer our prayers (Mark 11:24); he will help remove obstacles (Luke 17:6); he will give us spiritual fullness and light (John 6:35; 12:46), provide power for service (John 14:12), insure our salvation (Rom. 1:16), and give us eternal life (John 3:15).

Now that's quite a list of promises! The choice is ours. To trust in our own understanding or to place our faith in One who has never lied, never failed, and who offers continuous help and security. Keep in mind, he doesn't promise to eliminate the problems in life, but to help us work through them to his glory.

Acting on New Thoughts

The next step in reorienting a client's perspective on worry or overdependence on a spouse is to help her act upon her knowledge with a renewed mind. Philippians 4:9 says, "Whatever you have learned or received or heard from me, or seen in me—put it into practice. And the God of peace will be with you." Faith is of no value unless we act upon it. The Philippians 4 passage ends with an emphasis on *action.*

First we are to think on those things that are good, and then we are to act on what we know. The same principle is seen in Abraham. Look at the action words present in the biblical account of the sacrifice of Isaac. Abraham *rose* early and *went* to the place of which God had told him.

He told his servants that he would *go, worship,* and *return* to them. Abraham then *took* the wood, fire, knife, and Isaac, and the two of them *walked* on together.

When they got to the place of sacrifice, Abraham *built* the altar, *arranged* the wood, *bound* and *laid* Isaac on top of the wood. Then he *stretched* out his hand and *took* the knife to *slay* his son (Gen. 22:3–13).

God then intervened and provided a ram which Abraham *took,* and *offered* in place of his son.

Because of his faith in God, Abraham was able to take action. And because of the righteousness of God, any act of faith done in his name is valid, profitable, and useful for instruction.

Changing one's thinking does not make the beatings go away. But if a wife has fallen into the habit of passive rather than active responses to life's problems, this type of encouragement and instruction can be very helpful.

TRADITIONAL VIEW OF MARRIAGE

There is nothing wrong with the "traditional" marriage, but there is a great deal wrong with a husband who uses violence to maintain his position within the marriage. Neither is it a defect in character for the battered wife to be committed to the sanctity and permanence of marriage. Her problem usually is that she hasn't been able to separate commitment from unhealthy tolerance. A good mother will not hesitate to discipline her children in love, knowing that any punishment she gives is teaching the child correct behavior. Yet that same person will be very reluctant to apply the same principle to her husband. Part of the reason, of course, is that a child will not knock your head off if sent to his room, while a husband may be able to carry out such a threat. The battered wife needs instruction and support on how to find the balance between commitment and correction.

One of the major issues for the Christian wife is the principle of submission. Many a battered wife has gone for help only to be told she was not being submissive enough. The concept of submission and its companion topic *headship,* are clearly biblical. The confusion comes because of the multitude of explanations as to their meaning. The most prevalent implication in much of Christian literature is that the secret to a happy marriage is for the wife to accept a dependent role to her husband. She is to adapt to him rather than try to change him in any way. She should not be the one who initiates changes in the family, but should cultivate her created nature to be receptive to her husband's requests. The husband is to be the focal point of the family. Events and decisions are to revolve around sacrificially meeting his needs. Ultimate responsibility and leadership of the family is ordained to the husband.

An abusive husband can place the wife in a dilemma. If she puts up with his violence she is the victim of pain. If she takes action to stop his violence, she is the victim of guilt for being outside the chain of command.

One of the most common faults of much instruction about submission and headship is the omission of the teaching of mutual subjection. The primary reference passage on submission is Ephesians 5:21–33. Paul begins with the explicit statement, "Submit to one another out of reverence for Christ." Paul realizes relationships in a family are meant to be reciprocal and accountable. There must be equal give and take in a family for growth to occur. No happiness is found when one member inevitably dominates without respect for the needs and feelings of the rest of the family.

Biblical submission also includes accountability, which involves being held responsible for what one says or does. It is something entrusted to another person. The husband asks his wife to hold him accountable, and she asks the same of him. It is love in action as the wife helps her husband grow toward wholeness by asking him to demonstrate responsibility. It is intended to work both ways.

Abusive relationships are not reciprocal. A healthy relationship requires that both parties desire to grow through mutual adaptation. The wife is not the only one who needs to adapt. The husband must find that love for his wife can motivate him to change. He may even learn to sometimes do what his wife suggests even if it conflicts with some of his own desires. The abused wife may need help to shift her perspective from the requirement that she do all of the adapting. If she never expects her husband to adapt to her needs, he is not likely to change.

Obviously, abusive marriages do not contain accountability. The husband blames his wife, economic problems, his job, or in-laws for his violent behavior. He doesn't take responsibility for his own conduct, but tries to point the finger elsewhere. Many battered wives, however, have bought into accepting the blame. Mutual submission shares accountability. The counselor needs to help the wife get rid of false guilt and unshared responsibility.

The goal of marriage is oneness (Gen. 2:24). With this goal in mind, Paul gave instruction to each marriage partner. To husbands he said, love your wives with Christ's love for the church and thus be subject to them and serve them. And to the wives he said, be subject to your husbands as to Christ and thus love them. If the concept of mutual subjection were incorporated into a violence-prone family, there is little question the violence would stop. If the couple can be instructed on how to work toward a mutual relationship, in which each is attempting to love Christ and have a servant's heart, there can be hope for the marriage.

The topics of headship and submission will be briefly developed in the next chapter dealing with treatment of the abusive male.

DEALING WITH ANGER THROUGH FORGIVENESS

There are two opposite mechanisms available for dealing with the pain and frustration of being a victim of violence. If a battered woman uses anger as her only mechanism for coping with that pain, bitterness is the guaranteed result.

On the other hand, if forgiveness is added to the initial pain, healing is the guaranteed result. What a difference! From victim to victor by the act of choosing to give up our right to judge the behavior of others, despite the severity of the injustice.

The issue of forgiveness should not be rushed. It is an important component of the healing process, but it usually should not be among the first issues to be addressed. The victim of abuse has been asked to forgive too many times already, only to be hurt again. Give her time to adjust to the many other changes taking place. Allow her the chance to develop some independence and emotional autonomy. Forcing forgiveness too early can foster a resumption of the destructive use of power by the offender. However, forgiveness is crucial to the total process and should not be ignored, just delayed.

Definition

Forgiveness includes awareness that violence inflicted by another person was definitely wrong. Legitimate anger can be directed at the injustice. A battered wife will need a degree of anger to energize her into making changes in the relationship. She should not be counseled to give up her anger. The healing comes by actively choosing to give up the desire to seek revenge or to impose and carry out the sentence. It requires giving up the right to impose justice. Forgiveness involves the canceling of a debt (Matt. 18:32–34).

A number of years ago, Mr. Floyd Pettingill, the father of a student of mine, was shot in the head during an attempted robbery of his drugstore. He survived, although a bullet destroyed the sight in one eye and remained lodged in his brain.

91

A young man, Mike, was later arrested, convicted of the assault and was sentenced to the state prison. Several people in the Christian community who were involved in prison ministries became acquainted with the assailant, and eventually one of them told Mr. Pettingill she had been writing to Mike.

Mr. Pettingill could have dwelt on his bitterness. He could have focused on how the incident had cost him half of his sight, considerable pain, and financial loss. But, instead, he chose to correspond with Mike and express his desire to see the young man get his life turned around. Later, when Mike was paroled, Mr. Pettingill witnessed to him face-to-face. That testimony—of the man who was left for dead—was that God had placed in his heart the ability to love and forgive, even though he still had the constant reminder of the traumatic incident.

To forgive doesn't mean that the guilty party should not face the legal or financial consequences of his action. The robber was serving time in prison as partial payment for his crime. But the victim of the shooting, Floyd Pettingill, could still have claimed an emotional right for further vengeance. Apparently, he didn't and, as a result, an angry and troubled young man was exposed to the unconditional love of Christ.

Forgiveness is an act of the will, not a result of feelings. Seldom will an abused wife *feel* like granting forgiveness to someone who has injured her. She should not cover over her feelings. It is very important for a victim of abuse to acknowledge her irritation, wrath, or indignation. But she should be encouraged to not stay fixed upon those feelings. The wrongdoing of the person who trespassed against the victim does not entitle her to the sin of revenge or continued bitterness.

I have heard battered wives report their rage and intense desire to hurt their husbands who had inflicted bodily harm and humiliation on them. While I can appreciate the source of the anger, their victim status will not be healed by their becoming the aggressor.

The use of anger logs, journals, diaries, or role-playing may be appropriate to help the battered wife articulate her anger. It is important the feelings be expressed. But then the process of healing should continue beyond the anger.

Someone Has Got to Pay

The major ingredient in being able to grant forgiveness is to satisfy the basic requirement that someone has got to pay. If a wife has been the victim of marital rape, beaten with a stick, or if she has seen her house destroyed by a raving maniac, she will want to be satisfied that someone is going to pay for that pain and loss. A sin has been committed and she wants a pound of flesh in return. She knows the facial scars will remain, the broken vase cannot be replaced. The human tendency is to want assurance that some legitimate sacrifice is endured by the one who committed the offense.

Against this desire for payment, the death of Christ on the Cross begins to take on new meaning. It was only when the substitutionary atonement of Jesus Christ is presented in a down-to-earth manner that victims can break free from the bondage of bitterness. Isaiah 53:10, 11 is a crucial passage in this discussion.

> *But the Lord was pleased to crush Him, putting Him to grief;* If He would render Himself as a guilt offering, He will see His offspring, He will prolong His days, and the good pleasure of the Lord will prosper in His hand. *As a result of the anguish of His soul, He will see it and be satisfied;* By His knowledge the Righteous One, My Servant will justify the many, As He will bear their iniquities (italics added, NASB).

The phrases in italics are crucial to this discussion. It pleased God that Christ was crushed and put to grief. Because God is just, and sin had to be punished, it was satisfying to God that the penalty for sin was paid. It cost God his only Son, but death, the ultimate price for an offense, was paid by the one least likely to deserve it. The punishment for wrongdoing was handed down by the ultimate Judge, God almighty. Jehovah God who had said, "You shall have no other gods before me" (Exod. 20:3) passed supreme judgment on sin in the world and found satisfaction in the fact that Christ's blood had been spilled.

It is at this point that an emotional breakthrough can be made by those who harbor great bitterness because of injustices inflicted upon them. Through the use of visualization, meditation on Scripture such as the Isaiah passage above, and even symbolic action, the burden of anger and rage can be vented toward Christ's death on the Cross. Clients of mine have written the offenses on paper and then burned them, or tied the paper to a rock and thrown the rock into a lake.

Yes, somebody has to pay for the offenses imposed upon the victim. And that "somebody" is Jesus Christ himself.

If a client has difficulty in resolving anger about past hurts, have her try dumping the load of anger and revenge on the thorn-scarred head of Jesus. Have her take the perspective of God for a few moments and place the source of her hatred on the Cross with Christ. Do not limit it to an intellectual experience, but encourage her to express her gut-level feelings. Have her vent her pent-up wrath in the direction of the wooden instrument of death planted on the hill called Golgotha almost two thousand years ago. When her desire is to strike out and physically injure her tormentor, have her imagine the pain suggested by this verse, "But he was wounded for our transgressions, he was bruised for our iniquities: the chastisement of our peace was upon him; and with his stripes we are healed" (Isa. 53:5 KJV).

The victim can actually find pleasure, just as God found pleasure, in the substitutionary death of Christ. Not in some morbid sense of seeing someone die on the gallows, but in the sense of knowing that justice has been served. Transgressions have occurred, but the price of pain and death has been paid. At this point the battered woman can be released from the stronghold of seeking her own revenge. Christ atoned for the person who offended her.

A young man came to see me because his girlfriend had been gang raped while she was at a party with another girl. He wanted to get even. He had several schemes for inflicting harm and damage to the group of jerks who had defiled his friend. But he was a fairly new Christian who knew his hatred was not good for his growth in the Lord. I shared with him the idea that his anger demanded that somebody had to pay for this

94

crime. I understood his feelings. His desire for revenge was natural. In fact, God had been similarly grieved millions of times over and had also demanded a just penalty. Then we discussed how the death of Jesus was not only for our sins of lying, petty thievery, jealous thoughts, etc., but that he suffered and agonized because those five drunken punks had raped his girlfriend. Someone, indeed, had already paid!

The young man's response was, "Wow, I'd never thought of it that way before. I'm still very shook up about this whole thing, but I'll think about what you have said." Later I learned his feelings did soften considerably, and the legal prosecution took care of the rest of the process.

Forgive, but Impossible to Forget

Another major roadblock is the false belief that true forgiveness requires forgetting. It is physiologically impossible to forget anything as long as the brain is intact. Every flower that has been seen, apple pie smelled, or victory celebrated is cataloged and entered into the computer banks of the mind. Technically, we do not forget anything, but the recall of that information is impeded by the collection of new and more recent experience.

A number of years ago, my grandfather had surgery on the left side of his brain to help control the shaking in his hands and arms that resulted from Parkinson's disease. The doctors cut a hole in his skull and, while Papa was completely conscious, began using electrical probes to map out the precise location of the part of the brain that controlled the muscles in his extremities. As they probed, my grandfather suddenly perceived colors and sensations that he had not experienced for years. The memory was there and the electrical stimulation activated that response in his awareness.

You may have heard the phrase, "If you don't use it, you lose it." The correct statement about memory would be, "If you don't use it, you misplace it."

If forgiveness occurs, the emotional sting or feelings of devastation are removed from the memory. To hang on to the memory without forgiveness is to nurture the resentment and allow the hurt to impede growth. If forgiveness has occurred, the recall is much different. It says, "I know what happened. It is a part of my experience, but it is over. It no longer has an emotional devastation for me. I am not going to be hindered in the present or the future by what happened. The fact of history remains, but I choose not to let the memory control me."

If a client says, "Well, I forgave him, but I can't forget," check out whether or not the task of forgiveness is complete. Forgiveness doesn't keep us from remembering, but it does keep us from dwelling on the pain.

These are the major counseling issues for the battered wife. They can be covered in either group or individual sessions. There are many other issues that will present themselves, such as coping with depression, finding employment, discipline of the children, helping the children cope with the changes, etc. But this discussion highlights the themes that seem most unique to battered wives.

Once the violence has stopped and the husband has made some efforts at learning alternative ways to cope, the attention can move to marriage counseling. At that point topics such as communication, conflict resolution, roles, and sexual adjustment can become a focus of discussion. Many sources exist for helping the counselor or pastor explore those topics, so no attempt will be made to treat them in this presentation. Authors such as H. Norman Wright, James Dobson, and David and Vera Mace are among many good sources for these areas.

CHAPTER FIVE

TREATMENT OF MEN WHO BATTER

JEFFREY ENTERED THE GROUP counseling room with an obvious chip on his shoulder. At six-feet-four and 230 pounds, who was going to argue? Almost a month earlier Jeffrey had beaten up his wife because he'd thought Beth was having an affair with a friend of his. She'd denied any involvement, but Jeffrey had lost control and Beth had ended up with forty stitches and a broken rib. Because this hadn't been the first time this had happened, Beth had called the police and Jeffrey had been arrested.

Only a few states have mandatory arrest laws. But Jeffrey's state did, so he ended up having to post bail and sign an order preventing him from having any contact with Beth until his case came to trial. His attorney had told Jeffrey the court would probably require him to complete a counseling program for men who batter. Since a new series was starting at a counseling center near his job, Jeffrey reluctantly decided to go check it out even though he hadn't been sentenced. "It never hurts to make a good impression with the judge," his lawyer had said.

As Jeffrey slumped down into a chair at the edge of the room, he surveyed the rest of the "Wife Beaters" out of the corner of his eye.

They all look like a bunch of jerks to me, he thought. *I wonder which one of these guys with the beards is the shrink?*

Before Jeffrey could ponder the situation much longer, a very ordinary man and woman entered the room and introduced themselves as Drs. Roberts and Tharrington.

GENERAL PRINCIPLES FOR TREATMENT

Men who batter their wives are also victims. They are victimized by their inability to channel their anger, lack of communication skills, fear of closeness, and their dependency on the women they abuse. The majority of abusive husbands are not monsters of the midway. In situations where emotional intimacy is not required, they do rather well. But in their marriage they are either very passive, with occasional outbursts, or continually explosive.[1]

While many social factors have been suggested as influential in causing men to be abusive, most pastors and counselors are going to have an impact on the individual level. It's at the therapeutic level that most of the following strategies will be aimed. This is appropriate because it's the individual male who transmits his violence to the next generation. The proper therapeutic interventions can help bring the disastrous abuse to an end.

There are several assumptions or principles that underlie the major forms of treatment described in this chapter.

1. Abusive anger is a learned behavior that stems out of the basic nature of humankind. As Christians, we know that all humans have sinned (Rom. 3:23). All of humanity is inclined to oppose God's plan. The form of that disobedience may change

slightly from one generation to the next. But a constant fact of history is humanity's tendency to inflict pain upon others.

Unless a person personally accepts God's work of grace, the patterns of violence and anger will continue. The abuser must move to a point where he takes ownership and responsibility for his violent expressions. The hope in this assumption is twofold. First, the consequences of sin have been paid by Jesus Christ (Rom. 6:23; 8:32). Second, if violence is learned, then it is possible to replace abusive behavior by new, constructive expressions of anger. There is a realistic hope for change.

2. The abuser is solely responsible for his own violence and abuse. No matter how many stressors there are, violence is never justified in a marriage. An argument can certainly be irritating, but no one is *made* to use violence. Choice is involved in violence, and each person must be held accountable for that choice. Most of all, the victim cannot cause or eliminate the violence of the abuser.

3. Abusive behavior may start small, but will eventually contaminate the entire relationship. Hebrews 12:15 gives us the "rotten apple" principle: "See to it that no one misses the grace of God and *that no bitter root grows up to cause trouble and defile many*" (italics added).

Abusive behavior starts in the heart of one person, but eventually the whole system is defiled. Within a violent relationship, the abuser becomes more skilled at violence and the wife becomes more skilled at being a victim. This combination of events changes how the couple thinks, feels, and acts. There are probably good parts in any relationship, but the uncontrolled anger must be stopped if the marriage is to continue. The agenda becomes one of identifying the cues, prompts, or button-pushing events that lead to violence.

4. Outward action is a product of internal thoughts. Proverbs 23:7 tells us, "For as he thinketh in his heart, so is he" (KJV). Abusive anger is a function of how a person perceives his situation and the nature of his internal self-dialogue. Violence is intensified by the self-talk of the abuser. For example, *She called me a dirty name. I can't let her get away with that*, will probably lead to some form of action to punish her. This silent

monologue and its interpretation is the mechanism that converts situations to angry feelings, and then to aggression.

5. Violent behavior is motivated by low self-esteem and a sense of powerlessness. Both victims and batterers usually will have histories of low self-esteem. This feeling of powerlessness often acts as a predisposing factor to violence. It's a vicious cycle. As a couple continues abusive interaction, the pain and frustration gets worse. This lack of effectiveness adds to their feelings of incompetency. These pessimistic feelings, in turn, create a more stressful, depressive atmosphere. The more negative the situation, the more probable abuse becomes, and the intensity of the violence increases.

Abusiveness is often an attempt to overcome personal feelings of powerlessness that lead to lowered self-image, guilt, and more feelings of powerlessness.[2]

6. Violence is likely when the couple does not have adequate problem-solving or conflict-resolution skills. Violence is used when a man doesn't know how else to solve a problem. It becomes essential for the couple to learn effective problem-solving techniques for use in their marriage as well as with relationships outside of marriage.

7. The problems of the relationship should not be the initial focus of therapy. Marriage or family counseling with the batterer present should not occur until the violence has stopped and the victim is no longer afraid. It's too dangerous to discuss the problems of the marriage until everyone is safe. Any problems with conflict resolution or communication cannot be realistically discussed while the husband is blatantly abusing power. Trust and confidence cannot be developed unless safety is achieved.[3]

THE USE OF GROUPS FOR TREATMENT

Most experts recommend a group format for working with men who are violent. Many treatment programs have emphasized separating spouses and providing separate group rehabilitation programs. Many of these programs have a strong bias toward helping the woman make a permanent break from the violent relationship. The emphasis on total separation may be based on the assumption that all battered wives wish to end their relationships. The research shows most women *do* return to their partners. Many wives want counseling help for their batterers, whom they still love.[4] Most women seeking assistance for abuse would stay in the relationship if the violence could be eliminated.[5]

Secular experience, along with the Christian value of marriage, suggests that when possible the relationship should be given a priority. The pastor or counselor should heed the warnings about starting marriage counseling prematurely, but not lose sight of the need to bring healing to the marriage.

Some counseling groups involve only men.[6] Other groups are intended to have both husband and wife as active participants.[7]

Some forms of treatment seem to focus all the blame on the male and on the society that taught him to be violent. The interpersonal perspective of spousal abuse assumes that violence occurs in the context of an ongoing relationship. The couple is not isolated from each other. The actions of the husband cause the wife to respond in certain ways, and vice versa. The entire family system, both current and historic, needs to come under inspection. Both husband and wife must take responsibility for their actions. They will both have to make changes in their reactions to each other to avoid old habits that lead to violence. The basic goal for this form of treatment is to replace abusive expressions of anger with positive expressions of anger. Anger itself is not to be eliminated. But the violent expression of anger must stop. The abusive behavior and the thoughts that produce it are the primary focus of attention.

One problem with the relationship approach is that after the crises about half of the couples are separated and/or one partner refuses conjoint counseling. Unless court ordered, or when both partners wish to work on the marriage, the counselor or pastor may find that only half of the couple is available.

Advantages of Groups

One advantage of the group approach is that members tend to confront each other more directly and perhaps more effectively than does a therapist. Many group participants have commented that they have benefited from learning that other men have similar problems. A group experience allows the members to see that their situation is not unique. Others in the group are found to be struggling with many of the same issues. Group members can serve as both positive and negative examples for one another. Having other men in the group saying, "I don't like what I'm doing and I want to stop," is a powerful model and counterconditioning to what an abuser is used to thinking.

A group experience also helps the men overcome some of the emotional isolation from other men. The group helps those who lack interpersonal skills enhance their ability to relate to others. However, some men don't want to join a group because of their shame. Professional men seem especially reluctant to join therapy groups.

After a group is established, members will often reach out to other members during times of crisis. They may find it very helpful to learn how to give and receive comfort or assistance. Often a group will choose to meet for informal support after the treatment ends. In fact, some programs now include these self-help groups, called Batterers Anonymous, as a vital part of the treatment process.[8]

Finally, group treatment is an efficient use of the therapist's time and can be less expensive for the clients.

Dealing with Resistance and Denial

Almost all clients can be expected to show some initial resistance to treatment. Resistance should be considered a natural phenomenon. As such, it should be accepted by the counselor and not opposed. Some signs of resistance can simply be ignored. Some people just need to express their individuality, test the limits, and then get on with compliance.

Sometimes a good way to approach resistance is to discuss that everybody probably has some initial reluctance to participate in treatment. Some of the sources of resistance might include:

1. Resentment. Since no one likes being told what to do without being convinced, the natural reaction is to dig in one's heels and resist.

2. Skepticism. Everyone tends to resist change. Change is unpredictable. It involves risk and uncertainty.

3. Pride. It's not easy for anyone to admit to making mistakes.

4. Embarrassment. It's difficult to talk about one's mistakes to others. There's also a tradition that a man's home is his castle; he shouldn't have to reveal to outsiders what goes on within his family.

5. Hopelessness. Many people have adjusted to frustration and uncontrollable circumstances by being apathetic, defeated, and hopeless. This is very common in victims, along with the fear that their participation in discussions will be seen as betrayal and lead to additional violence.

6. Anger. Sometimes people are mad about events occurring prior to the treatment program. They may be angry at the legal system, a mental health worker, or the police. Accept the client's complaints and move ahead with the content of counseling rather than defend the sources of anger.[9]

If the contents of the counseling process are positive and the abuser is treated with respect, the resistance will decline. Generally, don't attack resistance head on or try to argue with the client.

Denial is a very common defense mechanism used by abusers. Men who batter tend to minimize and deny their use of violence. The function of denial is to avoid responsibility for the violent behavior and the need to change. Denial can also protect the abuser from depression and guilt that can come from a serious look at his situation. Denial can be observed in the following ways:

1. Blaming the victim. If he can blame her for the abuse, then she is the one who has to change.

2. Justifying his violence. The batterer will describe an incident so the listener will conclude that his violent act was the only alternative. The focus will be on how good he is and how wrong the victim was.

3. Distorting and minimizing. The story will be accurate except that some facts will be changed to make him look good. If he broke her jaw, he will have only slapped her. If he was screaming insults for an hour, he only raised his voice a little.

4. Externalizing. He will place the reason for the abuse outside of himself. For example, he had a difficult day at work and

was stressed out, the chair got in the way, or she didn't move out of the way fast enough.

5. Omitting and lying. The story is not accurate because details are not told or fabrications are made.[10]

The denial must be broken. This can be done by asking direct questions. When blame is shifted elsewhere or there is an inconsistency, the counselor should point out the discrepancy or have the group comment. Often the group will do a better job than the leader in spotting lies and omissions.

The goal is to teach the batterer he is not in control of others, but he is always in control of himself. No one but himself can control his feelings, emotions, and thoughts.

The method suggested by Frances Purdy and Norm Nickle for breaking through the denial is to provide overwhelming information about the nature of violence, how the abuser learned to be violent and how he uses violence to control others. This process begins by defining the four types of violence: physical, sexual, emotional/environmental, and social abuse. Detailed instruction, with many examples, is given on each type of abuse and the continuum that exists from minor to major lethality. Purdy and Nickle point out the importance of distinguishing between destructive behaviors that control others, behaviors that are generally accepted by society as "not too harmful," and behaviors that endanger others.[11]

In the course of the discussion each man is asked to place himself on the continuum according to the amount of abuse he has utilized. This avoids the need to pin him down about each incident. It also helps him to focus on the specific behavior and real outcomes of his violence.

The second part of the informational process used to deal with denial is to explain the function of anger. The physical and emotional aspects of anger are detailed. Anger is often a response to other feelings or thoughts. Feelings of fear, hurt, insecurity, inadequacy, or being ignored are sometimes mislabeled as anger. Most batterers are not aware of the differences in feelings, or how to express those feelings. So they respond to all frustrations with only one feeling—anger. The only thing that varies is the intensity—moderately angry or very angry.

Initial Components of Treatment

Several activities have been seen as useful in moving past the resistance and obtaining motivation by the participants.

Most programs seem to start with an individual assessment and orientation interview. The counselor needs to accept and indicate an understanding of the man's feelings, but at the same time state the unacceptability of violent behavior. If both husband and wife are included, appreciation of the victim's feelings of fear and apprehension should be conveyed.

The preview of the process should include hope, while not making promises. The group leader can describe the possibility of learning to deal with anger and conflict in nonviolent ways. But care should be taken not to set up a situation where the batterer sets out to defeat the counselor by not living up to the promises. The responsibility for change must always come back to the abuser.

Placing a time limit on the group can be motivating to the participants. They know there are twelve sessions, each lasting two hours, and there are certain assignments and activities. Most groups for abusive men seem to have a fixed number of sessions, and a definite sequence of material. The most common topics are anger management, self-observation, cognitive restructuring of irrational belief systems, conflict resolution, assertiveness training, relaxation, interpersonal skills training, jealousy control, and alcohol and drug control.

Sometimes an incentive deposit is required. For example two hundred dollars is placed in deposit and a portion returned for each session attended. Another variation is to ask the participant to write a check out to his least favorite cause or organization. The check would be mailed by the counselor if the client did not follow through with his commitment.

For most men the strongest external motivator is to keep their wives. This is often the reality: Their wives have said, "You participate in counseling or else." To be lasting, the motivation must eventually move to a desire to change because they don't want anger to control their lives.

ANGER CONTROL

"Man is not disturbed by events, but by the view he takes of them," wisely stated the philosopher Epictetus. Anger control is developed through teaching the person how beliefs, values, and cognitions create anger. Most batterers have only two ways to handle their anger—hold it in (at least for a while) or express it in a hostile and abusive form. The goal is to teach them not to get angry in the first place, or to express anger in non-violent ways.

Several sources contain complete programs and details for leading groups of batterers or couples. These materials can be consulted for specific procedures and instructions. The following discussion will highlight the common features of the better programs along with comments for application with Christian clients.[12]

Emotions do not have an independent existence. Feelings cannot endure for very long unless there is perception of an event followed by interpreting and continuing to think about the incident. It's not the event itself but the interpretation of that event, accompanied by internal messages to ourselves, that results in emotions and feelings. All anger is preceded by a thought process in which the event is perceived, interpreted, and then acted upon. Anger has many forms and varying degrees. It is a strong, usually temporary, feeling of displeasure or irritation. Anger is an emotional reaction that is aroused when a person is interfered with, injured, or threatened.

Even anticipation of an unpleasant event can trigger an anger response. Anger can be based on an actual or imagined threat. But it is real in the eyes of the beholder either way. Anger is an immediate response to our senses or mind telling us there is trouble ahead.

It is not necessarily wrong to be angry. Some aspects of initial anger, such as adrenaline flow, increased heartbeat and breathing, and pupil dilation, are automatic. In that case, we are not so much responsible for *being* in a state of anger, as we are accountable for what is *done* with the anger.

A frequent comment made by men who batter is "All of a sudden I find myself in a blind rage and I'm out of control." For

abusive men (and women) the events leading to a violent incident are unclear. They seldom connect a sequence of events
and thoughts to the eventual lashing out at their spouses.

Anger Log

The first step in many treatment programs is to start training
in self-monitoring or self-awareness. Clients are assigned an
anger log or journal in which they describe an anger-producing
incident and how they reacted. The anger log should include:

1. Date and time. When are the high risk times for anger?
2. Incident. Clients need to distinguish between actual
events and interpretations of those events. Description should
be as objective as possible.
3. Level of anger. Apply a value from zero to one hundred,
with one hundred representing total rage.
4. Outcome. What happened as a result of the incident? Describe the behavior and consequences.
5. Thought patterns. This will be, initially, the most difficult aspect to capture. Clients will need practice in describing
their internal processes in thoughts that can be recorded.
The goal is to have clients be able to describe their automatic
thoughts and to identify rational and irrational patterns of
thinking.

Ground Rules

Particularly if the couple is being seen in conjoint counseling, it is important to identify early some ground rules and
procedures for handling their anger. The husband needs to establish an early warning system to assist him in preventing violence. This *cueing* can consist of a verbal cue and sign that
clearly indicates he is angry. The words can be "Time out,"
"I'm too angry to talk," or "Time to stop." The physical sign
can be a gesture such as the time out signal used in sports. The
cue should remain the same until there is a mutual agreement
to change.

The one who is angry should then remove himself from the
situation and go to an agreed upon place. He should stay there
until he has calmed down, is in control of himself, and no
longer needs to control others by violent means.

Self-Talk

Before, during, and after an anger situation, it's important for each person to become aware of what he or she is thinking. This silent monologue and its interpretation is the mechanism that converts impressions into anger and, subsequently, into violence. The process is to first identify the destructive or irrational thought patterns, and then substitute ways of thinking that do not escalate into aggression.

Three particular irrational beliefs seem to have a great effect on abusive males. They are:

1. One must have certain and perfect control over things.

2. One has little control over emotions and cannot help feeling certain things.

3. Human misery is forced on one by outside people and events.[13]

As the man of the house, a batterer often believes it's his role to have total control over his wife's behavior. Although this is seldom true, such a belief will lead to confrontations over any and all issues where there is a difference of opinion. Thus, for the abuser, violence is justified in pursuit of certain and perfect control.

The second belief is almost a contradiction of the first. Many men justify their battering by attributing it to their temper. "I just blew my top. I couldn't control myself. Things just got out of hand. I know I have a temper, but so did my father. My wife has to learn to live with it. My mom did."

This belief combines with the first in such a way as to justify both the man's expectation of compliance from his wife, and his use of violence. A double standard is created where perfect obedience is expected of the wife, but violent behavior is justified for the man.

The third belief regarding outside influences helps the man avoid responsibility. This attitude works to justify his violence. Often a batterer will blame his wife for *making* him have to hit her. "She caused me to hit her." Abusers will also blame alcohol and other addictions for their violent behavior.

David Burns has identified several types of cognitive distortions that frequently accompany anger.

1. Labeling. Labeling involves categorizing someone as totally negative. Rather than thinking of people as having both good and bad qualities, they are reduced to objects bearing a single label, such as *jerk* or *idiot*.

2. Mind reading. This is assuming one knows the reason why a person acted in a certain way without checking out the assumption. Usually the motives attributed to others explain their actions to the mind reader's satisfaction.

3. Fortune telling. This is predicting the future. Because an event has occurred in the past, one decides it will continue forever. For example, "She'll never change. Even if I did my part, it wouldn't do any good."

4. Magnification. This is catastrophizing or exaggerating the importance or consequences of a negative event. "It's awful"; "I can't stand it any longer"; "She's driving me crazy" are exaggerations that serve to heighten the level of anger.

5. *Should* statements. These are cognitive distortions that translate preferences ("I would like to leave for church on time") into commands or demands ("We *have* to leave by ten o'clock"). *Should* statements imply that one is entitled to pleasure and satisfaction and that it's not fair if one doesn't get them. *Should* statements lead to inflexible rules.[14]

Use of the anger logs, along with detailed group discussion of self-talk and types of distortions, will naturally lead to discussions of how clients can refute their most frequently used irrational thoughts. Here are some suggestions for refuting self-talk or changing those destructive thoughts.

1. Labeling. Describe the behavior, not the person. Be specific and avoid overgeneralizing. Use the person's name to avoid reducing him or her to an object. Ask *yourself* if the label is totally accurate and always fits. Instead of thinking, *John is a jerk*, substitute *I don't like John's taste in music.*

2. Mind reading. Assumptions about motives are always speculative. Focus instead on behavior. Assumptions should be verified and held in check until confirmed. Instead of thinking, *She's doing this to hurt me*, a better way would be to think, *I don't like what she is doing. But since I can't read her mind, I really don't know why she is acting that way. Maybe I will ask her.*

3. Fortune telling. Be aware of the self-fulfilling prophecy: If you are convinced things won't change for the better, they probably won't. Instead of thinking, *My life is a shambles and won't get any better,* try, *If I make some changes, my life may become better.*

4. Magnification. Quantify statements by indicating precisely how often something happens or how undesirable it is. Terms such as *always, never, everybody,* and *nobody* should be avoided. Instead of thinking, *I can't stand the way she acts,* try, *I don't like it but I can stand it.*

5. *Should* statements. Rewrite the rules that include *should, ought,* or *must.* The result will be more flexible standards for oneself and others. Think of at least three reasons why other people "should" have done exactly what they did. Try not to translate preferences into demands. Instead of thinking, *She should not treat me this way,* try thinking, *It would be nice if she didn't treat me this way.*[15]

The point of this analysis is to suggest that people can think in a variety of ways. Abusive clients have a choice in how they think, and the type of self-talk they choose to use influences the emotions they will have.

Relaxation

One alternative to hurting someone is for men who batter to use the cue of being angry as an indicator for the need to relax. God gave us this precedent when he told Ezekiel, "Then my wrath against you will subside and my jealous anger will turn away from you; I will be calm and no longer angry" (Ezek. 16:42).

There are several relaxation techniques that are simple to learn. A sample progressive relaxation sequence is presented below. Practicing this technique twice a day will gradually help reduce daily tension.

The relaxation response is a physical and mental technique that counteracts the stress response. You cannot truly relax and experience psychological stress or anger at the same time. The two responses are incompatible. Complete relaxation involves learning how to recognize and feel tension in the muscles of your body and then how to release it.

Four basic elements are required to learn the relaxation response:

1. A quiet place to practice. Pick a time and place where you are unlikely to be interrupted for twenty to thirty minutes. It helps to use the same location, at the same time, and to tell those around you what you are doing. The place you choose should be as quiet and comfortable as possible. Dim the lights and loosen any tight clothing. Avoid practicing immediately before retiring or after a meal.

2. A comfortable position. Use a favorite chair or sofa which supports your body evenly. Avoid lying down on the floor or a bed so you aren't as likely to fall asleep. Your head should be supported, so you can relax your neck.

3. A phrase or words to help you concentrate may be helpful as you learn the technique of relaxing. Some suggestions include:

I am relaxing.	Relax
I feel peaceful.	Peace
My mind is quiet.	Quiet
I am calm.	Calm

After you have mastered the skill of relaxing, your word or phrase will be your key to activating the relaxation response. At any time you will then be able to say this word or phrase and your mind will work with your body to produce a relaxed state in five to ten minutes.

4. A passive attitude is the last element needed to learn the relaxation response. Follow the instructions and allow the relaxation to develop. Allow the tension to flow out of your body, effortlessly. Do not try to force yourself or work too hard.[16]

The following fifteen-step instructions can be memorized, tape recorded, or read aloud by a friend. It is important to practice at least once a day for fifteen to thirty minutes. It should take about two weeks to become proficient, so don't rush.

After you have completed a practice session, remain in the relaxed state for as long as you wish. If any tension creeps in, simply let it go as soon as you notice it. When you want to continue with other activities, slowly open your eyes and continue to sit quietly for fifteen to thirty seconds. Then slowly move and resume activity. You should feel refreshed, awake, and calm.

After using the instructions or tape five to seven times, try relaxing without them. You will find that you can *mentally* progress through the process in less time. You should also be able to begin relaxing completely, without going through the tensing stage, by simply focusing on a muscle group and allowing it to relax. At the same time, allow the relaxation in one area to flow into another area. Eventually you should be able to use your relaxation skills at any time and place by simply repeating your relaxation word or phrase several times. Once activated, your relaxation response will take over and produce a relaxed state for you in just a few seconds or minutes.

1. Select a comfortable place. Remove your shoes, loosen your belt or tight clothing. Stretch out and place your body in a comfortable position. Your eyes should be gently closed.

2. Think to yourself, *I am now going to relax completely. When I am finished I will feel fully refreshed.*

3. Think about your feet; wiggle your toes; flex your ankles. Then "let go." Let go of all the tension, and let your feet rest limp and heavy. Begin using the key word or phrase to help your mind relax. Breathe as deeply as you can. Deeply and slowly.

4. Think of the lower part of your legs, your knees, and thighs, up to your hips. Imagine them just sinking into the chair, heavy and relaxed.

5. Now think of your hands. Wiggle your fingers and flex your wrists, then let go. Relax. Breathe deeply. Think calm, relaxed, and tranquil.

6. Think of your lower arm, elbow, and upper arm. All the way up to your shoulders. Picture all the tension just melting away.

7. Think about your abdomen. Let the tension go, and allow your breathing to flow more smoothly and deeply.

8. Think about your stomach and chest, up to your throat and neck. As you continue breathing more deeply, just imagine all the tension flowing out and you are relaxing more and more.

9. Now think about your throat, neck, and head feeling limp and relaxed. Relax your facial muscles. Drop the jaw, parting the lips and teeth. Picture yourself completely relaxed.

10. If you are aware of any remaining tension anywhere in the body, go to that area mentally and relax the tension. Scan your whole body.

11. Continue to remain in this completely relaxed state for five to ten minutes. You may picture pleasant thoughts, favorite scenes, uplifting Scripture, or review positive experiences. It is important to keep your body relaxed. Don't think of active scenes or memories. Focus on calm, tranquil, peaceful, and relaxing thoughts. Remember to repeat your key word or phrase frequently as you become more and more relaxed.

12. When you are ready to end the session, say to yourself, *I have been deeply relaxed. I am now ready to get up, feeling completely refreshed and relaxed. The tension has gone from my body.*

13. Begin to move around a bit. Flex your ankles; wiggle your toes; then wiggle your fingers. Gently shake your wrists.

14. Bend your right knee, and then your left knee. Now bend your right and left arms.

15. Open your eyes. Stretch each arm over your head. Then slowly sit up, stand up, and stretch again. You are ready to continue with your activities.[17]

Self-Care

As part of anger control, the person should give attention to proper nutrition, sleep, and exercise. Without proper sleep it is difficult to feel relaxed and to think clearly. Nutrition is important to evaluate to determine if an individual is affected by the large doses of sugar, salt, artificial food colors, flavors, and additives included in many foods. Eating a balanced diet and keeping weight under control are important factors also.

Men who batter should not use substances as a means of tension reduction. Drugs and alcohol tend to impair judgment. The man who has a history of violence needs as clear a head as possible to think through his options to abuse. Screening for substance abuse prior to counseling will be important, since progress in therapy will be sabotaged if addiction is present and active.

Poor nutrition, sleep, exercise, or substance abuse may not affect all people in the same way. But when violence has been present, reducing each potential source of stress helps make the goals of therapy more attainable.

FURTHER ASPECTS OF COUNSELING

Inability to Express Feelings

The abusive male has the entire range of feelings that are available to anyone else. He just doesn't know how to tune into his own feelings or those of others. No attempt will be made in this section to outline an entire program for teaching the expression of feelings. There are resources devoted entirely to this topic. The intent here is to mention the importance of including this aspect in a total program for abusive men or couples.

Most programs will begin with a focus on personal awareness. The work on anger management will overlap with this content. By using a journal or checklist format, the individual is taught to identify, label, and discriminate his different feelings. I often use an adaptation of the Awareness Wheel to help a client understand the context of feelings.[18] This tool for instruction is divided into five parts:

1. Sensing. You see, hear, smell, taste, and touch. This is the beginning of most messages. You hear what somebody says, and you see the expression on his or her face. You also process the tone of voice and many other nonverbal cues.

2. Thinking. This happens automatically. You make an interpretation of *what* it is the person is saying or intending. Sometimes the understanding of the message is different from what the sender intended. Most of the time an assumption is also made about *why* the person said or acted the way he or she did. Often assumptions are not correct, but we act on those assumptions anyway.

3. Feeling. As we saw earlier, our feelings usually are a product of how we think about a situation. If we believe the person is giving us a compliment, we *feel* good. If we believe the person is criticizing us, we *feel* bad and defensive.

4. Wanting. The reason we feel good when a person compliments us is because we *want* affirmation and recognition. We don't expect to be downgraded and rebuked. Generally, if our

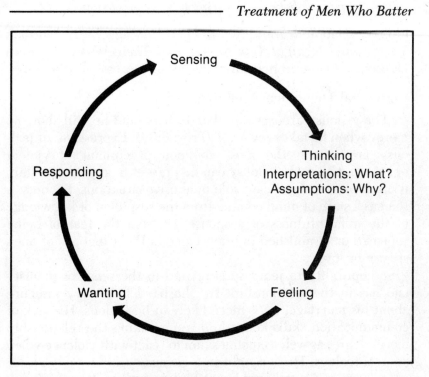

The Awareness Wheel

wants and our thoughts match up with each other, we will have positive feelings. If our expectations do not line up with our interpretations and assumptions, we will have negative feelings.

5. Responding. Based on how we feel, in the context of our beliefs and wants, we take *action*. I like being complimented. I like this person who likes me, so I will smile and be friendly.

This kind of internal information can be used to teach the person how to transmit clear and correct messages. When sending or receiving messages he needs to learn how to describe clearly and completely, as well as to check out what he is receiving. He can learn to express his feelings, to listen actively to the feelings of the sender, and to state his own needs in a nonthreatening manner.

Each of the programs mentioned in footnote 12 contains sections on expression of feelings for use with groups of men or couples. Books by Christian authors such as *Just Talk to Me* by André Bustanoby, *Caring Enough to Confront* by David Augsburger, *Communication: Key to Your Marriage* by H. Norman Wright, and *Straight Talk to Men and Their Wives* by James Dobson, all contain helpful material on expression of feelings.

Emotional Dependence and Jealousy

"For jealousy arouses a husband's fury, and he will show no mercy when he takes revenge" (Prov. 6:34). Expressions of jealousy are among the most common precipitant of violent episodes. Although jealousy can be present in any relationship, it often plays a significant role in abusive situations. Jealousy is seen as a state of mind coming from the suspicion or knowledge of the unfaithfulness of a spouse, or from the fear of being replaced or diminished in importance in the affections of one's spouse or lover.

Susceptibility to jealousy is related to the sense of security one has in the relationship. If a husband feels very insecure about his marriage, he is more likely to be jealous. His lack of communication skills keeps him from making the relationship more secure, as well as inclines him to react with violence when he gets jealous. He is caught in a vicious cycle.

Jealousy needs to be addressed in counseling. Because it can be an explosive issue, it should be dealt with carefully. Start with discussions that do not directly relate to sex. Present examples of jealousy unrelated to sexuality. An example might be the experience early in marriage of deciding to spend a holiday at home or with the wife's parents. Another might be the feelings of the husband when the wife has spent countless hours caring for a new baby.

Power is also an important ingredient in jealousy. Marriage is usually most satisfying when there is an even distribution of power—when neither spouse's desires automatically prevail. The concept of mutual submission, again, comes to mind. If the couple can learn to share and compromise, they will be doing a lot to inoculate against harmful jealousy.

Jealousy can have some positive functions. It tends to define the limits of the relationship. It can communicate one really cares about the relationship. And it can serve as an early warning flag of insecurity about the relationship.

The man or couple can be helped to put jealousy in perspective. It becomes a problem when it is expressed indirectly, becomes irrational, or leads to high levels of control.[19]

Low Self-Esteem and Lack of Assertiveness

Self-esteem is a function of success. If other parts of the program for abusive men are working, he should be gaining some measure of satisfaction and pride. This sense of increasing competency will greatly improve the self-image.

The components of a Sense of Being, Sense of Purpose, and Sense of Ministry as presented in chapter 4 are just as relevant to abusive men. That same material can be used with the man if he has a Christian perspective.

Assertion training consists primarily of rehearsing, modeling, and role playing a variety of situations in order to enable people to overcome social inhibitions. It starts by distinguishing among assertive, nonassertive, and aggressive behaviors. The different forms are discussed and demonstrated. The purpose is to teach a skill that can substitute for aggression.

Less threatening situations, such as work, shopping, or social activities, are used before working on family situations. Different kinds of assertive skills are used, such as coping with criticism, making requests, saying no, and stating needs and expectations.

Assertive action involves awareness of one's own needs as well as the needs of others. Assertiveness includes being honest and direct with one's feelings and desires. It may involve persistence when someone else does not agree. An assertive person respects the rights of someone else to deny his requests. Being able to propose compromises is an important assertive skill. It also involves confident body language: posture, gestures, and voice. Assertiveness usually results in feeling good about oneself because it is a more effective way to meet one's needs. That results in more self-confidence and others then respond better to a confident attitude.

Rigid and Domineering Application of Sex Roles

For the Christian, the "traditional" roles in marriage are still perfectly valid and functional. The problem is in the inflexible and demanding position taken by most men who batter. This is true whether the husband has an aggressive or passive style. For the outwardly aggressive husband, there is probably a direct relationship between his level of insecurity and the intensity with which he demands authority in the home. If the husband makes a major issue out of headship, submission, and obedience, he probably has questions about his own emotional status. A man with a poor self-image is going to look for affirmation of himself by exerting power over his family. He may use tradition and religion as a source of authority. But the primary motivation comes from his own insecurity. The more intense his demands, the greater his insecurity.

The rigid approach to roles in the family will be softened when the abuser learns to love himself as discussed previously. The need to dominate will also lessen as the husband learns to express his feelings and resolve conflict through negotiation. The discussion in this section will focus on the batterer's misuse of headship to rationalize his yearnings for power.

Desiring a place of power and authority is risky business. Internal conflict is likely because the man believes he must maintain his status as head of the household even though experience tells him he cannot always be superior. For the abusive male, this creates resentment which leads to more violence to regain his dominant position.

The basic therapeutic intervention in this area is to discuss whether or not the husband should always have to be dominant. For the Christian man, the primary source of his *should* is found in the teachings about headship and submission.

In the fifth chapter of Ephesians the notions of headship and submission seem to come together. The idea of mutual submission is the basis for Paul's presentation (v. 21). We discussed the application of mutual submission earlier in the section on helping battered women. Now we will look at the rest of Paul's argument.

Based on his initial comments, Paul expands on the meaning of headship. He fills it with new meaning and expands its emphasis toward the oneness which God initially intended for marriage (Gen. 2:24). The emphasis on headship is no longer to be a matter of rank or power. *Headship* is to take on a new meaning—not only as a superior leader, but as a *self-giving servant*.

Paul uses the example of Christ's self-sacrificing action on behalf of the church. This example defines the meaning of *headship*. The example does not mean that the husband should become a Lord and Master, like Christ. The purpose of the comparison is to show headship becoming a means of responsibility and initiative—responsibility to act in love and initiative to act in service. As Christ gave himself in love and humbled himself, so husbands are to take the initiative in building an atmosphere of loving, self-sacrificing service.

The comparison between the husband and Christ shows that headship for the husband is not defined in terms of singular responsibility for making decisions. Rather, the picture is one of love and service. Leadership may be more clearly seen as a type of catalyst or facilitating activity. The leadership of the husband is to be a matter of facilitating a family toward its goals.

The idea of the body of the church being composed of many parts, each fulfilling a unique function and purpose, seems to apply in this context. Because individuals in any family have widely varying skills and abilities, it may be that at different times particular persons will provide the leadership which moves the group forward. Headship in marriage is seen as accepting the responsibility and performing certain functions so that the relationship is advanced toward the goal of oneness.

This passage does not suggest any one person is most accountable to God. Nothing is said or implied in the model of Christ that would convey the idea that one partner is made more responsible for the actions of the family. Paul gives emphasis to the principle of oneness in Galatians 3:28, "There is neither Jew nor Greek, slave nor free, male nor female, for you are all one in Christ Jesus." The members of the body of Christ are individually responsible and accountable to God for their own actions. Nothing in this passage suggests that either partner is made more responsible for achieving creation's goal of oneness. A different function is given to each person, but two independent, equal people are to become one.

Leadership is intended to be a self-sacrificing love, which directs the husband to take an active involvement in encouraging his wife. The husband is free to give leadership in a dynamic manner without being threatened when his wife, who is equally involved, also gives leadership.

The husband's image as head moves him to become a servant to his wife in the same way as Christ is a servant to his church. Just as Christ creates conditions whereby the church may become whole and clean, so the husband is to create opportunities for his wife to move toward maturity and fulfillment as a person. There is no place for thinking that the wife should be forced to do something, just for her own good.

What does the Bible say about submission? Within the bounds of the servant type of headship, wives are to submit to their husbands. This subjection must allow her to retain her respect for her husband, since the subjection is to be of similar quality and nature as the church being subject to Christ. Several points seem important to highlight from Paul's discussion.

First, the woman is subject to her husband, not to all men. There would seem to be no justification in interpreting this passage to suggest that women must always act through the opinions of any man simply because of her sex.

Second, the woman is to be active, responsible, and involved in a positive and creative way. Although the church is to be subject to Christ, we find that a great deal of freedom and initiative is given into the hands of the church. The church is to use every resource and gift at its disposal to maintain a relationship with God and to fulfill the Great Commission. The church is to be active and energetic in its outreach. The wife is also to be active, not passive.

Third, the wife is to be honest and genuine in her relationship to her husband. She is not to use any ploys or forms of manipulation to get her husband to fulfill her selfish wishes. Submission is not a sophisticated form of manipulation.

Fourth, the wife is not under responsibility to obey her husband if he asks her to commit immoral or illegal acts. The example of Sapphira in Acts 5 demonstrates this. She was brought before Peter and quizzed as to whether or not she had agreed to her husband's deception. She was judged upon her own action, and not because she was just carrying out her husband's wishes.

Fifth, the wife is commanded to respect her husband. You can only respect someone else if your own self-image is positive. Behaving exclusively at the command of the husband does not allow a woman to maintain any self-dignity. Respect can come only when one acts in fairness and competency. The husband is to cultivate his wife's gifts and personality, not demand allegiance. You cannot demand respect. This is another area where the action of an abusive husband is counterproductive. Submission does not include the blotting out of the wife's personality or feelings. To do so would deny the gifts God has given her to be used to foster and nurture the marriage relationship.

In the final analysis, the acting out of mutual subjection, headship, and submission within a given marriage is an open and creative matter. There is no single mold to be used to determine how each couple should act. *Headship* means that both husband and wife live under the headship of Christ, submitting to him, and discovering his guidance for their marriage.

Again, the principle to convey to the violence-prone couple is *choice.* Given a variety of options for growth, a couple is not as likely to get boxed in by their history and resort to power plays for resolution. To be submissive means to yield in humble and intelligent obedience to a power or authority that God has ordained. This is to be done out of freedom and love, and not from fear or command. Both the husband and wife are free to choose the pattern that best fits them, just as we are free to choose Christ. Then, if a wife does not submit to her husband in the way that God intends, or when the husband does not demonstrate servanthood love to his wife, a spiritual, as much as a marital, problem may exist.

Drug and Alcohol Dependency

In 60 to 80 percent of battering incidents, alcohol or other drugs are used during or prior to the violence. There is no conclusive evidence that alcohol or other drugs cause violence. It is the problems that cause a person to abuse alcohol or drugs that also cause a person to be violent. Men need to learn to control their substance abuse *and* their violence. Therefore, a discussion of alcohol and other drug use is important in order to explore the role these substances play in the lives of the men. Some may see their use of alcohol as a social lubricant, with the implication they need to work on developing social skills. Others may see they have tried to use alcohol to control feelings of anger or depression, only to find it always backfired. Some may admit to using alcohol as a socially acceptable excuse for their aggression.

This aspect of treatment may need to be accomplished along with participation in Alcoholics or Narcotics Anonymous, and Al-Anon for the family and friends of alcoholics. In the instance of severe alcohol or substance abuse, treatment for the battering should not begin until significant progress has been made on the addictive problems. This might require a residential, hospital-based, or outpatient drug treatment program.

The possibility of the wife being a coalcoholic should be explored. The major feature of a coalcoholic is that she continues to try to help the alcoholic long after it has become clear the alcoholic does not accept the help. Coalcoholics tend to be rescuers. They try hard to be supportive and helpful to their alcoholic spouses. But their efforts are ineffective and they may even wind up supporting the habit of substance abuse. Coalcoholics have many fine personal qualities such as loyalty and responsibility. They also tend to have low feelings of self-worth and a need to be needed. Just as the alcoholic is dependent on the bottle, the coalcoholic is dependent on the alcoholic.[20]

This chapter summarizes the most important components for working with abusive men or couples. At the same time, some specific and practical ideas were included. Several important topics were not covered due to limitations of space. A decision was made to include some of the most important components in sufficient detail as to be useful for the practitioner. Stress management, coping with separation or divorce, divorce and remarriage, career and financial planning, combating cultural norms that sanction violence, and building a social network were not discussed. All of these aspects need attention somewhere in the long process of helping a family. It is anticipated the experienced counselor or pastor will have additional knowledge and resources that will apply to working with violent men and their families.

Families who have experienced violence will not simply go through this material and live happily ever after. The goal is to give them the ability to make a choice not to be violent. They may not always make the right choices. But there is no reason, with continued effort, spiritual guidance, and the support of a caring community, they cannot overcome their cycle of violence.

PART II

CHILD ABUSE

CHAPTER SIX

UNDERSTANDING PHYSICAL AND EMOTIONAL CHILD ABUSE

WHY DO BABIES CRY? When they cry, babies are telling the world they are hungry, wet, sleepy, or cutting teeth. It's natural for babies to cry.

Sometimes the cry of a child takes on a sinister significance. Those muffled screams of terror can be the result of deliberately broken bones or burns from a cup of scalding coffee or a lighted cigarette. The silent tears may represent livers and spleens ruptured by repeated blows or skin that is welted and bruised by whippings. The child may have inflamed sexual organs, or a pathetic body starved to sickness. For these things, too, a child may cry.

To a loving parent, the cry of a child elicits comfort and

125

concern. But the cry of an abused child is often met with more violence or neglect. Those of us who are given the responsibility of listening to the hurts of our society must hear these cries of abused and neglected children. We are obligated to do all we can to stop those who intentionally hurt and kill the children entrusted to their care.

It is to this end that part II of this book is devoted—equipping the counselor and pastor to be able to identify a family in which a child is crying. In this chapter I will present a brief look at the history of child abuse, then current incidence figures—to call attention to the magnitude and scope of the problem. I'll give definitions of the major categories of abuse, along with specific symptoms for the categories of physical and emotional abuse and neglect. Sexual abuse, because of its devastating effects, will be given separate attention in the following chapters. Before we can counsel with child abusers and their families, it is helpful to understand general descriptions and characteristics of parents that abuse their children. This information is presented in the first portion of this chapter.

HISTORY AND INCIDENCE OF CHILD ABUSE AND NEGLECT

"What that kid needs is a good crack on the head!" How literally do parents take such advice? Since time immemorial, children have been treated with incredible cruelty. Children have been tortured, burned, terrorized, and flogged in the name of "discipline." They've been dipped in ice water and rolled in the snow in order to "harden" them. They've even been buried alive with their dead parents.

Parents have been "beating the devil" out of their children since colonial times. Many communities enacted "stubborn child laws," which gave parents the right to kill children who were beyond their ability to control.[1]

Parents have exposed children to weather, starved or abandoned them, in order to avoid the burden of rearing them or having to divide property among too many heirs. Adults regularly succumbed to urges to mutilate, burn, freeze, and drown infants. The Huns used to cut the cheeks of newborn males. Italian Renaissance parents would burn a newborn's neck with a hot iron or with a burning wax candle. It was common to cut the string under the newborn's tongue, often with the midwife's fingernail. In every age, the deliberate mutilation of children's bones and faces prepared them for a lifetime of begging.

In many cultures, infants were not born with the right to live. Fitness to live was sometimes defined in terms of ability to survive. Germans threw infants into an icy river and saved them if they cried. The North American Indians hurled children into a pool. If they rose and voiced their screams, they were saved.

Certain characteristics have historically contributed to the value of an individual child. First born, healthy males have always held a higher value. Girls were more likely to be left exposed or to be killed than were boys; it was rare for more than one girl in a family to be spared. Children found to be mentally retarded, physically handicapped, born as a twin, conceived out of wedlock, or just born into a poor family have been in most jeopardy throughout history.[2]

The killing of babies has been so common in centuries past that many rivers, dung-heaps, and cesspools used to be littered with dead infants. Christians were considered odd for their opposition to infanticide. Polybius blamed the decline in population of Greece on the killing of legitimate children. As late as 1527, one priest admitted that "the latrines resound with the cries of children who have been plunged into them."[3]

With such beginnings, it's not surprising the eighteenth-century pediatrician William Buchan said, "Almost one-half of the human species perish in infancy by improper management or neglect."[4]

In Roman law, the power of the father over his children was absolute. He could kill, sell, or offer them to sacrifice. Because children were seen as chattels of their fathers, society gave sanction to child abuse. Even Aristotle, a major proponent of democracy, affirmed the lowly status of children. He said, "The justice of a master or father is a different thing from that of a citizen, for a son or slave is property, and there can be no injustice done to property."[5]

A child's life prior to modern times was very bleak. Most every child-rearing manual from antiquity to the eighteenth century recommended the beating of children. It was common at home or school. One nineteenth-century German schoolmaster even kept score of his actions. He administered 911,527 strokes with a stick, 124,000 lashes with a whip, 136,715 slaps with his hand, and 1,115,800 boxes on the ear.[6]

Fairy tales, folklore, and nursery rhymes are full of violence against children. Hansel and Gretel's parents left them to starve in the forest when money got scarce. Snow White was taken to the forest at the orders of the wicked queen. The huntsmen were told to cut out her heart because the stepdaughter was more beautiful than the queen.

The incidence of physical abuse to children is also found in both the Old and New Testament. The Egyptian Pharaoh first asked all the midwives to kill every Hebrew boy (Exod. 1:16). When that didn't work due to lack of cooperation, Pharaoh then demanded that every boy be thrown into the river (Exod. 1:22).

In Judges 9:5 we read of Abimelech murdering seventy of his brothers. There is also the account of Ahaz sacrificing his sons in the fire (2 Chron. 28:3).

A passage in Ezekiel makes reference to the pagan practice of abandoning and exposing infants to the elements, "Rather, you were thrown out into the open field, for on the day you were born you were despised" (Ezek. 16:5).

Finally, out of fear of the Messiah, Herod ordered all boys two years old and under who lived in and around Bethlehem to be killed (Matt. 2:16).

The treatment of children today is more humane than at any other time in history. However, it's possible the functional equivalents of earlier modes of neglect are still with us. We don't send infants out to wet nurses at birth or to be servants at age seven. But we do abandon them to hosts of nurseries, preschools, teachers, camps, and baby-sitters for a major part of their young lives. We don't throw dead babies into latrines or rivers, but we abort the lives of fetuses by the thousands, sometimes using back alley garbage bins for disposal.[7]

Have we really come that far? Abusive parents still find ways to restrict their babies' movements, much as swaddling and corsets did in years past. Parents continue to emotionally abandon, betray, bruise, and batter their children in both direct and indirect ways.

The heart of humankind seems to be very resistant to improvement, in spite of legal reform or advanced technology. Let's move from a historical perspective and look at the level of treatment for today's child.

According to the most recently published study of the American Association for Protecting Children (AAPC), over one million reports of child abuse or neglect were documented in 1983. These one million reports represented one and one-half million children. The national rate of reported child maltreatment is 23.8 children for every one thousand children living in the United States and its territories. Estimates are that the actual rate of child abuse is closer to seventy-five children out of every one thousand. Child abuse is a problem of monumental proportions.[8]

Estimates of the extent of child abuse vary because of different definitions and reporting procedures. The National Center on Child Abuse and Neglect (NCCAN) estimates that over one million children are abused or neglected each year. Of these, one hundred thousand to two hundred thousand are physically abused, sixty thousand to one hundred thousand are sexually abused and the remainder are neglected. Between one thousand and two thousand children die each year because of abuse or neglect by their adult caretakers. Ninety-five percent of these caretakers are the child's parents.[9]

Interviews with a random sample of parents in 1975 suggested between 1 and 1.9 million children were kicked, bitten, or punched in that year. Between two hundred seventy-five thousand and seven hundred fifty thousand children were "beaten up" in 1975, and approximately forty-six thousand children between the ages of three and seventeen had a parent use a gun or knife on them.[10]

Major physical injury seems to be concentrated among very young children. Sixty percent of major injuries occur to children under the age of four. Forty percent of sexual maltreatment involved children over twelve years old, but one out of every four involved victims under five years of age.[11]

Only 50 percent of the families in the AAPC study had both

male and female caretakers. Forty-three percent were headed by a single female compared to only 19 percent of all U.S. families with children.

Abused children can be found in all income groups, although 47 percent of the households in the AAPC study were receiving public assistance, while such families represent 7 percent of families across the United States. For each major form of maltreatment, the incidence rates for white children are much higher in families with income less than fifteen thousand dollars than in high income families. However, abuse incidence rates are constant and at a relatively low level across income levels for nonwhite children.

No geographic setting is free of child abuse and neglect. In fact, overall incidence rates are similar for urban, suburban, and rural communities. There were some variations within specific categories. For example, the incidence rate for sexual abuse is higher in rural counties than elsewhere.[12]

Although a little out of date, an interesting study was reported in 1973 by a researcher at the University of Southern California. He compared 674 abusive parents with a control group of 500 nonabusers. Two major differences emerged. Sixty-five percent of the abusers reported they had been exposed to violence when they were children, compared to 43 percent of the nonabusers. While the abusive parents had a higher level of childhood violence, what is troubling is the total incidence of violence for both groups. If the percentages are combined for the abusive and nonabusive samples, a total of 56 percent of the parents had violence in their background. That doesn't speak well for the amount of violence that pervades our society.

A second finding of the study was that 80 percent of the abusers claimed religious affiliation, compared with 62 percent of the nonabusers. As we continue to find, having some kind of religious affiliation does not ensure freedom from violence.[13]

DEFINITIONS OF CHILD ABUSE AND NEGLECT

In 1974, the U.S. Congress passed the Child Abuse Prevention and Treatment Act. This legislation is a milestone in the history of child protection because it was the first time parental abuse and neglect of children had been dealt with at a national level. The primary purpose of the legislation was to establish a national system to facilitate the conducting, compiling, analyzing, publishing, and dissemination of research into the causes, prevention, identification, and treatment of child abuse and neglect. Child abuse and neglect was defined as:

. . . The physical or mental injury, sexual abuse or exploitation, negligent treatment, or maltreatment of a child under the age of eighteen, by a person who is responsible for the child's welfare and under circumstances which indicate the child's health or welfare is harmed or threatened thereby.

There are four types of abuse included in the federal law:

1. Physical abuse. Includes violent assault with an implement such as a knife or strap, burns, fractures, or other actions leading to possible injury to the child. "Spanking" for purely disciplinary reasons generally is not seen as child abuse.

2. Neglect. Physical—includes abandonment; refusal to seek, allow, or provide treatment for illness or impairment; inadequate physical supervision; disregard of health hazards in the home; and inadequate nutrition, clothing, or hygiene when services are available.

Educational—includes knowingly permitting chronic truancy, keeping the child home from school repeatedly without cause, or failing to enroll a child in school.

3. Emotional abuse. Includes verbal or emotional assault; close confinement such as tying or locking in a closet; inadequate nurturance such as that affecting failure-to-thrive babies; knowingly permitting antisocial behavior such as delinquency or serious alcohol/drug abuse; or refusal to allow remedial care for a diagnosed emotional problem.

4. Sexual abuse. Includes sexual molestation, incest, and exploitation for prostitution or the production of pornographic materials. This form of abuse will be discussed more completely in the next chapter.

Legally, a *child* usually means a person under age eighteen. What makes child abuse and neglect different from crimes committed against children by strangers is that the abuser is a parent, custodian, or guardian and is someone with the duty to protect and guide the child to normal adulthood. Child maltreatment is a sign of a family in trouble.[14]

CONSEQUENCES OF PHYSICAL AND EMOTIONAL ABUSE AND NEGLECT

It is very difficult to separate out the impact of abuse and neglect from other factors in a child's life and family. But child maltreatment does touch every part of our society. It has an affect on our economic structure as well as our collective mental and physical health.

Physical abuse may result in permanent damage to either limb or body function. It can affect the central nervous system, resulting in seizures, mental retardation, cerebral palsy, hearing or visual damage, or learning disabilities.

Neglect, in the form of undernutrition, or lack of medical care may leave long-term effects on the normal development of the brain. Maltreated children have been found to have a much higher likelihood of significant illnesses in infancy. Anemia and its related aspects of apathy, poor learning ability, listlessness, and exhaustion appear to be common in abused children.

Other researchers have found victims of abuse and neglect had more behavior, discipline, and school attendance problems, as well as delayed language development.[15]

Mistreated children have lower IQs, poorer language skills, and show less competent academic progress than other similar children.[16]

The abused child lives in an unpredictable, unhappy, confusing world that may be violent or simply grossly inadequate. Survival may take all the energy a child has. The child may be excessively withdrawn, aggressive, or fearful of other people. Abused and neglected children have difficulty in forming healthy relationships with others.

The issue of self-esteem is very important. One study found a high incidence of attempted suicides and self-mutilative behavior among battered children whose average age was only eight-and-one-half years old.[17]

One of the most consistent and insidious findings in the

study of abused children is that abusing parents often report having been abused themselves as children. Abusive parents raise their children as they were raised.[18]

Having learned violence at home, abused children may act out their lessons against their own children or against society in general. Among the infamous adults who were abused as children are Charles Manson, Sirhan Sirhan, James Earl Ray, and Lee Harvey Oswald.

This doesn't mean that abusive parents cause their children to be abusive when they grow into adulthood. There is a strong relationship, but it is not always true. Some abused children do not act in violent ways as adults. And there are violent adults who were not abused as children.

Researchers have been curious to find out why abuse may or may not be transmitted across generations. One investigator found that nonabusive families have a broader network of available resources and better family interactional patterns than the abusive families. Nonabusive families are more likely to have available to them friends or an extended family. They were also more likely to participate in religious or other social groups, and were more skilled at using the services of community agencies.[19]

While some abused and neglected children do seem to survive, we cannot stand by and hope that all of them make it with no lasting scars. As concerned professionals we must learn how to identify the symptoms of abuse and then make the most appropriate intervention. We must also look at ways to prevent the pain from ever occurring.

A familiar verse in Ephesians 6:4 tells Christian parents not to provoke their children to wrath or not to exasperate them. The implication is that exasperated children are not the best kind of youngsters to have. The parents (here represented by the father) are instructed not to break the spirit of their children by severe, unjust, partial, or unreasonable use of authority. The consequences of abusive parenting will result in either an angry, vengeful, acting-out child, or a passive, broken spirit. Neither of these outcomes fulfills the admonition to the parent to bring up their children in the training and instruction of the Lord.

IDENTIFYING PHYSICAL ABUSE AND NEGLECT

Inflicted physical injury often represents unreasonably severe corporal punishment. This often happens when the parent becomes frustrated and angry, and shakes, throws, or strikes the child. Intentional assault, such as burning, biting, cutting, poking, twisting limbs, or otherwise torturing a child, is also included in this category.

The general clinical signs of abuse, in the absence of a reasonable explanation, include:

- damage to the skin and surface tissues, such as bruises, burns, abrasions, lacerations, or swelling
- damage to the brain, as evidenced by convulsions; altered mental status, such as coma or irritability; retardation of developmental progress; or change in the rate of head growth
- damage to other internal organs, as suggested by shock, abdominal pain or distention, or bleeding within the organs
- damage to the skeleton, as evidenced by swelling, pain on movement, or deformity

Indicators of reportable suspected physical abuse would generally fall into the following categories:

- a child claiming that injury was caused by abuse
- any injury unusual for a specific age group (e.g., any fracture in an infant)
- a history of previous or recurrent injury
- unexplained injury (e.g., parent unable to explain reasons for injury; discrepancies in giving explanations; blame placed on a third party; explanations inconsistent with medical diagnosis)
- bruising in an unusual area, other than on shins, elbows, or knees, for example. Certain specific bruising patterns also indicate child abuse, such as belt buckle marks, handprints, bite marks, and pinches.
- evidence of poor supervision (repeated falls down stairs; repeated ingestions of harmful substances; a child cared for by another child)

- evidence of neglect
- any indication of sexual abuse
- verbal threats against the life of a child made by a parent or caretaker

Indicators of Suspected Physical Abuse

There are many signs of physical abuse. Some of these indicators will only be seen by a physician when he or she examines a child. Others can be noted by a more casual observation.

Burns. Burns are often difficult to evaluate. However, the location of the burn and its shape, depth, margins, etc., may indicate abuse. It's important to keep in mind that children instinctively withdraw from pain. Burns without some evidence of withdrawal or retraction are highly suspect.

One burn characteristic of abuse is that which has the shape of a recognizable object evenly burned into the victim's skin. Such burns indicate forced contact or "branding" with something like the grill of an electric heater, element of an electric stove, a cigarette or an iron.

Another burn that does not appear to be accidental is a scald burn between the shoulder blades. Such burns can result from immersion of a child's upper back in hot water.

"Zebra" burns also indicate abuse. Such burns result when a child is held by his or her hands and legs under a running hot faucet. The tissue on the child's abdomen and upper legs folds up, preventing burning in the creases. The resulting "zebra stripes" from scalding of exposed tissue are clearly evident.

A child's natural response when stepping into a tub of water is to sit down. This may result in burns of the feet and the entire surfaces of the buttocks if the water is hot. The child will then usually try to escape. That will result in splashes, uneven burns, and sometimes burns on the hands. In contrast, when children are forcibly held in hot water, there are often sharply demarcated burns.

If held in water in a "jackknife" position, only the buttocks and genitalia may be burned. If held down forcibly in a sitting position, the center parts of the buttocks (if pressed tightly against the tub) are spared from burning, thus resulting in a "doughnut" shaped burn.

If the extremities are forcibly immersed in hot water, "glove" or "sock" burns to the hands or feet may result. The burns are often symmetrical and an immersion line is readily evident.

Abuse should also be suspected when burns are pointed or deeper in the middle. This indicates that hot liquid was poured on, or that a hot object, such as a poker or utensil, was pressed into the skin. Cigarette burns are usually multiple and are often found on the palms or soles. There is a searing effect with charring around the wound.

Rope burns appear around wrists or ankles when children are tied to beds or other structures.

Bruises. Inflicted or nonaccidental injury should be suspected when:

Bruises are either multiple and all of the same color, or multiple and of different colors. (Differences in coloration reflect various stages of healing and indicate that the injuries were sustained at different times.)

The child is less than twelve months old. (Children this age would be unlikely candidates for multiple bruises.)

Bruises are found on multiple surfaces of the body, particularly on the back, genitals, or mouth.

Bruises have a characteristic pattern (outline of hand, paired bruises from pinching, loop from a cord, etc.) or clearly resemble an impression of an item of jewelry, such as a ring.

Bruises are on both sides of the face. (Two black eyes would be highly suspect, unless in the case of a proven accidentally broken nose.)

Timing or age dating of bruises can be an important factor. While the following colorations are only approximations, they can serve as a rough guide to determine when the injury occurred:

- immediate—within a few hours: red
- soon—from six to twelve hours prior: blue
- later—from twelve to twenty-four hours prior: black–purple
- four to six days prior: green tint, dark
- five to ten days prior: pale green to yellow

Bite marks. Bite marks, which may be found on any part of the body, may be described as doughnut-shaped or double-horseshoe-shaped. Occasionally, as many as twelve or more tooth impressions will be seen and in some cases as few as one or two.

Time is of the essence in recording bite marks as they become less distinct with time. Photographs, impressions, and salivary swabbing can be used to collect suspected bite mark evidence. Human bite marks can be used to reveal the identity of the abuser, due to the uniqueness of the human dentition.

Abrasions, lacerations, and scars. Like bruises, the multiplicity and location of wounds should be considered. For example, lacerations under the tongue or those of a torn frenulum (the small piece of skin connecting the gum to the lip) could be caused by falling with an object in the mouth, or by excessive force during feedings. Both are suspicious injuries, particularly before an infant can stand.

Whipping. Linear marks or strap marks sometimes covering a curved body surface (wraparound) are evidence of intentional abuse. Belt buckles cause a "C-" or "U-" shaped dark wound called a "gull wing" laceration. Belt buckles can cause other wounds with distinctive shapes as well. Loop marks on the skin may be caused by a doubled-over electric cord or rope.

Head injuries. Whenever abuse or neglect is suspected, a careful examination of the child's eyes and nervous system should be performed, looking for signs of intracranial injury. Serious intracranial injury may occur without visible evidence of trauma on the face or scalp.

Skull x-rays should be performed in all abused children with evidence of trauma to the head, as well as in all small infants in whom abuse is suspected. All types of skull fractures should be carefully evaluated, especially when the explanation of the injury is not consistent with the presented trauma. Head injuries are the most common cause of child-abuse related deaths.

"Whiplash shaken infant syndrome." The essential elements in this syndrome present an apparent diagnostic contradiction, in that intracranial and intraocular hemorrhage occur in the

absence of signs of external injury to the head. Shaking, using excessive force, may produce not only these injuries, but also lesions of the long bones.

The injury may go undiagnosed for years and perhaps first show up in school as minor neurological deficits or learning problems. More severe deficits, such as blindness, deafness, or paralysis, generally appear sooner. Death can be caused by this type of abuse.

Pummeling. Blows from a heavy blunt object, such as a baseball bat or fist, on soft tissue results in deep muscular bruises or hemorrhage. These are rarely discolored. In time, such a collection of blood may be seen on x-rays. Blunt blows to the body may cause serious internal injuries to the liver, spleen, pancreas, kidneys, and other vital organs. Detectable surface evidence of such trauma is present only about half the time.

Fractures. Any fracture in an infant or toddler is suspect. Long-bone (arm and leg) fractures that are the result of twisting are called "spiral" fractures and are almost always due to inflicted trauma.

Other fractures that raise suspicion are "chip" fractures at the end of long bones, particularly when they occur in an infant; fractures resulting from yanking and jerking; rib fractures, especially back rib fractures; and healing or healed fractures revealed by x-rays.

Additional signs of physical abuse. Some additional factors that should raise suspicion and trigger further investigation include the following:

The child is generally fearful of adults, is nonspontaneous, and refuses to speak in front of parents.

The child is overly eager to please adults when asked to perform menial tasks.

Parents over-react and are extremely nervous.

Parents bring child to medical facility for unneeded treatment.

Very young children with injuries on the back surfaces of the body from the neck to the knees. This is the primary target zone for infliction of physical injuries. Such injuries constitute the largest percentage of identified abuse.

Bruises, scars, and wounds on the backs of arms and hands, which are called "defense" wounds.

Excessive layers of clothing, especially in hot weather, should arouse curiosity since clothing may be hiding wounds.

One of the most important indicators is when a child tells someone. The child should not be ignored, nor the gravity of the situation minimized.

Indicators of Emotional Abuse

Just as physical injuries can scar and incapacitate a child, emotional cruelty can similarly cripple and handicap a child. Excessive verbal assaults, such as belittling, blaming, sarcasm, unpredictable responses, continual negative moods, constant family discord, and double message communication, are examples of ways parents may inflict emotional abuse on the child.

Emotional abuse may be suspected if the child:

- is withdrawn, depressed and apathetic
- "acts out" and is considered a behavior problem
- is overly rigid in conforming to the instructions of teachers, doctors, and other adults
- displays other signs of emotional turmoil such as repetitive, rhythmic movements, inordinate attention to details, no verbal or physical communication with others.

These behavior patterns may, of course, be due to other causes, but the suspicion of abuse should not be precluded.

Indicators of Emotional Deprivation

Robert Mulford of the American Humane Association has defined emotional deprivation as ". . . the deprivation suffered by children when their parents do not provide the normal experiences producing feelings of being loved, wanted, secure, and worthy."[20]

For normal development, children need emotional involvement from their caretakers as much as they need proper nutrition. Infants who do not experience any affection are subject to mortality in spite of their physical needs being met. Emotional starvation is one of the most difficult types of abuse to detect and is perhaps the most tragic.

Emotional deprivation should be suspected if the following is observed:

The child refuses to eat or eats very little, and is very frail.

The child is not thriving in general (unable to perform normal learned functions for a given age, e.g., walking, talking, etc.).

Child displays antisocial behavior, i.e., aggression, disruption, etc.

Child displays delinquent behavior, i.e., drug abuse, vandalism, theft, etc.

Child constantly seeks out and pesters other adults for attention and affection.

Child displays exaggerated fears.

Indicators of Physical Neglect

Physical neglect is the failure of a parent or caretaker to provide a child with adequate food, shelter, clothing, protection, supervision, and medical and dental care.

Physical neglect is suspected if the following conditions exist in a home:

- Unsanitary conditions, i.e., garbage, animal, or human excretion
- Lack of heating or plumbing
- Fire hazards or other unsafe conditions
- Cold, dirty, or otherwise inadequate sleeping arrangements
- Infestation of insects or rodents
- Poor nutritional quality of food
- Meals not prepared; children snack when hungry
- Spoiled food in refrigerator or cupboards
- Insufficient medical or dental care for child
- Child always sleepy or hungry
- Clothing always dirty or inadequate for weather
- Child under fourteen left alone in home or unsupervised for long periods of time

While some of these conditions may exist in any home environment, it is the extreme or persistent presence of these factors that indicates neglect.[21]

CHARACTERISTICS OF PHYSICALLY AND EMOTIONALLY ABUSIVE PARENTS

Child abuse occurs in all cultural, ethnic, occupational, and socioeconomic groups. There is a proportionately higher incidence of abuse reported in minority and low-income families, but it is also true that these families have more contact with social service agencies, which increases the chances of detection of abuse within the home.

Many of the battering parents were battered children themselves. Consequently, these parents use the same destructive techniques on their own children as their parents practiced on them. Despite their intentions and efforts to be good parents, they end up repeating the type of maltreatment they experienced as children. Because they have never been exposed to proper parenting practices, the cycle is not interrupted and these violent patterns are transmitted to the next generation.

Also, in some families a role reversal occurs. The parent becomes the child in order to find the love and acceptance he or she had missed as a child. The child is then placed in an adult role, with the parent expecting the child to take care of him or her. The parent sees the child as having capabilities far beyond what is appropriate for his or her age. When the young child does not meet these expectations, violence can occur.

Parents of abused children are often described as being immature, dependent, impulsive, self-centered, rigid, and rejecting. They tend to lack nurturing and coping skills and have a relatively low frustration tolerance. Violence is a part of their history, so they use it as a frequent option.

Abusive parents are often socially isolated and distrustful of their neighbors. Many abusive parents had troubled childhoods and learned very early that they could not rely on others for emotional support. As a result they never learned the social skills necessary to form solid relationships with relatives, neighbors, and friends. They seem to reject offers of help, having learned to be suspicious of the good intentions of others. When faced with a stressful situation, such as a fussy baby, they feel totally alone and trapped and may react with violent abuse or neglectful depression.

Isolation can be related to the decline of the extended family. An extended family is one in which a number of immediate relatives reside in the same household or live close by and are readily available in time of need. The typical family today consists of a mother, father, and child with few relatives close enough to provide immediate support. There are fewer sympathetic ears listening and helping with frustrations and fewer potential baby-sitters or persons to assist parents with child raising. Mobility and the degree of transiency characteristic of the nuclear family also means the parents have fewer close friends upon whom they will depend.

Abusive parents often live in high-risk neighborhoods, and have a high level of stress. Even without children, adults encounter many stressful situations—unemployment, poverty, illness, or divorce. For abusive parents, these conditions can be doubly traumatic, because there is no vacation from parental responsibilities. When a parent with lowered coping skills has to deal with any of these stressful situations, there is little time or energy left for the children. Also, when the tolerance for stress is exceeded, the slightest misbehavior of the child can lead to a violent attack by the parent.

Studies have shown that a mother who has little or no contact with her infant immediately after birth may be more likely to abuse or neglect her child. Children born prematurely, by Caesarean section, or with an illness may run a greater risk of maltreatment because the early bonding between mother and child may be disturbed by the physical separation.[22]

Also, a child born with defects or other disfigurements is often singled out for emotional or physical abuse. A child who is viewed as different or slow often becomes a scapegoat for other family problems.

Alcohol abuse on the part of the parent is often a factor in situations of abuse and neglect. One study found an association of abandonment with alcoholism of the mother and an association of sexual abuse with the factor of a promiscuous and alcoholic father.[23]

A variety of skill and knowledge deficits has also been suggested as characteristic of abusive parents. These deficits are found in parenting skills (including overuse of physical punishment), life coping skills, self-control skills, marital skills, general interpersonal skills, and knowledge of child development. By not knowing the normal phases of child development, for example, abusive parents will tend to have inappropriate expectations for their child.

Abusive parents are also characterized by negative child rearing attitudes, inability to distinguish feelings of self versus others, and failure to take responsibility for one's own actions.[24]

The child abuser tends to repeat the abuse. It doesn't just happen once and go away. If it has happened once, it will probably happen again. The abuse will also tend to escalate in the amount and severity of the abuse. Because of these characteristics, it is very important for the helping professions to identify high-risk families and provide them with the resources to control their violence.

It is not possible to predict exactly if or when child maltreatment will occur in a given family situation. However, a family may be a high risk if the parent:

- is a loner; feels isolated, with no family to depend upon, no real friends; does not get along well with neighbors.
- has no understanding of the stages of child development and does not know what to expect of a child at a given age.
- has a poor self-image, feels worthless, with a pervading sense of failure.
- feels unloved, unappreciated, unwanted, with a great fear of rejection.
- has severe personal problems, such as ill health, alcoholism, or drug dependency.
- feels that violence can often be the solution to life's problems, or has not learned to manage his or her anger in a socially acceptable manner.

- is experiencing a time of severe stress (sudden unemployment, painful divorce) without any coping mechanism.
- has been abused or neglected as a child.

The following are added high-risk factors if the child:

- is "different"—smaller than average, sickly, disabled, considered unattractive, or born prematurely.
- resembles or reminds the parent of someone the parent hates (takes after a disappointing spouse or relative).
- is more demanding or active than other children in the family.
- is unwanted—seen as a mistake or burden, having ruined things for the parent.[25]

Child abuse is seldom the result of any single factor. Rather, it is a combination of circumstances and personality types that come together to bring about acts of abuse. For example, during a period of unemployment, a parent who had been abused as a child, resulting in a strong belief in corporal punishment, and who had a limited ability to manage her anger, might "lose it" and batter a clumsy child who drops the mother's favorite vase.

Finally, there are some indicators that may become apparent while interviewing the parents of a suspected abused or neglected child. The pastor or counselor should look for these responses. They do not guarantee the existence of abuse, but, if present, should lead to further investigation. If a parent cannot be located that is a red flag also. The response indicators are as follows:

- a contradictory history given by the parent or caretaker
- a history that does not adequately explain the nature and extent of the given injuries
- a reluctance on the part of the parent or caretaker to give information or participate in the history-taking process
- a history of repeated injuries or accidents to the child
- a statement that others caused the injury to the child (brother, sister, or playmate)

- an undue and unexplained delay in bringing the child in for medical attention
- a history of skipping from one health-care facility to another
- detachment by the parent from the child and from the interviewer
- under- or overreaction to the situation at hand
- information presented by the parent or child that indicates chronic family discord or inordinate amounts of stress within the family
- drug or alcohol abuse
- refusal to give consent or to participate in further evaluation procedures

We have seen how extensive the problem of battered children continues to be in our society. The indicators of abuse for both children and abusers have been summarized. The discussion has been limited to physical and emotional abuse and neglect. Sexual abuse will be the next topic. Because of the conspiracy of silence that has surrounded this form of maltreatment for both Christian and secular communities, along with the emotional scars inflicted on its victims, this topic will be the major focus of the rest of the presentation on child abuse.

CHAPTER SEVEN

SEXUAL ABUSE OF CHILDREN

BETH WAS NINE YEARS OLD when her father first began sexual contact with her. Keith, Beth's father, would touch Beth's genitals when the two of them were tickling and roughhousing in the family room. This early play progressed to fondling when Keith would tuck Beth into her bed at night. Beth found the experiences strange, but pleasurable.

Keith and his wife, Heather, had a strained relationship throughout their marriage. Although both parents were active in their local church, they seldom did things together. Whenever they had a major fight, Heather would refuse to have sexual relations with Keith. The couple became more and more distant in their relationship. By the time Beth was eleven,

Heather spent many evenings away from home, attending church and civic meetings.

Keith's sex play with Beth progressed to oral copulation by the time Beth was twelve years old. At this point, Keith attempted to restrict Beth's contact with her friends. She resented his restraints and became increasingly uncomfortable about the sexual activities with her father. Beth never told her mother about her experiences, although during a disagreement with her mother, Beth had shouted, "If you and Dad got along better, maybe he would leave me alone!" Her mother never asked Beth what she meant by that statement. Beth didn't think her mother would believe her anyway.

INCIDENCE AND HISTORY OF SEXUAL ABUSE

It has been estimated that one in every six people has been involved in some form of incestuous relationship. A random survey of women in the San Francisco area indicated that intrafamilial sexual abuse was experienced by 16 percent of the women before the age of eighteen and by 12 percent of the women by the age of fourteen. Sexual abuse by persons outside of the family was experienced by 31 percent of the subjects before the age of eighteen and by 20 percent before fourteen years of age. When both categories of sexual abuse were combined, sexual abuse occurred among 38 percent of the women before they were eighteen and among 28 percent before they were fourteen.

Only 2 percent of the cases occurring within the family were reported and only 6 percent of the cases of abuse by persons outside of the family were ever reported to the police.[1]

These figures indicate that almost one out of three females has been sexually abused by the time she is eighteen years old. If this were a disease, like the chicken pox, we would declare it an epidemic bordering on a national disaster!

Eighty percent of the victims of child sexual abuse are female, although it is expected that abuse of male children is underreported. The embarrassment and shame that tends to deter girls from reporting such abuse has an even greater effect on boys, since the abuse is often homosexual. Because girls are much more frequently the victims of sexual abuse, according to the reports available, the feminine pronouns will be used in most references in the balance of this discussion.

The National Center on Child Abuse and Neglect estimates that at least one hundred thousand cases of sexual abuse occur every year. Many experts believe two hundred fifty thousand cases per year is a conservative estimate.[2]

The initial sexual abuse may occur at any age, from infancy through adolescence. However, the largest number of cases involve females under the age of eleven. The sexual activity is usually repetitive and progressive. There is no escape for the victim until he or she is old enough to realize that incest is not a common occurrence and is able to obtain help outside the family.

Child sexual abuse is one of the most underreported forms of child maltreatment. It often remains undetected and the impact may not become obvious for many years. Other factors contribute to this lack of reporting. The family is often reluctant to report such incidents to the authorities for fear of social censure, public scrutiny, and removal of the family breadwinner. There being no physical, tangible evidence of harm or trauma also contributes to the underreporting of this form of abuse. In addition, children do not report incidents of sexual abuse because of ignorance, fear of reprisals by the offender, fear that their parents will blame them, or guilt over any pleasure they may have experienced. For the most part, then, the incidence of sexual abuse remains locked in a conspiracy of silence.

This conspiracy is also present within the church community. The evidence suggests the incidence of sexual abuse is every bit as high in Christian homes. Admittedly, the data is limited, but the informal evidence of the extent of abuse within the church is very convincing.

My own awareness has been heightened by the increasing number of children referred to my practice for suspected sexual abuse. Many of these children were abused by adults active in their own churches. In addition, I have seen a large number of adults, mostly women, who were abused as children. My impression is that there are as many victims from church as from nonchurch families.

It's difficult to measure someone's level of Christianity, but many counselors, therapists, and researchers do report that among churchgoers the adult male offenders tend to be very devout, moralistic, and conservative in their religious beliefs.[3]

I have talked to personnel at sexual assault centers, college counselors, therapists, and researchers throughout the West Coast and Midwest. They are unanimous in their conclusion that the rate of sexual abuse is no less in religious or Christian homes than the general public. One counselor from a Christian university told me a major portion of his caseload of students was for problems related to sexual abuse. He felt that one out of ten was a conservative estimate for abused female students on his campus.

Alice Huskey, herself a victim of incest by a father who was an active member of a fundamentalist church, reports a survey of two hundred forty-seven female students at a Christian liberal arts college. Ninety-six of the students responded to the survey, and more than half said they had been abused as children. Almost all of those students had been reared in Christian homes.[4]

A study completed at Fuller Graduate School of Psychology surveyed nine hundred Christian counselors and pastors on the subject of family sexual abuse. The majority of those who responded to the questionnaire felt that incest occurred as often in Christian as in non-Christian homes.[5]

Another example occurred several years ago when a Midwest family physician was arrested on charges of aggravated sodomy and taking indecent liberties with a fourteen-year-old girl. That same person had previously coauthored a book about baby and child care "for the Christian parent."[6]

While we might not like to admit it, this form of family violence may be even more prevalent within the church community than any other kind of abuse. Somehow, the good news of Christ and the grace of God have not sufficiently impacted this insidious but devastating form of sin.

Sexual abuse is not a recent phenomenon, however current the media attention may be. Incest was strictly prohibited in the Old Testament Law (Lev. 18:6–18). Rape was forbidden and death established as a consequence (Deut. 22:25–27).

As early as Genesis 34:2 we are told of Dinah being raped by Shechem. And later Reuben slept with his father's concubine, Bilhah (Gen. 35:22). Another form of incest is presented when we learn of Amnon raping his stepsister Tamar in 2 Samuel 13:14. Tamar's rape is followed by an early example of the minimizing of the trauma, so common in recent generations. After Tamar reports her attack and subsequent shame to Absalom, her brother, he tells Tamar not to make a big thing out of her situation (vs. 20). Although Absalom later had Amnon killed for molesting his sister, Tamar was still left with the scars of her abuse.

One reason for Absalom's initial minimizing of the rape may have been his own susceptibility to sexual temptation. Later, we read about his own violation of the law when he commits incest with his father's concubines in 2 Samuel 16:22.

Another instance of rape involved the Levite's concubine (Judg. 19:25–28). Abused by a gang of angry young men, she died from the ordeal.

Many prostitutes have been abused as children. It is estimated that over 75 percent of all adolescents involved in prostitution, both male and female, were victims of prior sexual violence, rape, incestuous abuse, or molestation.[7] It is assumed that traumas of this nature led to their decision to work the streets.

Although this passage is probably an allegory of the unfaithfulness of Israel, Ezekiel 23:3, 8, and 21 describes two adulterous sisters, Oholah and Oholibah, young prostitutes in Egypt. Each of those verses tells that their breasts were fondled and their virgin bosoms caressed during their youth. Even as a parable, the inference could be made that there were such women who were abused as young girls. Those early violations set the stage for their uncontrollable lust in later life.

Secular history is replete with child sexual abuse. Greek poetry abounds with men swooning for "the tender flower of youth." And the technological inventiveness of the nineteenth century, along with the Victorian males' interest in female children, helped spur the production and distribution of child pornography. The desires of men have always found ways to take advantage of the status and availability of children.

DEFINITION OF CHILD SEXUAL ABUSE

Legally, child sexual abuse can be described in several ways. It can be called *rape* if physical force is used and penetration takes place, or *statutory rape* if force is not used and the victim is underage. Sexual abuse without penetration, such as touching, fondling, masturbation, etc., usually is defined as *indecent liberties.*

From a psychological perspective, child sexual abuse is the sexual exploitation of a child who is not developmentally capable of understanding or resisting the contact, and/or who is psychologically and socially dependent on the offender. It may involve fondling, exhibitionism, masturbation, and/or genital penetration.

The National Center for Child Abuse and Neglect, and many state statutes, also includes commercial exploitation for prostitution or the use of children in the production of pornographic materials, in the definition of child sexual abuse.

Two criteria establish child sexual abuse as a form of violence. The first is the lack of consent on the part of the victim. For children, the lack of consent is a given. They cannot give or withhold consent when approached sexually by an adult, because they are immature, uninformed, and usually dependent on the adult. They lack any real power to resist or make choices.

In the example to follow, Courtney, who at age ten was seduced by her father, admonished him in a letter when she reached adulthood. She asked him the question, "Can you understand how ironic it is being in my position where I kept my mouth shut about your sexual abuse of me to protect you from the destruction of our family?" She then further detailed the double bind which fed her anguish:

> Since I was a little ten-year-old child, I had to deceive and hide from all the world and my mother that my father took a sexual interest in me and initiated sexual activities with me. Remember how you taught me that art of deceit? First you put me in a situation that had to be kept secret (for your protection) and then you pledged me to secrecy. . . . As a ten-year-old child, what was I supposed

to do? You are an intelligent man—you figure out the options available to a ten-year-old in that position.[8]

Of course, a ten-year-old child who is exploited by her father has no options. If the person who is supposed to be her prime protector is also her seducer and exploiter, where can she go? This is the power an adult, and particularly a parent, has over a child. The element of choice in the matter of sexual relations between adults and children rests with the adult.

The second criterion for seeing sexual abuse as a form of violence is the resultant injury to the victim. The sexual use of a child disregards the child's best welfare. The child becomes an object exclusively to meet the needs of the offender. The act is exploitative and, therefore, damaging to the child.

Katherine Brady, in her book *Father's Days: A True Story of Incest,* describes some of the emotional disturbance brought on by her incestuous experience:

> Each increase in my guilt, shame and disgust caused an equal increase in my need to create a glossy pleasing surface. The darker the inside the brighter the outside must be to hide it. . . . By the time I reached high school, I had two absolutely separate personalities. The public one, exhibited to family and friends alike, was friendly, stable, honest, thoughtful, courteous, trustworthy, reliable, and cooperative. The private one was fearful, isolated, anxious, and depressed.[9]

A common consequence of sexual abuse is the sharp sense of betrayal of trust. By turning the trust of a child into corrupted obedience to meet selfish desires, the adult creates a legacy of suspicion and hurt. The child will never have an earthly, loving, caring father. It can take years of therapy before a woman can learn to order her life with that reality.

CONSEQUENCES OF CHILD SEXUAL ABUSE

Sexual abuse does not affect every child to the same extent. Responses to sexual abuse may vary according to a number of factors: the child's age and developmental status; the child's personality and general level of adjustment, the nature and type of the offense; the relationship of the offender to the child; the frequency and duration of the abuse; the degree of felt shame or guilt; the type of threats used to maintain secrecy; and the reaction of the parents when the sexual activity is discovered.

Most experts believe sexual abuse is nearly always a profoundly disruptive, disorienting, and destructive experience for the child who has experienced a degree of stimulation that is far beyond his or her capacity to encompass and assimilate. As a result there is interference with the accomplishment of normal developmental tasks. The progression of mastery of one's self, environment, and relationships with others is significantly disrupted by the child's permanently altered awareness and new role with the perpetrator. The child is in conflict and frustrated by contradictions: "Is this man my lover or my father? Am I my mother's mother? How can I participate in this activity which keeps my family together, when I feel wrong and the outside world feels it's wrong? How can I be loved and avoid the sexual activity?"

The child has a secret she cannot share. This situation leads to feelings of alienation and separation from her family and friends. Although confusing, her special status may lead her to feel she has an inordinate sense of power. She may manifest this power via an air of superiority or haughtiness. Or she may perceive herself as having an evil power to corrupt or to contaminate.

Another result of her alienation may be blaming herself, both for the event and for its consequences. Mixed with her guilt and her alienation is the compounding factor that, at some level, she has enjoyed the sexual experience. The longing to return to these experiences, at least in fantasy, can only intensify her ambivalence.

The sexually abused child is depreciated in value and becomes more of an object than a person. She may feel burdened with the responsibility of holding the family together through her relationship with the perpetrator.

Child sexual abuse is disorienting because profound blurring of boundaries inevitably follows when someone in a power position exploits the child by making her a sexual partner. These children can't avoid questioning limits set for them and for others. They will be confused about the appropriate uses of power and authority. Their very identities are at stake when they ask, "Who am I, that I am both a child and a sexual partner of someone who is supposed to be parenting, nurturing, or protecting me?"

These dilemmas create guilt, shame, fear, and anxiety. For an estimated 20 percent of sexually abused victims, severe depression may follow and may be associated with suicide attempts. For 40 percent of the victims, problem behaviors develop, including irritability, school truancy, deteriorating school performance, somatic complaints, sexual promiscuity, running away from home, lying, etc. For another 20 percent, frigidity in adult life seems to be the consequence of this awkward initiation into adult sexuality. Probably only 20 percent come through the incest experience unscathed.[10]

Many sexually abused children have very poor self-images, possess very poor social skills, and are reluctant to trust any other human being.

Many adults who were abused as children describe serious difficulty in attaining a satisfactory level of emotional self-sufficiency or independence as adults. Nearly all attribute a lack of confidence to their childhood victimization. They may become dependent on drugs or alcohol, or become carbon copies of their mothers.

Two final consequences are noteworthy. Childhood sexual victimization may increase the likelihood that an individual will become a perpetrator as an adolescent or adult. It is also disturbing to note the tendency of women who were sexually abused in childhood to select mates who, in turn, are likely to abuse them and sexually exploit their children.

These results of sexual abuse leave no doubt about its negative long-term effects. This serves to underscore the seriousness of this silent conspiracy. It must be identified and treated.

IDENTIFYING SEXUAL ABUSE

Following is a list of symptoms often found in sexually abused children. They are presented in three areas: behavioral, medical, and familial. As is true of other lists of indicators relating to child maltreatment, most of these indicators are not, of themselves, absolute proof of sexual abuse. But if any obvious symptom or several of the possible indicators are observed, an immediate attempt should be made to investigate further.

Behavioral Indicators

These apply to the child's daily pattern. An occasional occurrence does not immediately suggest abuse. Look for repeated patterns unless it is a direct statement.

- indirect hints or open statements about abuse
- difficulty in peer relationships, i.e., violence against younger children
- withdrawn, less verbal, depressed, or apathetic
- self-mutilation
- preoccupation with death, guilt, heaven, or hell
- retreat to fantasy world, dissociative reactions—loss of memory, imaginary playmates, referring to herself by more than one name
- fear, clinging to parent, requires reassurance
- unwillingness to participate in physical/recreational activities
- refusal to undress for gym class at school
- sudden increase in modesty
- fear of bathrooms and showers
- anger, acting out, disobedience
- refusal to be left with potential offender or caretaker
- lack of trust
- runaway behavior
- refusal to go home or stated desire to live elsewhere
- extreme fear or repulsion when touched by an adult of either sex
- touching to either extreme
- inappropriate dress; use of clothing to reverse roles—child looks like sophisticated adult, mother like teenager
- sophisticated sexual knowledge
- precocious, provocative sexual behavior

- seductive, indiscriminate display of affection
- regression to earlier, infant behavior—bed wetting, thumb sucking
- sleep disturbances, nightmares
- inability to concentrate in school, hyperactive
- sudden drop in school performance
- overly compliant or almost compulsive in action
- arriving early at school and leaving late with few, if any, absences
- excessive masturbation
- combination of violence and sexuality in artwork, written schoolwork, language, and play
- hysterical seizures
- attempts to establish boundaries, such as wearing clothing to bed
- total denial of problem with total lack of expression or feeling

Medical Indicators

These indicators will be documented by a physician, but are included here to give a full representation of all types of symptoms.

- passive during pelvic examination. A nonabused child will be more agitated during her first pelvic exam. A raped child will yell and scream, while a repeatedly abused child will quietly spread her legs.
- bruises and hickeys, or both, in the face or neck area or around the groin, buttocks, and inner thighs
- torn, stained, or bloody underclothing
- bleeding from external genitalia, vagina, or anal regions
- swollen or red cervix, vulva, or perineum
- positive tests for gonococcus or spermatozoa
- pain or itching in genital areas
- venereal disease or gonorrhea infections
- pregnancy
- abrasions and erythema of the vulvar area, laceration of posterior fourchette

- small perihymenal scars and scarring of posterior fourchette
- abrasions and laceration of hymen with tearing between three o'clock and nine o'clock
- scarred and thickened transected hymen with rounded redundant hymenal remnants with adhesions sometimes binding hymen laterally and distorting the opening
- complete or partial loss of sphincter control
- fan-shaped scarring extending out from anus in six o'clock position
- pain on urination
- penile swelling and penile discharge
- vaginal discharge and urethral or lymph gland inflammation[11]

Familial Indicators

The following symptoms apply to the rest of the child's family. It is always important to keep the entire family perspective in mind when making any kind of assessment.

Sibling behavior:

- brother and sister behave like a girlfriend and boyfriend
- child fears being left alone with sibling
- children appear to be embarrassed when found alone together
- child is teased or antagonized by sibling but does not retaliate
- siblings report another child is favored by parent

Parental behavior:

- dysfunctional family system, blurring of generational lines
- strained marital relationship
- parent often alone with one child
- favoritism by parent toward one child
- overly protective or jealous parent

CHARACTERISTICS OF THE INCEST OFFENDER

Those who commit incest cannot be distinguished from those who do not on the basis of any major demographic characteristics. Such offenders do not differ significantly from the rest of the population in regard to level of education, occupation, race, religion, intelligence, mental status, etc. They come from all socioeconomic classes. They do differ from nonoffenders in the fact that when faced with overwhelming life stressors, they seek relief from the situation through sexual activity with children.[12]

The incest offender is usually a male (98 percent) who is insecure and socially immature. He does not have social skills for relating to adults, particularly in intimate situations. He has trouble sharing feelings because of both lack of personal awareness and lack of ability to express congruently how he feels. Some offenders appear to be comfortable with their peers in social settings and may even have positions of leadership. However, they do lack the ability to satisfy their affection and attention needs through adults.

The Pharisee Connection

You hypocrites! You clean the outside of the cup and dish,
but inside they are full of greed and self-indulgence . . .
on the outside you appear to people as righteous but on
the inside you are full of hypocrisy and wickedness.

> (Matt. 23:26, 28)

Like the Pharisees denounced and rebuked by Christ, many incest offenders have rigid beliefs and authoritarian manners. They want to be the head of the household and in control. For some, this is accompanied by strong alleged religious beliefs which are very opinionated and divided into clear but simplistic compartments.

Dr. Henry Giaretto is founder of Parents United, the nation's largest treatment program for incest victims and their families. I asked him to describe his impressions of the religious component in incest offenders. While acknowledging the lack of hard data, he readily affirmed the fact that some of the most serious cases in his program have come from the highly dogmatic, religious family.

Dr. Bob Rencken, director of the Family Development Center in Tucson, Arizona, also verified the overrepresentation of rigidly religious fathers involved in incest. His experience, based on a large multi-disciplinary treatment program, is that a typical offender is likely to have a rigid, highly structured, religious style. Often the offender is extremely regular in church attendance, but has no sense of community or participation in the fellowship of the church.

Psychological test data was gathered on a small sample of male offenders from families where children had been sexually abused. The test profile showed offenders to be very conscientious and moralistic yet frustrated, when compared to nonoffending males.[13] This data also suggests there is a tendency for offenders to be strongly opinionated, and with an outspoken view of right and wrong, regardless of the behavior in private.

Richard Butman, a professor at Wheaton College, described incestuous fathers as coming from all areas of society. As a rule, he is intelligent, between thirty-five and forty years old; he is perceived by others to be a good provider, religious, an active church attender; he has a poor self-concept and lacks full control of his impulses; he is socially isolated, feels needy and neglected, lacks intimacy in his life; his marriage is not satisfying; and he was abused or emotionally neglected as a child.[14]

Incest offenders have very rigid moral codes, particularly regarding sexual behavior. Many of them would never go outside the family to obtain sexual satisfaction. They tend to not view their incestuous behavior as "immoral" or unacceptable because it occurs within the family.[15]

Parent-child sexual behavior serves partially to gratify a need, to defend against anxiety, and to express an unresolved conflict. The incestuous offender becomes dependent on sexual activity to meet his emotional needs. He finds adult sexual relationships, which require negotiation, mutuality, reciprocity, and shared commitment, either unavailable or overtaxing. So he turns to his child for sexual gratification of his emotional needs without the demands of adult responsibility. Although it is a sexual offense, incest, like other forms of sexual assault, is not motivated primarily by sexual desire. The sexual offender is not committing his crimes to achieve sexual pleasure any more than the alcoholic is drinking to quench a thirst. Incest is sexual behavior in the service of nonsexual needs. It is the sexual misuse of power.[16]

Types of Offenders

Nicholas Groth suggests that sexual offenders against children can be divided into two basic types based on their level of socio-sexual maturation.

Fixated offenders. Some males at the onset of their sexual maturation develop a primary or exclusive attraction to children. Children, often male victims, become the preferred subjects of their sexual interests. Although these men may also engage in sexual encounters with agemates, and sometimes even marry, such relationships are usually initiated by the other partner and result from social pressures or constitute a means of access to children. Psychologically their sexual preference remains predominantly cross-generational. Their sexual orientation is fixed on children. Fixated child molesters are drawn to children sexually in that they identify with the child and appear in some ways to want to remain children themselves. They tend to adapt their behavior and interest to the level of the child in an effort to have the child accept them as an equal.[17]

Regressed offenders. The second type regresses to sexual encounters with children as the result of conflicts or problems in their adult relationships. These persons fail to cope with life stressors and impulsively offend against children when crises arise in their lives. Although they offend against children, these persons are predominantly sexually oriented toward adults and the majority of them are married. When they offend, they will suspend their usual value system or rationalize that what they are doing is allowable. They are distressed by their abusive behavior and do experience guilt, shame, and remorse after an incident much like alcoholic or other addictive personalities. Regressed child molesters are drawn to children sexually in an attempt to replace their adult relationships which have become unfulfilling or conflictual. Such offenders select a child as a substitute and tend to relate to the child as if the child were a peer or agemate.[18]

Gaining Access

Offenders use variations of two methods to gain sexual access to children. The first method is enticement, encouragement, or instruction. For example, "I'm going to teach you a special game that will be our secret," or, "Feel my penis. It is all right to touch it. It makes me feel good," or, "If you let me just lie here a while I'll buy you something nice." The offender explains that what is important to him about the sexual relationship is that he feels special to the child and he wants the child to love and appreciate him.

The second method used to gain sexual access to children is through force, including threats, intimidation, or physical duress. This is usually found with the less skilled and tactful perpetrator. For example, an offender may tell a child to do what he says or he will beat the child, or throw the child out of the home.

Threats are also used to buy the child's silence if pressure does not work. For example, "If you tell, our family will be split up and it will be all your fault."

Incest offenders project their needs onto the children they abuse. They may fantasize that a child is lonely and needs companionship, while it is the abuser who needs the companionship.

CHARACTERISTICS OF MOTHERS OF INCEST VICTIMS

The mother, who normally would be expected to protect the child, may purposely try to stay isolated from the problem of sexual abuse. Sometimes she is distant and uncommunicative or so disapproving of sexual matters that children are afraid to speak up. Sometimes she is insecure and the potential loss of her husband and the fear of scandal are so threatening that she cannot allow herself to believe or suspect that her child is at risk.

She may have been a victim herself of child abuse and rejection and may not trust her judgment or her right to challenge the male authority. Some mothers actually know of sexual abuse but, for whatever reason, look the other way.

If a child does not tell her mother of the incest, it is usually because she does not perceive her as a person who can assume an assertively protective role. This is an example of the common role reversal between child victim and mother in incestuous families. The child is protecting the mother by not telling her of the incest, and is, in essence, parenting the mother. In such cases, the child keeps the incest a secret, choosing to protect the mother's well-being instead of her own. When the child can no longer tolerate the abuse, she reports it to someone outside the family. The child sacrifices herself for the mother's sake.

What personality types have been identified for mothers in some incestuous families? It should be emphasized that not all nonoffending mothers are expected to share in any type of pathology. Many mothers genuinely do not contribute to the problem in any direct way. There are some, however, who do fall into these categories.

The Passive Child-Woman Mother

This person is extremely dependent and immature. She relies on her husband or other adults to make decisions for her. Often she has not learned to drive a car or balance a checkbook. She tends to relate to her oldest daughter as a peer, confiding intimate matters and delegating many maternal responsibilities, such as child care and grocery shopping. This type of woman assumes an attitude of helplessness and apathy to any form of conflict. Her husband is likely to be authoritarian and abusive. She embodies the victim role.

Passive child-woman mothers have probably been severely abused or emotionally deprived as children. Their fathers were most often the source of the physical abuse. Many of these mothers report incest or molestation in childhood. Their relationships with their own mothers are described as poor. Memories of their childhood elicit feelings of anger and pain. Their mothers are said to have been emotionally unavailable to them. Their mothers often modeled a victim role, and the children grew up assuming abuse was part of how a woman had to live. These women embody the term "learned helplessness."[19]

The Intelligent, Competent, Distant Mother

This woman appears to be a model mother. She is charming, runs her home efficiently, and espouses the typical American middle-class values. She knows exactly what to say and to whom to say it. Her verbal skills allow her to manipulate professionals successfully with her sophisticated rationalization of the incest report. She avoids relating to people on any but an intellectual level. She uses logic to block interventions aimed at uncovering her role in the incest. She is charming and likable, and professionals will tend to rescue her. She is usually married to a man who is not as well-educated as she, but who is warm and nurturing.

This woman often describes her own mother as assertive, high achieving, competitive, and emotionally distant. She is likely to feel closer to her father than to her mother. She is often active in civic and church affairs, and she is away from home quite often. Her husband is the children's caretaker and nurturer. This affords the husband ample opportunity to molest them.

Because she has associated males with nurturing, she often has more male than female friends. Sometimes her distrust of women may be expressed as open hostility. She may even treat her sons more warmly than her daughters.[20]

The Rejecting, Vindictive Mother

This woman is openly hostile and threatening. She is also intelligent and resourceful. She will do anything to avoid admitting incest has occurred, even when her husband admits it. This is why she is so dangerous to the child. She would rather have her children taken away from her than admit the incest report is true. This type of mother disowns her child on learning of the incest. She may threaten never to speak to the child again or start giving the child's things away. Such vindictiveness usually results in the child recanting her report of incest. This is just what the mother wanted. This woman is glad her daughter assumed some of the mother's responsibilities as wife and mother. She is disgusted with sex, considers it a duty not to be enjoyed. She is usually married to a passive, meek man who is more afraid of her than he is of jail.

The rejecting, vindictive mother usually has an aggressive and controlling mother with whom she has a mutually dependent relationship that continues into adulthood. She was probably raised to view men as vehicles to respectable womanhood, but not as emotional partners. Her disdain for men is often thinly veiled. She tends to relate to women in a superficial manner, with an everpresent smile, even under strain. She is often accompanied by her mother to official appointments related to the incest. If the child has been taken out of the home, the mother may insist on having no one else present when she visits with the child. She will attempt to prevent social workers and other professionals from seeing her husband unless she is present to control the interview.

This type of mother makes it very difficult to intervene in the situation because the children and husband are so afraid of her rejection and anger.[21]

The Psychotic or Severely Retarded Mother

Psychotic mothers are unable to protect their children. Their emotional status incapacitates them. Their illness severely limits their effective functioning as a parent. These women are more likely than any other type to participate in the active molestation of their own children.

Psychotic mothers may be amenable to treatment, depending on their condition. If they are in remission, they can be receptive to treatment. The bulk of treatment energy should initially go into protecting the child. This can be done by either teaching the child how to protect herself (or himself, since some disturbed mothers are more likely to abuse their sons) from future sexual assaults, or by placing the child in a safer environment until the mother is not at risk to abuse again.

A severely retarded mother with no awareness of the inappropriateness of incestuous behavior may condone and actively participate in the molestation. If she is unable to protect her children and cannot learn to take proper care of them, the children should be placed elsewhere.[22]

DYNAMICS AND SEQUENCE OF SEXUAL ABUSE

Sexual encounters between adults and children usually fall within a predictable pattern. This seems particularly true of incest within the family. The discussion will continue to focus primarily on incest, because of its widespread incidence, particularly within the church community. The activity usually occurs in distinct phases.

Engagement Phase

Child sexual abuse is not an accident. Most of the time, the perpetrator is known by the child and has ready access to her. The offender and the child need to be alone—in a room, a house, or secluded place out of doors. Although the circumstances of access and opportunity may be accidental on their first encounter, the perpetrator can be expected to create opportunities for private interaction with the child thereafter.

The dynamics of child sexual abuse most often involve a known adult who is in a legitimate power position over the child and who uses that authority to engage the child in sexual activity. Almost always it is someone in the child's own family who has access and opportunity by residing in the home or family circle. If not a relative, the offender may be someone within the child's daily sphere of activities, such as babysitters, coaches, teachers, or youth leaders.

Inducement is usually done in a low-key, nonforcible fashion, possibly by presenting the activity as a game or something that is "special" and fun. This entails misrepresentation of moral standards, either verbally or implicitly. The power and authority of the adult conveys to the child that the proposed behavior is acceptable. Rewards or bribes may be offered. More often than not, the opportunity to engage in activity with a favored person is sufficient incentive for the child to participate.

The successful perpetrator will manage to be coercive in a subtle fashion. Threats are seldom used, if the offender is skilled. Physical force is rarely used to engage a child, in the intrafamily situation. However, when sexual abuse of a child occurs within the context of a violent family, there is strongly implied force or threat of force.[23]

Sexual Interaction Phase

This phase does encompass a progression of sexual activity. The progression of exposure to fondling to some form of penetration is very predictable. Sexual activity between an adult and a child may range from exhibitionism to intercourse, often progressing through the following spectrum of behavior: nudity, disrobing, genital exposure, observation of the child, kissing, fondling, masturbation, fellatio, cunnilingus, digital penetration of anus or rectal opening, penile penetration of anus or rectal opening, digital penetration of vagina, penile penetration of vagina, and "dry intercourse."[24]

Secrecy Phase

After the sexual behavior has taken place, the primary task for the perpetrator is to impose secrecy. Secrecy eliminates accountability. The offender does not want to be caught and held responsible for the abuse. Secrecy also enables the behavior to continue. Since the needs of the offender are likely to continue, he wants the child to be available. Thus, secrecy is essential. The perpetrator must persuade or pressure the child to keep their activity a secret over time.

The child usually does keep the secret. Some children never tell anyone. Others keep the secret throughout their childhood and disclose the sexual behavior many years later. The child may keep the secret because she has been offered rewards. The child may also keep the secret because she enjoyed the activity and wants the behavior to continue. This premature introduction to sexuality by a "significant other" may feel good to the child on several levels: pleasurable sexual stimulation, enhancement of self-esteem, feeling grown up, having a special relationship, and so forth.

Threats may have also been used to reinforce secrecy. Threats may include: the prospect of anger by a third party ("If you tell Mommy, she'll be awfully mad!"); separation ("If you tell anyone, Mommy may divorce me or I may be sent to jail"); separation of the child ("If you tell anyone, you'll be put in a foster home"); self-harm by the offender ("If you tell anyone, I'll kill myself"); harm to someone else ("If you tell anybody, I'll hurt your sister or your dog"); violence against the child ("If you tell anybody, I'll hurt you or kill you").

The secrecy phase can last for months or years, especially if it occurs within the family. The sexual behavior progresses over time, usually in the direction of greater intimacy. As the child grows older there may be an increase in the frequency of incestuous sexual activity. Whenever the situation comes to the attention of outside professionals, it's unlikely to be the first and only incident of sexual activity for the child.[25]

Disclosure Phase

There are two types of disclosure of child sexual abuse: accidental and purposeful.

Accidental. In this type of disclosure, the secret was revealed accidentally, because of external circumstances. The key factor is that none of the participants decided to tell. Instead, the secret was revealed in one of the following ways: observation by a third party; physical injury to the child; sexually transmitted disease; pregnancy; precocious sexual activity initiated by the child.

Accidental disclosure most often precipitates a crisis. Depending upon the people involved, a state of chaos, high anxiety, hostility, and fear may predominate. The immediate task of a pastor or counselor, if involved at this point, is to diffuse the anxiety, reinforce the reality that sexual abuse does exist, participate in fact finding, direct the validation process or refer to appropriate agencies for that purpose, and assist in the initial intervention planning.

In spite of the confusion and anxiety, there are several advantages in the crisis situation. First, it brings the situation out in the open so intervention and treatment can take place. Second, it takes the decision to tell off the shoulders of the child. The child did not have to take the initiative to reveal the family secret. Third, the crisis situation can allow a pastor or counselor to come into the family system and provide concrete supportive assistance.

Purposeful disclosure. In this type of disclosure, a participant consciously decides to tell an outsider. It is often the child who decides to reveal the secret. A young child may tell the secret to share an exciting or stimulating experience. An older child tells for different reasons. When she enters adolescence, a youngster who used to regard her father as a warm and loving person may see him as a self-centered, controlling individual. In earlier years she could be totally preoccupied by his attentions; as a young teen she is more interested in peers and group activities outside of the family. Her father, however, limits her social activities and she rebels against his restrictions. As her frustration mounts, she may finally reveal the secret in order to gain more freedom.

After the disclosure, the child may experience a sense of relief by having rid herself of a long-kept secret. She is also likely to experience guilt for any feelings of enjoyment, and feelings of disloyalty for betraying her father. There may be other reasons for telling. Fear of pregnancy or concern for a younger sister have motivated some children.

It is important to find out why a child decides to disclose her abuse. The child may have very unrealistic expectations about the consequences. She is probably looking for a magical solution to her problems. The child wants the situation to change without confrontation, outside interference, or separation. The child's reasons must be understood. If she has unrealistic expectations, the counselor should try to help modify those toward a more realistic direction. If this isn't done, the child will likely recant her story when things don't go the way she expected.

The child needs immediate and ongoing support. If unprotected, the victim is often subjected to more abuse, threats, and coercion. If unsupported the child may give in to the pressure and retract the accusation.

If a report has been transmitted to the proper agencies, an opportunity exists to capitalize on the child's conscious decision to seek help. The professional can then meet with the child and proceed with the fact finding and validation of abuse. This gives the child an opportunity to express her concerns and explore with the counselor alternatives which are in the best interest of the child and the entire family system.

The family reactions to disclosure will range from denial and hostility to protection and concern. The offender is likely to react with alarm and denial. Child sexual abuse is a crime, and the prospect of publicity, loss of status, and criminal charges will motivate the perpetrator to react defensively in order to protect himself.

After disclosure, the offender can be expected to exploit his power position to the fullest, to control the child and other family members, while undermining the credibility of the allegations.

Mothers of victims of incest have many pressures to face. Some mothers have been aware of the abuse, but have done nothing about it. Now they have to deal with their guilt. Even if they were not knowingly involved, mothers of victims must sooner or later face the consequences of siding with the child. If the offender provides the primary means of economic and emotional support or social status, this may be a very difficult choice. If the abuser has been violent toward the mother in the past, she will fear physical retribution along with everything else.

It's not unusual for mothers to collapse under these combined pressures, abandon responsibility, avoid decisions, and withdraw from the situation. This only serves to give the abuser more opportunity to exert control over the family's response.

Siblings of victims may react protectively and with concern, or they may react defensively. Children fear disruption and separation of family life, even if the situation has been traumatic. Fear of the unknown can lead siblings to attack the victim, even if they agreed with her need to disclose the abuse.

All family members can be expected to react to disclosure of abuse with one perspective: "How will these events affect me?" Only those with a great deal of strength and security can be expected to sustain continuing concern and support for the victim.[26]

Suppression Phase

Following disclosure, the dynamics of most cases tend to enter a suppression phase. Even if the abuser was from outside the family, the child's family is likely to react by trying to suppress publicity, information, and intervention. The suppression can lead to minimization of the abuse, saying, in effect, "It's nothing to worry about. She'll forget about it soon."

In a case of incest, the perpetrator can be expected to exploit his power by pressuring the child and any other family members who appear to be cooperating with outside authority figures. There may be attempts to undermine the child's credibility. The child may be described as a pathological liar or crazy. Prior school problems or difficulties with peers may be cited as evidence that the child is untrustworthy.

Feeling isolated, fearful, and guilty, the child may give in and withdraw the complaint or simply stop cooperating with the process.[27]

Repression or Recovery Phase

The last phase in the progression of child sexual abuse can have one of two endings. If the suppression phase was successful, everything may return to "normal." The family system will lapse into its old habits, and nothing will have changed. The abuse may even begin again, sometimes with a new victim, perhaps a younger child in the family. This is the *repression* component. The crisis has come and gone. The social service agencies have done all they can, and moved on to other cases piling up on their desks. The family is left to suppress its awareness of the problem. The power demands of the offender have succeeded in overwhelming the pleas for help.

The more desirable conclusion, of course, is *recovery*. The attempts to suppress the child's disclosure are not successful. Through the efforts of many, the necessary changes in the family system begin to take place. The road to recovery is long and difficult. Treatment takes at least one year, and frequently two or more. In spite of its difficulty and cost, this is the outcome to which the Christian pastor or counselor should be committed. We should not be lulled to inattention just because the crisis has died down. We must work with all the appropriate agencies to make sure the cycle of abuse is stopped, and that the family gets the help it needs.

This chapter gives the pastor or counselor a basic foundation for the understanding of child sexual abuse. Next, I'll discuss how to interview and treat both the victim and the offender.

CHAPTER EIGHT

EVALUATION AND TREATMENT OF SEXUALLY ABUSED CHILDREN

Dr. Marshall gave Jill a piece of paper and a box of crayons, and told her she could draw anything she wanted. Jill enthusiastically began drawing a picture of "Uncle Frank" and herself.

This was the third interview between Jill, an eight-year-old girl who was acting out at school, and the psychologist. The parents had consulted with Dr. Marshall because Jill's teacher reported her classroom behavior had become a major concern since Christmas vacation. Until recently, Jill was an average student who usually got along well with her classmates. Now she was disobedient and often seemed quite angry. Her attention span had also declined, and she daydreamed far more

172

than usual. The parents were mystified about the reasons for Jill's decline in performance.

Jill seemed comfortable with Dr. Marshall now, after shedding a few tears in the first session. Her drawing was fairly simple. It included a large male figure sitting on a chair and a little girl standing nearby. Jill identified the adult as Uncle Frank and then added a television set to the picture, saying she used to like to watch television at Uncle Frank's house.

During the initial interview, Dr. Marshall recalled, the parents had mentioned that Uncle Frank and his wife had often taken care of Jill and her younger sister when the parents went out of town. So the counselor asked Jill about her visits to Uncle Frank's house. At that point, Jill put down the crayons and said, "I don't want to draw anymore. I'm tired."

Dr. Marshall assured Jill she did not have to draw, but he would like her to tell him about the picture she had made. After some additional conversation, Jill picked up a black crayon and quickly added a narrow slit to the front of Uncle Frank's pants. She then scribbled over the entire drawing, and said, "But, I don't like Uncle Frank anymore. He's naughty."

Further investigation revealed Uncle Frank had molested Jill when the parents had gone skiing a few days after Christmas.

As a professional counselor or pastor, you may be consulted about the source of behavioral problems in children. Sometimes those problems will be triggered by sexual abuse. The pastor and counselor will also likely see adults who acknowledge having been abused as children, or who present symptoms often found in adults victimized as children. This chapter deals with the task of investigating and treating children who are suspected of being sexually abused.

Although some of these principles will apply to adult victims of rape, adults abused as children, and victims of similar forms of violence, the scope of this chapter will be limited to sexually abused children. Particular attention will be given to incest and abuse by persons known to the child.

The first step is to identify for sure that the child has been victimized. In come cases, a referral may be made to you by a case worker after the initial investigation has already been completed. The appropriate social service agencies may have determined the facts of the abuse, and you are contacted to provide counseling for the child and/or family. In this case, you will get the background reports and proceed on with the long-term intervention. The crisis phase may already have passed.

You may be involved at the very early stages of the process, and must be prepared to help determine the nature of the problem. This is a difficult task. Sexual abuse is usually a silent and secret crime. The offender seldom admits his guilt. In the case of incest, the mother tends to deny the reality of the situation. A physical examination of the child will often prove to be negative. There are hardly ever any witnesses to the abuse.

The pressures working against disclosure are probably greater with sexual abuse than any other problem confronting the pastor or counselor. For this reason, self-awareness, prior training, and experience are most crucial for the Christian counselor. Without proper knowledge and experience, the well-meaning but uninformed counselor or pastor can do more harm than good.

COUNSELOR ATTITUDES AND EXPERIENCE

One of the major barriers to effective work with sexually abused children is the attitude of you, the counselor. Many otherwise professional workers are uncomfortable with the subject of sexual abuse in general, or incest in particular. While experience with abuse can help desensitize the embarrassment, if you are not able to overcome the discomfort, you should refer the case to someone else. Righteous anger over the crime of abuse can be appropriate motivation for a counselor, but watch out for hostility, insensitivity, or biases that would prejudice the direction of the intervention.

As a counselor, you should be comfortable with your own sexuality and be able to discuss any issue relating to human sexuality in terms understandable to children and adults. Clients often report the counselor's ability to talk freely about sex and sexual abuse helped them overcome their own anxiety about the topic.

The counselor needs to be comfortable with both slang and anatomically correct terms for sexual behavior. This is particularly important for Christian counselors whose everyday language may be very moderate. If you blush, clear your throat, pause, or stammer over certain words, the child is going to assume something is wrong and clam up.

A counselor who is going to work with abused children needs to enjoy children. Establishing a good relationship with a child requires the adult to be able to convey interest, warmth, sincerity, and respect for the youngster. If you are a "natural" at working with children, this part of the process is easy. Here are some questions to ask yourself about your inclination to work with children:

Do I like being with children?

Do they make me nervous, or am I exhausted after being with them?

Do I reach out and communicate with children?

Do I spontaneously stop and talk with children when I meet them?

Do I really care about what a child is thinking?

Do I like to play games with children?

Am I willing to sit down on the floor with a child and play games?

Am I able to look at a child's drawing and talk to him or her about what it means?

Do I tend to spontaneously praise a child and focus on good behavior?

Do children interest me? Do I find myself wondering how they are unique and different from adults?

Do children have a tendency to make me angry?

Do I resent the extra effort it takes to communicate and respond to their needs?

Does a child's behavior often lead me to feel out of control with a situation?

If most of your answers to the positive questions are *yes*, and to the negative questions, *no*, you are probably effective with children. If your answers don't follow this pattern, consider the following alternatives. If you aren't naturally inclined to adapt easily to children, chances are good you can learn to relate on their level if you observe others who can. It takes practice, but can be enjoyable. However, investigating possible sexual abuse is not the place to begin. If you are not comfortable with children, refer the case to someone who has had experience with them.

OTHER ISSUES FOR THE THERAPIST

Anger

As a counselor you can have strong beliefs about the abusive situations. But your feelings of anger must be monitored. Your goal is to be objective in order to help the victim sort through her options and begin to make healthy decisions. If you are biased, and it shows, your professional stature is compromised.

The anger of the counselor toward the abuse may influence you to recommend more immediate or drastic measures than are needed. "Throw him out of the house," and, "I hope the judge puts him in the slammer for the rest of his life," are some examples.

Yes, the safety of the victim is of top priority. And, indeed, it often takes legal action to get the offender into therapy. But you must be careful to model a balance between constructive suggestions that have the potential to bring about healing and harsh recommendations that only serve to seek revenge.

Sexual Arousal

Whether we admit it or not, sexual content appeals to our basic nature. It is the rare counselor who has not found him or herself being at least slightly aroused by the sexual descriptions of a client. You must continually ask yourself if the continued exploration or discussion of sexual material is for the benefit of the client or yourself.

This can be an issue with both child or adult victims of sexual abuse. He or she has come to you seeking help. Some level of trust is developed between you and the client/victim. This initial trust may be similar to that which existed between the victim and the offender. There is often a grooming phase in sexual abuse where subtle language, conversation, and nonverbal sexual advances are made. Your goal is to help the victim identify and deal with this type of thing, not to fall prey to it again in your office.

On the other hand, do not deal with your own sexual issues by totally avoiding sexual content in the counseling process. Sexual issues, whether with victims of abuse or other types of clients, will often be present. You must learn to be comfortable with sexual content and not respond with either extreme.

As Christian counselors we must maintain the highest level of standards, and not let anything we do become a stumbling block for others in our influence (Rom. 14:13, 1 Cor. 10:32, 2 Cor. 6:3).

Blaming the Victim

You must also be on guard against getting trapped into using explanations that result in blame being laid at the feet of the victim. Children have the right to expect that adults will not take advantage of them. Many times, offenders will allege that the victim was partly to blame for the abuse because he or she behaved in a provocative or seductive manner. If the child behaved in a sexually inappropriate fashion, why didn't the offender correct the youngster? If a child behaves in a sexually explicit manner, a responsible adult will not encourage or take advantage of such behavior, but will try to rectify it.

Be careful not to hook into the offender's tendency to blame the victim and begin to view the client as somehow responsible for the abuse. If you find yourself thinking the victim is guilty of misconduct related to the sexual abuse, an immediate reevaluation or consultation should be made.

Creating or Extending Client Dependency

Dependency is a very real issue in the counseling process. You have been consulted to help the victim and her family deal with the trauma. A certain amount of trust or dependency is needed in the therapeutic process. Once the victim learns to trust the therapist, she may become somewhat dependent. If you have a strong need to be depended upon, another form of abuse can be imposed.

Pastors and other counselors in the helping professions all like to be needed. We find fulfillment in seeing people grow, learn to make better choices, and find meaning for their lives. That is a legitimate part of being in a ministry that contributes to the building up and edifying of the saints (1 Cor. 12:7; 14:12). But you should remember your goal is to work yourself out of a job. As soon as possible, the client needs to have enough tools to cope with the stressors of life on her own. Any activity that detracts from the client moving toward a self-sufficient life should be identified and altered. If you find yourself wanting to hang onto a client for either personal or financial reasons, an ethical issue is present, and an immediate change in strategy should be imposed.

Victim Experiences of the Therapist

A major issue for the counselor of sexual abuse cases is to know yourself. If you have been victimized in some way, it is crucial for the grief process to have been completed. If you are stuck at a certain point in dealing with pain, loss, sorrow, or grief, your clients will often not progress past that same point.

This is not to suggest you must be pain-free to qualify as a healing servant. But you must have worked through the pain and be well on the road to reconciliation and strength before you have any right to sell your services to those who are in the middle of their own trauma and confusion.

An important example would be the issue of forgiveness in an abused client. If you have not adequately dealt with events and persons needing forgiveness in your own life, then the process of forgiveness will not be handled well with your clients. The topic of forgiveness will be avoided or covered in a superficial fashion. Because it is unresolved for you as a counselor, there will be a tendency to move to forgiveness before the client is ready, or to delay too long. This will allow bitterness and anger to take a stronger hold. Either way, the client is not receiving the help she needs in a timely fashion.

The admonition is for you to know yourself, and to seek healing before trying to be a servant of healing to others.

PREPARING FOR AN INTERVIEW

The procedures and content of an interview or series of sessions with a sexually abused child will vary, depending on the purpose. If outside circumstances and symptoms strongly suggest abuse, then obtaining a disclosure may be a goal for the session(s). Once a disclosure is made, additional information is needed to ensure safety and treatment for the child and offender.

The initial interviews may be investigative in nature. There may be suspicion or knowledge of sexual abuse, but the specifics—of who, what, when, and where—need to be determined. The information may then be used for prosecution of the offender and/or protection of the child. Generally, there are *founded* and *unfounded* types of investigations.

In a founded investigation, someone believes there has been sexual abuse. It has probably been corroborated, but for some reason the victim is denying the abuse.

An unfounded situation exists when the investigation shows there has been a false allegation, usually by another adult. For example, a divorced parent is trying to gain changes in custody or visitation, and accuses a spouse of sexual abuse. This can also include false allegations made by the child or teenager. It is possible, of course, for an investigation to yield insufficient evidence to confirm or prove abuse.

If the child has already told someone else all of the facts, the child may need a chance to deal with her feelings, not give more details. The focus of this type of session will be on feelings of anger, embarrassment, guilt, ambivalence, regret, etc., not on more fact finding.

An interview or series of interviews may need to focus on the emotional consequences of the abuse. In this situation, the facts of abuse are known, but the question remains, how deeply affected is the child? One child may see a man expose himself in the park and run home, eager to tell his parents. Another child may experience the same event, become withdrawn, feel guilty, and have nightmares for a year.

If all of the investigative work and legal process is complete, treatment becomes the focal point of the sessions. This is probably a longer term focus, and the content becomes different, tailored to the needs and symptoms of each victim.

Another purpose of an interview may be to determine readiness for visitation or contact with the offender. If the child was abused by her father, and the father was removed from the home, there may come a time when it is appropriate to introduce him back into the home. The focus here would be on the child's feelings, such as fear, ambivalence, anger, or anticipation over the father coming home.

Keep Family Perspective

Rarely is incest the only problem in a family. Some families are experiencing so many problems that incest is almost incidental. The counselor or team of professionals must be patient and persevering to untangle the complicated system of behaviors and thought patterns that characterize these families.

Incest activity is likely to be serving a useful purpose in the family. It is keeping the system in balance. It is a tenuous balance, and destructive to be sure. But the balance is there. Interrupting the activity without replacing it with something more useful and healthy may only serve to make things worse. For example, the mother–daughter roles may be reversed, and the daughter has functioned as the father's sexual outlet. Just to intervene and stop the father's sexual activity with the daughter will not solve the entire problem. The whole family system will need readjustment.

The interview process should include sessions with the parents present unless it is already known one of them is the offender. The counselor will also want to see the child alone, as well as with other children in the family, if a total assessment is desired.

Know Child's Developmental Level

A child's cognitive, emotional, and social levels will affect his or her ability to give the details of sexual assault. The counselor should be familiar with the developmental sequences of increasingly complex levels of behavior that occur in children. For example, infants (ages birth to two) comprehend the world primarily through physical observations and touch. They respond mostly to things they see, hear, or touch. Toddlers and preschoolers (ages two to seven) make sense of the world through language and fantasy. Although children of this age have the initial ability to make internal thought patterns, they are still more influenced by how an object or event looks than by logical explanations. Depending on the maturity level, many children at this early age have difficulty understanding that other people may think differently from themselves. They may also have difficulty distinguishing between real and pretend people and situations. The toddler will also not be able to think logically and clearly back to the beginning of a sequence of events over time.

Young preschool children are egocentric. They have little ability to identify themselves in a context. They are dependent on caretakers to meet all their needs and they give adults total authority to carry out that task. Young children often mirror the emotional climate of the family system. As they grow older, of course, children gradually shift to a greater reliance on peer relationships and emotional commitments outside the family.

Young children are spontaneous, impulsive, and unpremeditative. They start out with few internal limitations and only a vague awareness of external limits. They have short attention spans. They are most likely to express their feelings through behavior and actions, rather than with words. As children grow older, they acquire internal controls for their behavior and are able to establish a sense of identity and independence apart from their parents. Their peers and other adults, such as teachers or coaches, have an increasing influence on their behavior.

Primary school-age children (ages seven to eleven) understand the world through concrete thinking. Mental logic is available, but it is limited to situations that are real, concrete, and observable. Children at this stage are not usually able to understand problems that are primarily verbal or hypothetical. They tend to be very literal about rules and instructions. They pay attention to the details of a situation or object. And they respond with dichotomous, right or wrong, answers to social situations and problems.

By age eleven and beyond, the usual way of making sense of the world is through the use of abstract thinking. The preteen is able to think about the form of an object or problem without having it physically present or concretely represented. At this age, boys and girls have the ability for complete logical thinking. They can recognize several points of view simultaneously and identify conceptual, rather than just functional, relationships between those ideas. Logical thinking allows one to see various alternatives involving social problems, rather than black and white solutions. The intermediate-age child can think about thoughts and feelings and can understand cause-and-effect relationships between events spread over time.

These are only a few of the developmental considerations that will influence interviews with children. The counselor should have a sufficient background so the methods used are appropriate for the age and ability of each different child.

Obtain Background Information

Prior to talking to a child about suspected or known sexual abuse, obtain all the relevant information possible. Talk to the parents, Child Protective Services caseworker, physician, sexual assault center, or rape relief counselor whenever appropriate. Explain your interest and goals to these agencies, find out what has already been done, and enlist their cooperation. Obtain any reports that pertain to the case, making sure to have signed releases for all persons involved.

Do not try to deal with the case by yourself. Sexual abuse is so complex in both its cause and treatment, you need all the help possible so you are not led into a superficial resolution.

If you can, obtain background information on: the child's age; grade; achievement level; disabilities, if any; capabilities, such as ability to write, read, count, ride a bike, tell time, remember events; siblings; family composition; child's knowledge of anatomy and sexual behavior; and family terms for genital areas.

Ask the parents about behavior or mood changes, and whether or not these changes can be tied to any chronology of events or contacts with people. For example, did the child start having nightmares or wetting the bed after being with a new baby-sitter or after the mother started working evenings. In short, take a good social history of the child and the family.

If there has been a disclosure of prior abuse, review the circumstances of the assault. Find out as many details as possible—who, what, when, where, and to whom reported. Review the exact words used by the child, and to whom they were spoken. How many people have interviewed the child? What was the reaction of the child to the assault, as well as to having told about the abuse? Ask if there are any signs of anxiety, such as nightmares, withdrawal, regression, bed wetting, acting out, etc.

Determine the nature of any changes in the child's life since the disclosure. Who does and does not believe the disclosure? How much support exists in the extended family? Is there blaming of the child? Are the parents getting a divorce as a result of the disclosure? Has the child been taken out of the home, moved to a new house, or changed schools?

INTERVIEWING THE CHILD

The first goal is to make the child comfortable and relaxed. The room should be quiet, private, and attractive to the child, and I encourage the use of toys, drawing, dollhouses, dolls, pillows, etc. Having the art work of other children on the walls helps children begin to believe they are not alone in their situations. If possible, counsel children in a room separate from your "adult" office. If you have nice artwork or figurines sitting around your office, it's counterproductive to tell the child not to touch or play with them. Be flexible. Most children will want to move around the room, explore the toys, sit on the floor, or in your lap.

The attention span of most children is short. Keep interruptions to a minimum. The room should be private so the focus of the session is not diverted or so a self-conscious or apprehensive child will not withdraw.

The use of toys or activities occupies a child's attention, and provides a concrete focus. Such an activity allows the child to talk with more openness. Toys are necessary, but if a child has trouble attending to a task, too many toys can be an extra distraction. Learn to arrange the room for the needs of each child.

If the child wishes a safe parent or other caretaker present, it should be allowed. If there is any suspicion that a parent is the offender, of course, the parent should not be present. The child should be interviewed alone at some time in the interview process.

Usually a parent can enter the room with a hesitant child, join in the activity for a while, gradually pull back, and leave the room during the initial session. Find out from the parent if the child has a favorite toy or activity. The counselor can announce the availability of such a toy, and most children are eager to go find it.

Beginning the Interview

The counselor's task is similar to the perpetrator of sexual abuse, although with far different motives. The counselor must engage the child's interest, confidence, and cooperation.

Begin by telling the child your name. Be alert to cultural or family histories and your own preferences. Some counselors will tell a child to use their first names. Most children will not perceive "Miss," "Mr.," "Mrs.," or "Dr." as being unfriendly. If your name is difficult to pronounce, you may wish to tell the child to call you "Mr. G."

Demonstrate an interest in the child. Ask the child his or her name. Comment on a positive feature about the child, such as an article of clothing or a toy brought from home. You might say, "I knew you were coming today, so I got out some special toys for you to play with." Give the child a choice of things to do or toys to use. This also helps you begin to know something about the child's likes and dislikes.

Ask about the child's age, grade, school, family members, pets, friends, activities, favorite playthings, or television programs. When appropriate, share some of your own interests and activities. Questions should be asked casually. Don't give the child the third degree with rapid fire delivery and firm tone of voice. Listen attentively and let your body language and facial expressions reinforce your attentiveness along with your comments. Space and time the questions so they are not obtrusive. Watch for cues that a change of pace is needed. On the other hand, don't be afraid to be direct about the nature of the interview and the purpose of your meeting.

It is also important to clarify the purpose of the interview and what will happen. For the young child, it may be, "I'm here to talk to you about the things you told your teacher." The older child may need to know why the interview is taking place and how the information will be used.

Many older children will know the reason for the interview, and a discussion can then be held about how the child feels about talking to a counselor. Tell the child that most people feel uncomfortable and apprehensive in similar situations. Such reassurance is helpful.

Ask the child, "Why do you think you are here?" Young children, particularly, may think you already know their secret. Ask them if they think you know. At some point you should also ask if they have been told not to tell anything. Reassure them that if something "yucky" or uncomfortable has happened, it is better to tell someone so it won't happen again.

Be aware that the child who has been instructed or threatened not to tell by the offender will be very anxious. Look for a change in the child's mood or emotions while you discuss the abuse. These fears need to be allayed as much as possible. You can say, for example, "It's not bad to tell what happened"; "You won't be doing wrong by telling"; "You can help your dad (brother, uncle, etc.,) by telling what happened"; "It wasn't your fault, so it's okay to talk about it"; "You are not to blame if a big person makes you do something you don't want to do."

Also ask the child if anybody told him or her what to say or how to act while talking to you. Ask the content of the instructions. When appropriate, ask if the child has been obedient to those instructions. Sometimes it will be self-evident and you won't need to ask.

Realize the child may have real ambivalent feelings about the abuse. It may have been the only time the child received any sign of affection from a particular person—or from anybody. Acknowledge the child's feelings of pleasure and attraction and how confusing that may have been. Give an example, such as taking a cookie after Mother said not to eat any; the cookie tasted good, but the child worried about getting into trouble when Mom found out. Try to diffuse guilt at every opportunity.

Your responses toward the offender should be consistent

with the child's perception of the abuse. Don't talk about jail for the offender if the child has expressed positive feelings for him.

During the initial stages of the interview, the counselor needs to assess the level of sophistication and stage of cognitive development. Ask simple, direct questions. Don't ask two-part questions, unless the child demonstrates the ability to handle them. When speaking to the young child, for example, don't ask, "Where were you when he hurt you, and what did he do?" Ask the questions separately.

Determine if children can read, write, count, tell time, and know colors or shapes. Do they know the current day or date, or their birthdays? Do they remember past events, understand *before* and *after*, know about money, or have responsibilities, such as chores or pets? How much freedom do they have? Do they go about the neighborhood alone, stay at home alone, or prepare meals for themselves?

Child clients also need to know you are experienced and knowledgeable about the situation they have experienced. Tell them something like, "I have talked to many boys and girls who have had things like this happen to them." This establishes your credibility.

Do not make promises you cannot keep. Do not tell children you will keep everything a secret, because you can't. The information must be shared with the proper authorities. Do not tell them that if they tell you their stories they will not have to talk to anybody else. They may, indeed, have to tell their stories several times before the process is over.

If children have disclosed or do disclose their abuse, it is important to find out why they chose to tell the secret. This may have to be approached later in the interview, if the initial question is not answered clearly.

In working with children a standard task is to ask them to draw a picture of a person. Often victims of sexual abuse will not put hands or feet or even arms and legs on their people.[1]

The implication is one of helplessness to cope with the situation. Another variation is to draw exaggerated hands and/or feet. This might imply the extremities are viewed as intrusive or overwhelming tools of abuse. The drawings of children will

This drawing is by a six-year-old girl molested by her stepbrother. No arms or feet were included, even though she was a very bright student.

This is a drawing by an eleven-year-old boy abused by his father. Notice the attention to the genital area.

This drawing is by a four-and-a-half-year-old boy who was abused by his father. No arms, hands, or feet were included.

This is a drawing by a five-year-old girl molested by her father. There are no arms or hands on figure.

also often localize the place of abuse on the body. A large zipper or fly may be drawn on the front of the pants. A hand placed somewhere on the private parts is another example. Look for these clues. (On pages 187–190 the author has provided reproductions of four drawings by children who have been abused.) Don't overinterpret drawings which may be explained by poor motor skills, lack of opportunity, or other emotional factors. But do use the drawings of children as part of the information bank.

Conveying Desire to Help

The initial phases of the interview are intended to convey your willingness to help the child. You are interested in fulfilling the goals of the interview, such as validating abuse or determining the emotional impact on the child. On the other hand, the child needs to feel something is being done to help.

There are several ways to do this. You might give new or clarifying information to the child. An example might be explaining what will happen to Daddy if he has to go to jail or has to move out of the home.

Somewhere in the first or second session it is good to grant some type of request for the child. You can be on the lookout for something appropriate that the child wants. But, on the other hand, be careful not to make promises that would be difficult or unwise to fulfill. For example, do not tell the child the offender will go to jail and she will never have to see him again. There is no assurance the offender will, in fact, go to jail.

Children usually feel anxious or guilty about what has happened up to this point. As counselor, you can help them feel better by being supportive and reassuring.

Victims of sexual abuse are also very fearful. They may think they have been damaged, that no one likes them, or that their families will never be happy again. These fears are well founded. Although you should not promise to wave a magic wand and make everything go away, you can promise to help the child deal with her fears.

A final way to convey help is to believe in the child. Most victims have found that very few people will believe them. If you have reason to believe the child's story, say so. Your belief in the child may be one of the most therapeutic benefits of the child's disclosure.

Determining the Details of Abuse

After establishing a relationship with a child, begin to explore more of the details regarding the suspected assault or molestation. Careful record keeping is important. Be prepared to take good notes or tape record the interview. Video tapes of sessions can be helpful if the setting allows for unobtrusive recording. Check with legal experts about what type of recordings, if any, will be accepted in court.

Do not threaten or try to force a reluctant child to talk. Pressure only causes a child to clam up and may cause a further distrust of adults. Take your time. Engage the child in play activity. Don't avoid the topic because of your own biases or hesitancy to talk about sexual abuse, but if the child does not respond to reassurance, play, and firm but polite questioning, try again at a later time.

Again, remember to use terms the child understands. If the child looks confused or embarrassed, be ready to clarify and explore. Ask open-ended questions. Avoid questions that can be answered with a *yes* or *no.* Also do not ask *why* questions, such as "Why didn't you tell anyone?" which tend to sound accusatory and are often difficult to answer. Use *what* or *how* questions instead. They focus on behavior which the child can more accurately describe.

Make sure you understand the terms a child uses. Anatomically correct dolls or drawings can be used to label the various body parts. You can ask, "What does Mommy call it?" If the child uses a descriptive term, be sure to use that term in further comments. Don't correct the child or insist on the use of anatomically correct terms. If you are not certain what part of the body is being referred to, use the dolls or pictures and have the child show you.

If the child makes a disclosure or reveals some previously undisclosed details, make an appropriate response. Don't react with shock or horror, but don't be completely blank either. Try to empathize with the feelings of the child at that moment. "I bet that really scared you didn't it?" or "I'm glad you told me about what happened. I'm sure it wasn't easy to do," are examples of responses that may fit a situation where a child reveals part of a secret.

The nature and extent of the abuse can be explored by following the what, who, when, and where outline. It may take several sessions for the child to become comfortable enough to talk about the details. A child will go in and out of the main content of a session. Allow for that pattern and for a short attention span. Don't rush to fill silent periods. If a child starts to cry, be careful not to smother. The tears may be needed. Allow some time or go ahead with the play activities until you sense the child is ready for more questions. It may be appropriate to take a walk or go get a snack. Watch the pacing. Don't hustle or hurry a child. Be patient, but persevere.

What? Questions that might elicit the nature of the abuse include: How did it begin? Can you tell me what happened? I need to know what the man did. Did he ever touch you? Where? Where did he put his finger? Have you ever seen him with his clothes off? Did you ever see his penis (thing, pee pee, wiener) get big? Did anything ever come out of his penis?

Other questions might include: Did you ask him to stop? What did he say? Did he say anything while he was doing it? Did it ever happen before?

Explore whether or not there was a progression of sexual activity from grooming to physical contact. Distinguish between touching on top of the child's clothes or underneath them. Use drawings or dolls to determine exactly which areas of the child's body were involved.

Once some initial information is obtained, ask about other types of sexual activity. You can describe sexual contact in a general way and note the child's reaction. Sample comments for the major types of activity are: Sometimes men ask children to lick them or suck them. Sometimes people try to stick their fingers inside of someone. Sometimes people put their mouths on a little girl's bottom.

Determine if there was any injury as a result of the abuse. Was there ever any bleeding, pain, irritation, swelling, or interference with the ability to urinate, defecate, or menstruate?

What was done about these problems? Did the child ever have a sexually transmitted disease? How was it handled? For the older female victim, was there any form of birth control? Did she ever get pregnant? If so, what happened? Has the child or teenager been sexually active with other adults, boyfriends, or girlfriends?

Explore whether or not there were any other victims known or suspected by the child. Questions might include: Do you think Daddy might have done this to Sally, too? Has anything happened to anybody else you know?

Remember to ask about pornography. Ask questions such as: Has anybody ever taken any pictures of you? Were you ever on television or in the movies?

Keep in mind older children may also be victimizing other children. They may have something to tell about their being abused, as well as their abusing others. If an abusing child has been victimized by someone who has already been prosecuted, the child may be extraordinarily fearful about a personal offense coming to light. Such a child may anticipate the same consequences as befell the original abuser.

Who? Most children will know the offender by name. Sometimes they will not know the exact nature of the relationship, such as whether the person is a relative, family friend, or boyfriend. You can use other sources to determine these details.

A sentence completion activity, such as "This person—." can be used as a nonthreatening way to glean information. Start by saying, "I may be talking about Mommy, Daddy, your teacher, your brother or sister, or anybody else. You guess whom I am talking about." Then ask questions such as: Who is always fun to cuddle? Who is always there? Who teaches me things? Who did something yucky?

Ask if there was anyone else. Was anyone else around? Were there any witnesses or participants? Where was the rest of the family when the abuse occurred?

When? Find out the general time of day or night or day of the week when the abuse occurred. The clarity of a child's response to this question will depend on the child's ability to tell and recall time. It will also depend on how recently the assault happened, and how often it occurred. Multiple occurrences result in the child confusing or blurring separate incidents. If a child is under six, his or her concept of time is unreliable. An older child can narrow down dates and times using familiar events or other activities as bench marks: Did you go the park before your birthday? After Christmas? Was it nighttime or daytime? Did it happen after dinner? After the television cartoons were over? After your mom left for the meeting?

Find out as much as possible about other family members' activity patterns, such as a mother's night-shift work. Look for times when the offender could have had private access to the child.

How long has it been going on? Grades in school can be useful measures of time. Try to determine the frequency: Every night? Once or twice a month? Every time Mom went out of town?

Where? Ask the child where the abuse occurred. If at home, find out which room, and in what part of the room: On the floor? On the bed? In the bathtub? On the couch? A dollhouse can be very helpful in determining locations. Let the child volunteer information and then ask more questions. Ask the whereabouts of other family members. Use doll figures and the dollhouse to position the rest of the family.

If the abuse took place outside of the home, ask how the child got to the location. Was there any reason for the site being used? Have the child describe any details of the setting, such as in a movie theater, in the bushes at the zoo, or behind the neighbor's garage.

How? Also find out what kind of force, threat, enticement, or pressure was used to obtain the child's participation and secrecy. You may approach secrecy in a general way by saying, "Sometimes people try to get boys and girls not to tell what happened." Then note the child's response. Then follow with questions such as: Did he tell you not to tell? What did he say? Did he say something bad would happen to you or someone else, if you told? Did he tell you it was to be a secret? Look for circumstances that are typical of sexual abuse, such as children being told they can't go out with their friends unless they comply, or children being told they're being taught how to act when they have a boyfriend or get married.

Was violence threatened against the child or anyone else, including a pet? Was any aspect of the threat ever carried out, such as the child's kitty disappearing and the child being told the same thing would happen to her if she ever told?

What is the child's emotional response to the telling of the threats? If very fearful, take time to reassure and comfort the child before going on to other details.

Did anyone else know? Has the child told anyone else? If not, why not? If so, what did the other person do? Look for others who may be able to corroborate at least part of the child's story.

Why is the child telling now? The timing of the disclosure can be very important. Was the disclosure accidental or purposeful? If purposeful, the counselor needs to find out what the child wishes will happen as a result of telling. If any of the expectations are unrealistic, the counselor should help introduce some realistic thinking.

How does the child feel about the offender now? Was it a special relationship that had good and bad parts to it? Be careful not to convey a strong negative attitude toward the offender because the child may still have enjoyed part of the activities or relationship.

Is the child angry at anyone? Whom? How has the child expressed the anger?

It might be appropriate at this point to ask the child, "If you could have three wishes what would they be? Responses may reveal feelings about the situation and people involved.

Assessing Credibility

Determining the validity of a child's allegation of sexual abuse is mostly a matter of belief. Most of the time there will not be any corroboration of the child's story by physical evidence, witnesses, or a confession by the offender. To make things worse, if the perpetrator or unsupportive family members perceive that the counselor or other investigators have not yet reached a conclusive decision about the allegations, they will almost always pressure the child to recant or deny the story.[2]

This places a great deal of importance on your obtaining reliable, accurate impressions about the child's credibility. The primary components in evaluating a child's story are: reports of multiple incidents over time, a progression from less intimate to more intimate sexual activity, revelation of direct or implied understanding between the child and offender that the activity should be kept secret, presence of elements of pressure and coercion, and explicit details of sexual behavior.[3]

If the child is going to be a witness in court, three conditions must be met. 1. The child must be able to receive and relay information accurately. 2. The child must be able to tell the difference between truth and a lie. 3. The child must know the importance of telling the truth in court.

The counselor should have a pretty clear understanding of the child's ability to meet these qualifications before proceeding with the process of preparing her to testify.

Children rarely fabricate stories of sexual abuse.[4] In the 1 percent to 5 percent of the cases when this does occur, the false report is an indication of another problem. Parents, church leaders, and professionals tend not to believe children because such adults do not want to believe them. Acknowledging the truth of what victims say forces us to admit an unpleasant reality. We don't like to acknowledge a society where such things can happen, let alone admit that it happens within the church.

The best stance is to assume that the sexual abuse is a fact until proven otherwise. Believe the child and support him or her in every way possible.

When false allegations do occur, it is usually a result of one of the following:

An opportunistic lie. The child got revenge or gained a privilege by making the accusation.

An adult confederate. The child was coached by a parent to lie as a part of divorce, custody, or visitation proceedings.

Prior history of sexual abuse. The child was abused by someone else, but generalized the events to an innocent party.

Serious emotional problems. The child may have experienced some kind of trauma that resulted in a personality disorder or a loss of contact with reality.

In around 30 percent of the cases, a child will either deny abuse ever took place (even though there is strong corroboration) or will admit the abuse and later say the story was not true. For intrafamilial sexual abuse, the following issues can put pressure on a child to falsely deny the abuse:

- threats by the offender to change her story or something bad will happen
- guilt about upsetting the family, perhaps because the father had to leave the home
- worry about the mother falling apart and not being able to care for the family
- rejection by the family
- infatuation with the offender. The victim may have very pleasant feelings toward the person involved. The abuse may have been the only source of nurturance for the child who doesn't want to lose that only good source.
- pleasurable feelings because she enjoyed certain aspects of the experience. The child may feel she is partly to blame; she may want the relationship to continue.
- fear regarding the court proceedings. The stress of the testimony process is greater than the desire to convince others of the truth.

Children recant not because they weren't abused, but because the need for acceptance and security is crucial to their survival. The counselor must help with these security needs if the child is going to hold up during the long and troubling process.

Closing the Interview

After obtaining all the information possible, you should praise and thank the child for cooperating. If the session has been emotional, take time to reassure the child. It may be appropriate for you to take the blame for difficult interviews. ("I'm sorry, Karen, that I made you cry by asking those hard questions." "I know today was hard for you. Maybe I didn't do a real good job, because you got very upset. But I'm so proud of how you kept going.")

Gradually moving from the detailed content to more light-hearted material is a good idea. The older the child, the more necessary it is to allow transition time.

Take time to explain what is going to happen next. It's a good idea to ask what the child would like to have happen. Do everything possible to carry out any reasonable and appropriate requests.

If a referral to another agency is going to be made, explain this. If a physical examination is to take place, explain the procedure. Although all details of the legal or social service process need not be given to the child, the events should be demystified as much as possible. Give simple, straightforward information to both the child and the parents.

The child may be fearful of someone talking to the parents or to the offender. This should be discussed and the child given reassurance about protective concerns. Illustrations of the success of other children in similar situations can be used to give confidence.

REPORTING AND CONFIDENTIALITY

If you are the first to learn about child sexual abuse, you must report your findings to the appropriate agencies. Some states exempt pastors from the reporting requirement. In most states, the report must be made within a certain time period, from twenty-four hours to seven days. If you are working with a child as part of an investigative or therapeutic effort, the reporting will already have been done. If in doubt, check with the other agencies involved.

Sometimes suspicion of abuse will arise while dealing with other issues. I once saw a child whose mother was interested in getting a professional opinion about her son's extreme reluctance to continue visits with his father. The child was very strong in his desire not to go visit his father, but was vague about his reasons. Later it was discovered the father was subjecting his son to extreme sexual abuse, including pornography.

If there is a reasonable basis for thinking a child has been abused, it should be reported. If there is doubt in your mind as to the appropriateness of a report, consult informally with Child Protective Services and/or law enforcement personnel.

Reports can be made by phone, in writing, or in person to a local law enforcement agency, Department of Social and Health Services, or Child Protective Services. Take the time to find out the proper procedures in your locality.

The report will consist of the name, address, and age of the child, name and address of the adult having custody, and nature and extent of the injury, neglect, or sexual abuse. Any other information that would help establish the cause of the abuse and the possible identity of the perpetrator should be included.

All fifty states mandate reporting of all types of abuse, including sexual abuse. For most social service, medical, and educational personnel, failure to report suspected child abuse is a misdemeanor. In most areas the responsibility for identification and reporting belongs to people who have direct contact with children as part of their job or profession. Although any citizen may report, most states name medical personnel, mental health workers, educators, and clergy. Those who report abuse are generally given immunity from liability and can remain anonymous, as long as the report was made in good faith. A report of suspected child abuse, sexual or otherwise, is based on concern for the health and safety of the child, not to punish his or her caretakers.

Privileged communication—between husband and wife, physician and patient, clergy and confessioners—normally protected in court procedure, is generally not protected in cases of abuse and neglect. The protection of the child is considered the overriding concern. In most states, only communications between attorney and client are deemed privileged.

The issue of mandatory reporting for pastors and clergy has created some controversy. Some pastors see the requirement of reporting to be in conflict with their function as a spiritual confidant. Many pastors do not want government to interfere with their functioning as clerical professionals. Neither do they want the relationship with their parishioners intruded upon by the state. These, indeed, are legitimate concerns.

But why wouldn't a pastor choose to report abuse, even when not required to do so? The reluctance of many pastors to use even a voluntary system suggests there are issues other than mandatory reporting.[5]

Secrecy involves a promise never to tell under any conditions. But in the case of abuse this involves supporting the secret of abuse and contributes to the perpetuation of the problem. Unless the secret is shared, the abuse will continue. A higher order of ethics mandates intervention to stop pain and suffering, even at the expense of breaking an implied promise not to reveal the disclosure.

Clergy confidentiality is intended as part of a process to help a person overcome personal problems so as not to cause further harm to self or others. Confidentiality is not intended to protect offenders from being accountable or from getting help. Protecting abusers from the consequences of their actions will deny them the opportunity for spiritual repentance and a chance to change.[6]

Another major ethical responsibility is to protect the victims of abuse. The Christian tradition has always included the responsibility of the community to protect those who are defenseless and vulnerable (Exod. 22:21–27; Matt. 25:34–45). The alien, widow, and orphan were particularly vulnerable to exploitation because they did not have any source of support. The greater community was responsible to protect them because they were without resources and power.

Today, the abused child is one who is most powerless to protect personal interests; the child needs the support of the church community. Maintaining an effort of confidentiality for secrecy's sake while ignoring the pleas of victimized children contradicts the entire message of Jesus Christ.

A final ethical consideration is justice. "Have nothing to do with the fruitless deeds of darkness, but rather expose them" (Eph. 5:11). "Those who sin are to be rebuked publicly, so that the others may take warning" (1 Tim. 5:20). "So watch yourselves. If your brother sins, rebuke him, and if he repents, forgive him" (Luke 17:3).

The perpetrator of sexual abuse must be confronted so he can seek repentance. Only with repentance can change occur. "Rid yourselves of all the offenses you have committed, and get a new heart and a new spirit . . . Repent and live!" (Ezek.

18:31, 32). When the offender is confronted with his sin and held accountable for his behavior, the stage is set for confession, forgiveness, and reconciliation. Maintaining secrecy does not bring about justice.

When deliberating the question of confidentiality, the pastor should keep in mind the following factors surrounding child sexual abuse:

Incest offenders will reoffend unless they get specialized treatment.

Offenders against children minimize, lie, and deny their abusive behavior.

Offenders cannot follow through on their good intentions or genuine remorse without help from the outside.

Treatment of offenders can be effective when it is ordered and monitored by the courts.

The secret of the child's abuse must be broken in order to get help to the victim and offender.

Clergy, generally, do not have all the skills and resources necessary to treat offenders or to assist victims, and they should not try to do it alone.

Quick forgiveness can be superficial in its effect and can get in the way of permanent changes.[7]

While confidentiality is important, the overriding principle is to protect those who are being victimized and to hold the perpetrator accountable. Confidentiality can be a pathway to help and restoration, rather than a cloak to maintain the secret of abuse. If you do not participate in the reporting process, ask yourself what good is being served by not doing so. Who benefits most by withholding the information, the offender or the victim?

COUNSELING THE SEXUALLY ABUSED CHILD[8]

Treatment of the sexually abused child can be divided into three phases: crisis intervention, short-term therapy, and long-term therapy.

Crisis Intervention

The disclosure of sexual abuse or incest throws the family into a crisis state. This is a difficult time for both the counselor and the family. The pastor or counselor must be prepared to help the victim and family cope with investigative interviews, a medical examination, visits with Child Protective Services and law enforcement personnel, interviews with attorneys, court appearances, and publicity following the disclosure.

If the immediate family has been disrupted by having the father removed, practical matters, such as food, clothing, shelter, money, and transportation, become critical considerations. The counselor, if involved in this process, will need a close networking of community resources.

The therapy, at this point, is very practical and includes a great deal of support and reassurance. After the physical and economic needs of the family are met, the family can move on to individual and group therapy.

One of the most important tasks for the counselor will be to prevent the suppressive forces from harming the child or building to a crisis point. Based on trust between the counselor and victim, the effort is to prevent threats, recrimination, badgering, and retaliatory measures from having a crippling effect on the victim. Predicting or anticipating such pressures for the child will be helpful.

If the victim does recant previous allegations, the counselor must quickly try to determine why the child changed the story. Most likely someone has frightened or pressured the youngster into changing the disclosure. The counselor's task at this time is to give the child enough support to outweigh the pressure from other sources and/or get to the source of the pressure and remove it.

Short-Term Therapy

This follows the crisis intervention phase and will be sufficient for some victims. Those who have not been subjected to severe physical and emotional trauma may require only one to six months of therapy. The greater the amount of familial support for the child, the more likely short-term therapy will be sufficient. If the child was abused by someone outside of the family, and the family remains supportive, the therapy will be short-term. Incest, involving a sibling or parent, greatly complicates the problem and will dictate a longer term project.

The following issues need to be addressed during this phase of treatment.

Damaged goods. A victim of sexual abuse feels damaged. If physical injury or pain occurred, the child has factual reason to believe he or she was damaged. Usually there is no physical impairment, but it is understandable that a child who experienced pain would expect there to be some kind of permanent damage.

Adolescent girls often ask, "Will I be normal when I grow up? If I have a baby, will it be all right?" If a victim has become pregnant, the experience provides concrete evidence of damage.

When the family and community learn the child has been prematurely introduced to sexual activity, the victim's perception that he or she has been mysteriously altered by the abuse is heightened. The youngster is likely to be viewed with intense curiosity, pity, disgust, or hostility by those who learn of the sexual abuse.

Treatment of the "damaged goods syndrome" should begin with a comprehensive physical examination of the victim, done by a physician who is knowledgeable about child sexual abuse. If physical damage did occur, it can then be treated. If there is no damage, this fact should be conveyed to the victim and the family. An authoritative statement that physical damage is absent or has been treated is a step toward convincing everyone that the victim has not been otherwise damaged.

Parents, siblings, teachers, and others should be made aware of how important it is *not* to treat the child differently from other children. The child needs to be viewed as a child and not as an adult or a sexually sophisticated child.

Guilt. Intense feelings of guilt following disclosure of sexual abuse are almost universal. There are three levels of that guilt.

1. Responsibility for the sexual behavior. As soon as they perceive society's response to their involvement, many children feel they are responsible for the sexual activity that took place.

2. Responsibility for disclosure. When the secret is told by the children, they are obviously responsible for the disclosure. Children may also assume responsibility when the dis-

closure was accidental or when someone else told. Under any circumstance, children may feel they have betrayed the perpetrator.

3. Responsibility for disruption. Disclosure of abuse leads to profound disruption for victims and everyone around them. If it is incest, the uproar is even greater. When children tell their secret, they can be expected to feel guilty about the changes that result. Usually the disruption is greater than they expected. Even when problems flare up weeks or months later, children may receive the blame and feel guilty.

The treatment consists of first helping victims identify and sort out their guilty feelings. You should consistently convey to the child, family members, and the perpetrator that a child can never be held responsible for initiating sexual activity with an older person. Your message should also be that a child has a right to expect protection from an offender, and that the child had a right to disclose the secret. The perpetrator is the one responsible for the sexual activity, including the disruption that followed.

Sometimes older children have taken advantage of the favored position with the offender. Or they may have acted inappropriately toward their brothers and sisters. In other cases, they may have become very manipulative or disobedient. Such youngsters may be experiencing some appropriate guilt for their conduct, and you need to help them sort through the distinctions. If there is legitimate guilt, the child should be helped to work it through and redirect their behavior.

Once a child has revealed the secret, he or she needs a great deal of reassurance. Youngsters need to be told that others believe the story, that they are not to blame, and that they will be protected from further sexual abuse and retaliation. Victims should be praised for their courage and assured that, in the long run, their confessions will help the whole family.

Fear. Child victims may fear future incidents of abuse as well as retaliation. Often these fears are evidenced by nightmares or dreams.

As counselor, you can help the child identify and determine the reality of such fears. It helps a victim to express the feelings associated with the fear. Realistic fears of reprisal and separation can only be alleviated if concrete assistance is available. The Christian counselor can talk about God's protection, but the victim's experience to this point has been contrary. The child's living situation should be made to feel as safe as possible, and steps should be taken to build trusting and safe relationships within and outside of the family.

Depression. Most victims will exhibit some signs of depression after disclosure. There may be overt signs of sadness and withdrawal or indirect symptoms, such as chronic fatigue and physical illness. Some children may act out their despair with self-mutilation or suicide attempts.

Counselors of sexually abused children should be alert for signs of depression. Some of the feelings can be alleviated by talking and expression through art, music, or activity. As children perceive they are believed, supported, and loved unconditionally, their depression can subside. Serious cases may need intensive therapy, hospitalization, and sometimes even medication.

Low self-esteem and poor social skills. All of the preceding influences tend to undermine the child's self-esteem. Seeing oneself as spoiled or damaged tends to undermine self-confidence. The child, therefore, does not take many risks, and as a result does not learn new skills and does not grow. A vicious cycle is started that is very hard to break.

Additionally, many victims of incest have been limited in their exposure to outside relationships. As a result, they have limited social skills. The few times a child victim tries to make friends are often unsuccessful, and the failures reinforce the low self-opinion. Victims often feel helpless and are not able to assert themselves.

Treatment can include both individual and group therapy at this point. Individual counseling can focus on learning new and positive ways to view oneself. The fact of God's unconditional love, even to people who hurt, can be introduced and emphasized. Christ's suffering and anguish can be used as a bridge for the feelings associated with being a victim. Don't rush too quickly to Christ the Victor, but give the child time to identify with Christ the Victim.

Group therapy can also be helpful in building self-esteem,

particularly for adolescent victims. The group provides both peer support and identity, as well as a basis to try out new social skills.

Long-Term Therapy

Victims who have experienced severe physical and emotional trauma will probably be candidates for therapy lasting up to two years or more. The smaller the base of support, the longer it will take for a child to develop strength on his or her own. If the family is not making progress as a whole, the child will also be slower to grow.

If the offender is a parent or parent-figure who lives with the victim, it will take longer to overcome the problems of trust, security, role confusion, and so forth. Besides the five areas covered in the short-term discussion, an additional five impact issues need to be attended to in the longer term setting.

Repressed anger and hostility. Although they may appear passive and compliant, most child sexual abuse victims are inwardly seething with anger and hostility. They are angry at the one who abused and exploited them. They are also angry with parents or family members who did not protect them. Their anger may be expressed in depression or withdrawal, physical complaints, and aggressive fantasies, stories, drawings, or behavior.

Treatment must help the victim get in touch with repressed feelings and learn to express anger in healthy, nondestructive ways. Children should be encouraged to be assertive in their expression. Their feelings need to be supported, and they need to hear the basic message that anger is not wrong. It is okay to feel angry; the goal is to learn how to handle it well. A group therapy context for older children and adolescents is good for providing a safe setting to learn nondestructive ways to express anger.

Inability to trust. A child who has been victimized by a trusted person will have difficulty trusting anyone else in the future. The degree of impairment will depend on how traumatic the consequences of the shattered trust. Often the child learns not to trust because of broken promises and betrayal.

A child will develop trust slowly and only with positive

experiences. By having satisfying relationships, the child's feelings of alienation can be overcome. Both individual and group therapy are likely to be more successful than individual therapy alone, when it comes to encouraging the child to try new relationships.

Blurred role boundaries and role confusion. Victims experience role confusion due to the blurred boundaries between the offender and the child. If an adult in a power position takes advantage of a less powerful child for a sexual relationship, there is a crossing of the usual societal role boundaries. Although the sexual activity, for the adult, is primarily in the service of nonsexual needs, the sexual experience generates a great deal of confusion for the child. The confusion is magnified when the perpetrator is a family member.

As counselor, your task is to help the victim resolve any role confusion. It is important to have at least one adult family member confirm your statements about appropriate boundaries.

If at all possible, at some point the offender should explain to the child how the boundaries were crossed. The offender should acknowledge that he or she was responsible for the abuse, that the sexual behavior was inappropriate, and that it will not be repeated. This may be a good time to approach the topic of forgiveness between the offender and the victim.

If the family is working toward reuniting, this may be a good time to work out detailed agreements on respect for boundaries. This might include rules for entering occupied bedrooms or bathrooms, borrowing of possessions, and assignment of shared tasks and responsibilities.

Pseudomaturity and failure to complete developmental tasks. Abuse is disruptive because the stimulation of the sexual relationship interferes with the accomplishment of age-appropriate developmental tasks. Role confusion often leads to the child taking on an adultlike role. For example, it is common in father-daughter incest for the mother to relinquish her role as spouse, parent, and family caretaker to her daughter.

As victimized children take on more adult responsibilities, the gap widens between them and their peers. They don't have any opportunity to be age-appropriate children. The victim is left with no appropriate interactions with peers and is more vulnerable than ever.

Treatment requires that the sexual abuse stop and that the child's parents acknowledge the victim's right to behave as a child. The overly mature victim must be allowed to give up inappropriate responsibilities and act like a child. This requires changes by all members of the family. The roles of each person must be examined for appropriateness, and then the mechanics of implementing changes discussed. Unless the entire family system changes, the child cannot change in this area.

Self-mastery and control. Sexual abuse involves a violation of the victim's body, privacy, and rights of self-mastery. The child has been forced, by someone in a more powerful position, to do something that was wrong and unhealthy. The right to make decisions about one's own space or territory was violated by someone who was supposed to be trustworthy.

The result is often a child who avoids decisions or resists the decisions of others. The effects can be long-lasting and very destructive.

You must help the victim learn self-mastery and control over elements in the child's world. This involves accountability, behaving responsibly toward others and oneself, and finding the freedom to make one's own choices.

Victims need opportunities to test their capacity for decision making. They need the freedom to make mistakes and to learn from them. Good judgment is achieved through practice. A person needs the chance to make choices, be responsible for personal actions, and get feedback that is not harsh or punitive. A good treatment plan will provide this type of structured opportunity.

The family should be involved in the victim's progression toward greater independence and self-mastery. If the whole family system is not becoming more flexible, the growth of the victim will upset the balance and cause more tension.

MOTHER–DAUGHTER DYAD THERAPY

In cases of father–daughter incest, it is important to have some sessions with the mother and child together to discuss their relationship. It is important so both can understand why there was a communication breakdown between them and why the mother was not able to protect the child. Both mother and daughter need to examine how the role reversal took place, and why and how it needs to be corrected. The child needs to hear from the mother that she will be protected and that the incest was not the daughter's fault. Both parents were to protect the child and both failed.

There are three major therapeutic concerns in restoring incestuous families: the need to restrict and control the excessive power of incestuous fathers, the need to reinforce and foster the power of mothers, and the need to restore the mother–daughter relationship.

If the father has been absent from the home as a result of the incest disclosure, the mother–daughter relationship must be rebuilt before a permanent return is made. If the father does reenter the family, both the mother and daughter need to be assured of continued protection and support.

Children are often angrier at the nonoffending parent than at the perpetrator of incest. Victims tend to blame this parent for not protecting them, even if this parent was absent when the sexual abuse took place.

The anger will be even more intense if the daughter had told her mother but was not believed. This is likely to be a difficult and painful process for both mother and daughter, but an essential part of their recovery.

It is a good idea for the mother to be in a mother's group during this part of therapy so she can receive some feedback and peer support.

The emphasis in this chapter has been on identification and validation of abuse, since I believe this is the biggest need for the majority of Christian counselors and pastors. Many more aspects of counseling the victim on a long-term basis could be presented, but space does not allow.

The next chapter will focus on treating the offender of sexual abuse. Since the family perspective should always be kept, there will be some carryover between the counseling needs of children and their perpetrators.

CHAPTER NINE

TREATMENT OF THE SEXUAL OFFENDER

"WE'RE NOT JUST a churchgoing family. Our faith is very strong. I have been a Christian for years, and my husband even considered going to seminary. For our daughter to make these accusations about her father was a real shock. I couldn't believe what she was telling me. It was like watching a horror movie. Everything started happening in slow motion. I was in a daze, and couldn't think what to do next. I felt like I was in the bottom of a deep well, and nobody could hear my screams. But then my daughter told me she had been screaming silently for two years. Will our family ever be the same?"

This mother's statement illustrates the crisis condition a disclosure of incest or sexual abuse brings to a family. Usually, by the time the secret is revealed, the abuse has been going on for a long time. Whether known or not, the abuse has become an integral part of the family life. Disclosure disrupts whatever fragile balance existed. No element of family living is unaffected. Each person must come to terms with the changes necessitated by establishing new patterns of behaving and relating.

INITIAL CONSIDERATIONS

Pastors and counselors will increasingly find themselves in some form of intervention with a sexual offender. It may come about as a result of the offender's disclosure, because the offender has been accused or arrested, or because the child or wife has sought help.

Influencing Factors

While some of these characteristics have been stated before, the pastor or counselor needs to be aware of several factors that influence the counseling relationship with a sexual offender.

Sex offenders seldom tell the truth about their behavior. They will minimize, deny, and lie about what happened.

Sex offenders seldom express remorse or any sense of wrong-doing.

Sex offenders will be most concerned with the consequences of being caught. Therefore, they can be very manipulative and will try to mobilize a minister's support as a character witness in their behalf.

Sex offenders are repeat offenders and will continue to abuse others until they are stopped. The legal system provides the best leverage to get an offender into treatment and to keep him there as long as necessary.[1]

The pastor or counselor's role can be instrumental in working with other agencies to provide the offender with the consistent message that his behavior was wrong, that it must stop, and that there is help.

Marie Fortune, in her book *Sexual Violence: The Unmentionable Sin,* gives the following illustration of an appropriate pastoral response to a plea for help by a sexual offender.

A man came into his pastor's office looking for help. He told his pastor that he had been "messing around" with his nine-year-old daughter. In response to the pastor's questions, the man admitted that he had finally decided that this was wrong and he wanted to know if God and the pastor could forgive him. The pastor replied, "John, you know that God forgives those who are truly sorry for their sins, and I can certainly forgive you. We are going to pray about this right now together and ask God's forgiveness and as soon as we finish, we are going to call up a psychologist I know and get you into treatment."[2]

This was a very appropriate response for the pastor to give, although it probably wasn't what the offender expected. Most perpetrators of sexual abuse and incest want a quick fix. They want the pastor to pray with them, assure them of forgiveness, and stand up for them in court.

This pastor knew what the offender needed and dealt with his needs in a loving but direct manner. This man did go into treatment and the pastor met with him weekly for prayer and Bible study. This allowed the pastor to keep abreast of John's treatment as well as offer support and encouragement during the long road to restoration.

One of the main goals during the initial contact with an offender is to confront him and not become duped into also minimizing the offense. Most pastors are not trained to be the primary therapist for a sexual offender. They can be an important part of the total team, but it is unwise to try to deal with such a complicated problem without the input of professionals specially trained in this area.

Many counselors are also not equipped to work with those who have committed incest and other forms of sexual abuse. The typical offender has many psychopathic personality qualities, and the counselor should be comfortable working with multiple layers of denial and deceit before taking on such a client on an individual basis.

The state of the art in counseling offenders is still very much in development. There is no preferred mode of treatment. Some approaches focus on separate members of the family, using a combination of group and individual therapies. Other strategies spend most of the time working entirely with families. The following discussion will present some general recommendations for both types of involvement.

Why Does Sexual Abuse Occur in Christian Families?

First of all, Christians are still human. Being a sexual offender doesn't necessarily invalidate a person's faith. Such weaknesses, however severe, are clear reminders that we are fallen creatures in a fallen world. Although our faith does contribute to emotional well-being, it does not guarantee the absence of problems. We may have yearned that somehow our human inadequacies would disappear. The facts are that we all have enduring weaknesses. While it would be nice to be problem free, no one has yet succeeded. When we profess faith in Jesus, we bring our raw material with us, including our insecurities, need for personal power, and sexual drives. We also bring our personal history which may have included abuse of our own. While many abused children vowed they would never act in the same manner as their parents, unless something intervenes to significantly alter the habit pattern, the probability is that history will repeat itself. The model of a violent and abusive parent is tough to shake. And the Christian is just as vulnerable to that vicious cycle.

This is not meant in any way to excuse sexual abuse. Every effort should be made to prevent its occurrence and to make the offender accountable before the law, the victim, and God.

Second, the rigidity of many offenders gives evidence to the observation that it is much easier to *teach* the law than *live* in grace. The dogmatic, authoritarian personality is almost always covering over a strong sense of insecurity. This perceived lack of personal power and influence can often lead to direct or indirect attempts to dominate others. Religious dogma, doctrine, and protocol lend themselves to misuse by the insecure personality. Interpretation of selected Scripture can conveniently be used to maintain the balance of power in favor of the abuser, i.e., "Children, obey your parents," or "Wives, submit yourselves to your husband." The implication is "With God on my side, how can you ever question my authority?"

Fear of rejection predisposes a domineering or intimidating attitude and behavior: *"I'll overpower you before you have a chance to reject me. Then, if you avoid or resist me, it's because you can't stand the heat. I win!"*

A knife can be used to spread butter or take a life. So too can religion be inappropriately used to further selfish ends.

Third, many persons are unable to separate sexual behavior from emotional intimacy. One of the forms of love mentioned in Scripture is *storge* love, which means to cherish one's family. It is a type of reciprocal tenderness between parents and children (Titus 2:4). This kind of love, which is totally separate from romantic or sexual love, is misdirected by the incest offender. This love could be likened to a comfortable old shoe, which would describe a family relationship comprised of natural affection and a sense of belonging to each other. Most sexual offenders have not learned how to give and receive love of this type, so access and contact with a vulnerable child provides opportunity for the inappropriate expression of emotional and physical needs.

Fourth, although incest is sexual behavior in the service of nonsexual needs, part of the total dynamic for the religious offender is his difficulty in dealing openly with sexual matters. In spite of the attention given to the proper place for sex in the creation of God, many persons still are uptight about sex. This lack of ability to talk about sex in a healthy manner creates a type of tension which makes the forbidden expression even more desirable.

In a related vein, offending adults have often looked to sexual release as their major form of dealing with stressors. When the bills pile up, the car breaks down, work is frustrating, the marriage is a disaster, and there is no Monday night football on television, sex becomes the dominant way for many people to cope. Accompanied by fear of intimacy, insecurity, poor communication skills, and lack of ability to handle conflict, the tendency to resort to sex as a solution to emotional needs becomes very strong. This pattern remains present in many cases of sexual abuse.

Fifth, many offenders lack the social and communication skills needed to adapt in other than dogmatic and compulsive ways. If a person feels uncomfortable in open, two-way communication, he or she erects a defense system. A devout, rigid, moralistic, and conservative framework can become very comforting to one who lacks the ability to share and listen. The accompanying fear and suspicion of different points of view allow a protective shield to be erected which keeps the fragile psyche safe. Although all forms of growth are stifled, a comfort zone has been established and any changes are resisted with enthusiasm.

These reasons probably only partially explain why the incidence of sexual abuse is so high in certain types of Christian homes. But we must continue to postulate and test our hypotheses until sufficient knowledge is gleaned to allow us to stop this tidal wave of destruction.

Initial Intervention

The structure of treatment for families involved in incest begins with prevention of further victimization of the child; crisis intervention to help the family restructure their interactions; and individual and family treatment.

The first step in the process is to ensure the safety of the victim. Often this results in removal of the offending adult (usually the father or father figure) from the home. If the non-offending parent has not been able to prevent the abuse prior to disclosure, there is little reason to think she is any better equipped immediately after the secret is told.

Every effort should be made not to allow removal of the child victim from the home. This only adds to the child's trauma and feelings of guilt. Removal of the child, in a few instances, may be necessary because there is no support system left within the home.

Allowing the adult offender to remain in the home and removing the child is also risky because of the possibility the offender will start molesting another child within the home. The ideal is to reunite a family, but there usually has to be a time of separation to ensure that the abuse does not continue.

The second part of the initial intervention is to help the family deal with the immediate consequences of the disclosure.

Issues such as living and financial arrangements, social and medical assistance, publicity, legal process, etc., must be started. Large amounts of support are needed at this stage. The church community can be very helpful, as it would be if a member family had experienced a death. Baby-sitting, meals, transportation, and help with household chores are examples of practical services that will minister to a family during this crisis time. If the rest of the congregation is involved in ministering to the traumatized family, discernment should be used with regard to revealing the details of the abuse. The abuse should not necessarily be kept secret, but extensive particulars are private matters for the family.

Once the crisis begins to pass, the long-term treatment can begin. Experience suggests the treatment of an incestuous family requires close to two years of intensive, structured intervention. Generally speaking, the beginning phase of treatment requires that the victim (usually the daughter), her mother, and the father be treated on an individual and group basis. Later in the process, the father and mother can be seen for couple therapy, followed later by the entire family becoming involved in weekly family therapy sessions.

The discussion will now turn to treatment goals and general procedures for the offender and the family. Treatment issues for the victim have been presented in chapter 8. It is important to view sexual abuse in a family perspective, but there are unique issues for each of these therapeutic endeavors.

EVALUATING THE INCEST OFFENDER

Some of the basic problems for the incest offender are his inner feelings of helplessness, vulnerability, and dependency. As he tries to meet the daily stressors of marriage, parenthood, and vocation, his long-standing insecurities come to the surface. He feels overwhelmed and his usual coping mechanisms begin to fail him. As a result, he may use one of two responses to try to cope with his situation.

First, he may withdraw from adult responsibilities and adopt a passive–dependent role within his family. By becoming dependent, the offender gives over control to the rest of the family and withdraws from the demands and responsibilities of his marriage. The incestuous relationship becomes his substitute for meeting needs of success and control.

A second possibility is that he is overcompensating by adopting an excessively rigid, controlling, authoritarian position. He becomes the family patriarch, often using Scripture and concepts such as submission and obedience to support his position. This position of dominance allows the offender to rule and control the rest of the family and reassures himself of his adequacy and effectiveness. Incestuous behavior becomes his precarious attempt to compensate for feelings of loss or inadequacy.[3]

The counselor will find the passive–dependent type of offender looking to his therapist to cure him in some magical way. Sometimes this will take the form of requesting prayer for healing or other spiritual activity. This type of offender may appear to be cooperative but tends to view himself as a victim of forces, such as court action, a vindictive wife, or abusive parents, over which he has no control.

The aggressive–dominant type of offender may be more obviously resistant and continue to deny the offense. He will fail to keep appointments, actively sabotage the treatment, or even abandon the family.[4]

The incestuous offender usually becomes dependent on sexual activity to meet his emotional needs. The sexual relationship is used to express a variety of unresolved problems that are not just sensual in nature. Rather, the incest is more directly related to issues of competency, adequacy, worth, recognition, validation, status, affiliation, and identity. Incest is the sexual misuse of power.[5] There are a number of motivations the counselor should look for in the makeup of the incestuous offender.

- It may serve to validate his sense of worth and bolster his self-esteem.
- It may compensate for feeling abused or rejected by his wife, or women in general.
- It may serve to restore a sense of power.
- It may gratify a need for attention and recognition.

- It may serve to meet a need for affiliation and to overcome loneliness.
- It may temporarily strengthen his sense of identity.[6]
- It may be used to provide relief of pain.
- It can be used as an aid to reduce tension or deal with stress.

Offender Characteristics

There is no absolute set of personality qualities that distinguishes incest offenders from nonoffenders. There are, however, some general tendencies or traits that do seem to be pronounced across the many persons who have been treated.

1. Fantasy and submissiveness are more prevalent than assertiveness. The offender experiences himself as a helpless victim of outside forces. He does not feel much sense of personal control over his life. This produces:

2. A continual feeling of isolation from others. The offender feels he is alone. He lacks any consistent sense of intimate attachment or relatedness. This results in:

3. An underlying mood of emptiness, fearfulness, and depression. This combines with low self-esteem and poor self-confidence to make him oversensitive to interpretations of criticisms, put-downs, exploitations, and rejections from a hostile world.

4. This lack of security and comfort, along with his deficient empathic skills, leads him to avoid adult relationships. He substitutes fantasy for reality, and replaces adults with children who complement his own immaturity.

5. The offender becomes emotionally overinvested in his victim. He tries to monopolize her time and restrict her outside interests and activities. He regards her more as a peer than as a child. He feels a narcissistic sense of ownership or entitlement to her, and he projects his own needs and desires on her. He is preoccupied with sexual fantasies about the victim and develops a sense of pleasure, comfort, and power in the relationship.[7]

Many of the features of a incest offender are also seen in the addictive personality. A significant amount of child sexual abuse is perpetrated by individuals who are addicted to sex.

The features seem to apply to either the passive–dependent or the aggressive–dominant type of offender. These characteristics include:

1. A tendency to move from crisis to crisis never becoming settled in a satisfying day-to-day existence. There is a lack of any feeling of mastery over his environment. This results in despair, pessimism, and a sense of helplessness and self-doubt.

2. A dependent personality that cannot stand alone without continuous external support. He has difficulty handling problems on his own. He looks for outside support for many things he does, and can show a readiness to submit to outside powers, higher authorities, cults, or movements. This can occur even with the aggressive–dominant type of offender, although masked by a great deal of verbal hostility and aggression toward opposite points of view.

3. An impulsive nature. The sexual addict cannot defer gratification, yet he gets little long-term pleasure from life.

4. Low self-esteem. His parents may have been very critical or displayed sudden shifts from too much to too little affection. He is left with a core sense of worthlessness with an extreme vulnerability to criticism and a tendency to be motivated by shame and guilt. Often he will obsess on criticism while minimizing his strengths.

5. A history of untreated psychosocial trauma in his childhood which has left him emotionally immature, fearful, and unable to trust others. He often will be a victim of child abuse.

6. Needs the comfort of well-established and well-defined routines to provide the necessary reassurance to go about daily living. He goes to great lengths to maintain strict routines and rituals.

No one person necessarily shows all of these characteristics, but they are common enough across many offenders to be useful guidelines in the diagnosis and treatment process.

Content for Evaluation of the Sexual Offender

The offender has typically operated from a position of power over the victim of his abuse. It is important for the counselor, then, to operate from a base of authority. Knowledge is the best form of authority and power, so it is necessary to obtain an accurate and complete account of the offender's history and incestuous behavior.

Your position as an experienced professional in sexual abuse and/or skill in dealing with spiritual issues, gives you the authority to impact the offender. The goal is to combine a position of authority with affirmative support. You should be very direct, ask for cooperation in mutually examining the situation, yet draw on your authority to explore the facts of the abuse. Remember to never lose sight of the offender's responsibility, and do not allow him to minimize his behavior.[8]

As soon as possible, even prior to meeting with the alleged or known incestuous offender, the following information should be obtained: Police reports, victim counselor reports, background interview with wife, probation report stating conditions and requirements, and a complete description of the offense(s). There will be an official version of the offense, perhaps found in casework reports or court records, along with the offender's version. Check for consistency or discrepancy in the reports. If a polygraph or plethysmograph evaluation was done, obtain a copy of the results. This can be useful in working with the offender's denial. The offender will need to sign a release of information for most of this background material. Copies of the case history can usually be obtained from the offender's case worker, parole officer, or attorney. You also need to evaluate your counseling skills and make sure you are competent to work with this type of client. A referral to a specialist may be the most appropriate thing to do.

A mental status exam should be obtained. This can include psychiatric or psychological evaluations based on interviews and/or testing. The goal here is to rule out extreme mental illness and severe pathology, and determine suitability for therapy.

A complete sexual history, beginning in childhood and adolescence, should be obtained. This can be done during several interviews and/or have the client write out a detailed description. It should include normal and deviant experiences, other unreported offenses, the onset and specifics of any deviant behavior, sexual fantasies, nature and source of sex education, attitudes of parents, and any other sexually related information or feelings. Nothing should be left out.

Along with the sexual history, a complete developmental or social history should be secured. This should include any history of physical or sexual abuse, family abuse, antisocial or criminal behavior, violence or aggression patterns, school and work history, social and family relationships, physical health, and any past treatment for mental health issues.

Explore the presence of substance or chemical abuse, psychiatric history, suicide attempts, and how these problems were treated.

Examine the offender's current social situation, which would include employment, family relationships, including extended family, social support system, community involvement, and church participation.

Try to determine the offender's use of Christian or religious values, and how this fits into his coping pattern. Does he use certain ideas or values to justify or perpetuate his behavior? What are his sources of authority? For example, does he use concepts of headship and obedience to justify the victim's compliance with his wishes? Does he misuse certain biblical material?

What is the offender's attitude toward the victim and the offense. Does he take responsibility, minimize blame, or show any remorse or empathy?

The goals of this initial evaluation are twofold: to determine the offender's amenability to treatment and degree of risk to the community; to begin to formulate a prescriptive diagnosis and treatment plan. To accomplish this, you need to assess the offender's general level of functioning, his overall ability to think rationally, act purposefully, communicate effectively, respond appropriately, and deal adaptively to his environment. It is likely there will be significant deficits in many of these areas. The offender's level of reality testing, frustration tolerance, characteristic mood state, impulse control, empathic abilities, and self-image should be determined.

Of major importance is the nature and intensity of the offender's sexual behavior and its relationship to the fulfillment of his nonsexual needs.

As counselor, you must also consider the prospective living arrangements and environment in regard to the offender's coping style. A high stress environment will make treatment more difficult and will require immediate attention to how the stress impacts the offender.[9]

Assessment of Outpatient or Residential Treatment

If the offender lacks the motivation or the ability to control his incestuous behavior, strict limits and controls must be imposed. The following issues should be examined to determine if the offender can be treated in a community-based program or if a residential or institution treatment program is necessary. Usually this kind of decision is made by the courts or other agencies. The information is included here for your general reference.

Outpatient care may be advised when:

1. The incest did not involve physical force or threat of physical harm to the victim.

2. The offense seemed to be a regression under stress, rather than a chronic sexual fixation on children (see chapter 7 for discussion of these two types). Also the abuse occurred in response to specific and identifiable stressors which have diminished or are no longer present.

3. The offender does not have a criminal record, and has not led a criminal lifestyle apart from the incestuous behavior.

4. The offender acknowledges his responsibility for the offense, appreciates its inappropriateness, is concerned about the impact on the victim, and is genuinely remorseful about his behavior.

5. The offender has dependable social and occupational skills to manage most of his life demands in an adequate fashion. He does not show any evidence of major psychopathology such as psychosis, retardation, alcoholism, severe depression, organic brain dysfunction, and so forth.

6. There are strong support services available in the community. The offender has access to mental health services and

job opportunities. The rest of the family, including the victim, has support to work through the situation. Is there an appropriate place for the offender to live? This may be outside of the home if it is best for him initially not to reside in the same place as the victim, or if the marriage should terminate.

Residential treatment within a security setting would seem more appropriate when:

1. The threat of harm, or actual physical abuse and violence, played a part in the incestuous relationship. Did the offender use a weapon, alcohol, or drugs to incapacitate the victim? Did the sexual offense involve any bizarre or ritualistic acts? Was the victim forced into prostitution or pornographic activities? Or was there a progressive increase in aggression by the offender over time?

2. The offender has had multiple and chronic difficulties with the law in both sexual and nonsexual areas.

3. The offender's psychological adjustment has always been tenuous or borderline. Is his behavior compounded by serious psychopathology, such as psychosis, substance abuse, or organic brain damage which makes his conduct unpredictable?

4. The abuse reflects a chronic and persistent sexual attraction to children in general. If the incest is but one of many types of indiscriminate sexual activities, such as exposing, peeping, sexual contact with animals, etc., the condition is more serious.

5. The offender denies or minimizes his offenses or blames external events for his behavior. He is more distressed by what is going to happen to him than he is about the effects on the victim.[10]

Most experts agree that outpatient treatment is more effective when it is mandated by the court. If not, when the initial pressures following the disclosure subside, there is a strong chance he will drop out of treatment and the offender's abusive behavior is likely to reemerge.

If the offender is institutionalized, he will be relieved of many of the normal responsibilities, demands, and stresses of family living. His daily activities will be structured, other agencies will take care of most of his marital, parental, and financial obligations, and there are not temptations, such as alcohol or the presence of a victim. Under these conditions, his pathological behavior may diminish due to lack of opportunity or lack of stress, only to reappear again when he is released.[11]

There is still a lot of work to be done within the legal and social service systems in dealing with recidivism. There are no easy answers. Effective intervention requires a team effort with all disciplines involved. The issue is again raised—that until the spiritual condition of the heart is changed, there can be no permanent treatment. Confession and repentance, followed by a long-term commitment to change one's behavior is a basic requirement. The Christian counselor or pastor must be supportive of the spiritual dimension of an offender's life, but not be taken in by the offender's good intentions. Treatment is necessary, even if a life-changing step of faith is undertaken. Faith must be followed by consistent action.

Forms of Denial

Once sexual abuse has been reported, a variety of forms of denial may be used by the offender. Below are some familiar themes and examples.

Outright denial. "I didn't do it. She's lying."

Forgetting. "I can't remember." "Everything is just a blur." "I can't imagine that I would ever do such a thing." "The judge says I did it; you seem to think I did it; but I just can't remember doing it."

Avoidance. "I believe sex with my child is wrong. How could I ever do that to someone I love?" "I don't know if I did it or not." "I'm an elder in my church. How could you accuse me of so great a transgression against my own flesh and blood?"

Blame. "I'm being framed." "My wife is just putting my daughter up to this so she can get custody of the kids." "She seduced me into doing it by walking around in her nightgown." "She came up to me and started rubbing against me."

Indirect admission. "This would never have happened if my wife would have been more submissive." "I must have been drinking when it happened."

Mystical excuses. "I don't know what came over me. It must have been the devil himself." "I was under too much stress. Nobody could have handled it any differently."

Minimizing. "I may have hugged her, but I didn't touch her breasts." "It was harmless. I was just patting her on the butt to dismiss her from class." "It only happened once and will never happen again."

Grasping for straws. When confronted with the fact that sperm was found in or near the child's vagina: "Well, I had masturbated in the bathroom earlier, and she must have got it off the toilet seat."

Easy way out. "Yes, I did it. I feel so ashamed. But I prayed with my pastor and asked forgiveness. I know I have been released and it will never happen again."

Dealing with Denial

An admission of guilt is not necessary to start treating an offender or the incestuous family. If the investigation and validation by competent professionals suggests sexual abuse, the treatment is necessary even if the perpetrator is stuck on denial. The fact a child would choose this devastating thing to say about his or her family indicates something is seriously wrong. It is your responsibility to help determine what is wrong and to help with the intervention process.

During the initial session with the family or alleged offender, it is a good idea to anticipate denial. The offender will try to place blame and guilt on the child. Statements will be made such as, "I love my child, I would never do anything to harm her." "I don't know why she says these things, I've always tried to give her everything she needed." "Our family has never needed any help before. Now that these lies have come out, everybody is sticking a nose into our private affairs."

No single statement is going to break down years of denial. But the process can begin by making statements such as: "Sometimes parents force or beg children to change their stories. Many parents worry so much about the assault on their reputation in the church or community that they find it hard to admit to what really happened. Many fathers do not realize that the sexual behavior with a child causes severe psychological damage; they know they aren't hurting the child physically, so they think everything is okay. Let me tell you about some feelings that children who have been sexually abused by their father have shared with me. . . ."

Most sexual abuse offenders will deny their involvement. You can expect such offenders, whether they be adults or teenagers, to deny it and to greet you with hostility and suspicion, particularly if they have been ordered into treatment by the court.

One way to deal with this denial is to explain that all children make complaints about their parents. They tell their friends about how strict or stingy their parents are. After admitting that children do make complaints, the counselor might say, "Given the fact all children say terrible things about their parents, we know that when they say sex is involved, there are usually some problems in the family relationship. We are here to find out what is going on that would prompt such a complaint. I would expect as a parent, you are as concerned as I am. So I need all the information you can give me. After all, you know your child better than anyone else."

While not always conclusive, a polygraph or lie detector evaluation may be useful in confronting the denial pattern. A person must *voluntarily* agree to take a polygraph examination, so a guilty offender may not allow such an evaluation to occur. A refusal, while not legally incriminating, adds credibility to the child's disclosure. Even if positive, the results of polygraph testing cannot be used in court; it is simply a tool in the investigative process.

The offender may admit to his offense but qualify his admission by minimizing what he has done or direct the blame elsewhere. The most common type of minimizing is to allege the sexual abuse only occurred once. You might point out that experience indicates that such a single incident is extremely rare.

A more important response to the minimizing is to inquire about whether or not the offender saw the experience coming. Did he anticipate becoming sexually active with a child? If so, then he either deliberately permitted himself to become involved or he was unable to prevent it. Either way he needs help to avoid a recurrence. If he did not see the sexual involvement coming, then there is nothing to prevent it from happening again in a similarly unanticipated manner. Again, the offender needs assistance to gain awareness and control.[12]

The offender may claim his sexual offense was the product of intoxication. If drinking leads to incestuous behavior, why does he drink? Did he take any responsible action in regard to his drinking when he learned it resulted in sexual abuse? If he says the drinking wasn't bad enough to take action, then question his assertion that the abuse was caused by his use of alcohol. If the offender does have a drinking problem, the counselor should point out that alcohol addiction is not a cause of his incestuous behavior. Incest and drinking are usually two separate and independent symptoms of the same underlying problem which therapy hopes to uncover and help overcome.

The offender may allege that the victim was partly to blame because the child behaved in a provocative or seductive manner. If the child behaved in a sexually inappropriate fashion, why didn't the offender correct the youngster? If a child, in fact, behaves in a sexually explicit manner, a responsible adult will not encourage or take advantage of such behavior but will try to rectify it.

The offender may also blame a poor marriage as being responsible for his sexual abuse. If the marriage was that bad, why didn't he seek to improve the marital problems in a responsible fashion? He should have sought out marriage counseling.

Sometimes offenders will justify their actions as being a caring gesture to the child. They may describe incest as less serious than adultery or suggest the incest was a form of sex education. Many offenders have no appreciation of the traumatic impact of such behavior on the victim (even if they were victims themselves). In such cases, the offender needs to be sensitized and reeducated about the impact of sexual abuse. He needs to see and hear examples of abuse that led to impaired emotional and social development, such as sexual dysfunction, substance abuse, prostitution, depression, social isolation, suicide, etc. Confronting the offender with films or tapes made by former victims may be helpful here.

Be cautious about working through the offender's denial. If and when the offender stops his denial, admits his guilt, and allows himself to experience remorse and shame, he may experience a major depression. This could lead to heavy drinking, substance abuse, suicidal urges, or destructive behavior. The counselor should anticipate these possibilities and be ready to provide crisis intervention and support to the offender.[13]

TREATING THE INCEST OFFENDER

Treatment of the incest offender is properly viewed as helping the offender learn to accept his own responsibility for maintaining a conscientious and life-long effort to keep sexually abusive behavior under control. Treatment can focus on:

1. Helping the offender become aware of the major unmet needs that underlie this behavior; helping him find adaptive ways of satisfying these needs.

2. Helping the offender identify life-demand situations with which he has a particularly difficult time dealing; helping him find ways to lower the stress associated with those events or demands.

3. Helping him become more sensitive to environmental and internal events and messages that have been antecedents of his incestuous behavior. By becoming aware of these early warning signals, he can interrupt the behavior chain of the incestuous offense and take alternative action.[14]

4. Helping him bolster a fragile sense of self-esteem. His self-esteem will improve if the offender is able to demonstrate effectiveness in mastering control of his environment, living up to his values, and by developing a new identity.

5. Helping him develop the ability to delay gratification; supporting the client while he works on the achievement of long-range goals. Therapeutic goals will need to be divided into many short-term measurable objectives.

6. Offering new coping skills. The offender does not know how to manage high levels of anxiety in appropriate ways. Treatment must help provide practical ways for the offender to deal with daily demands.

7. Assisting in recovery from early life traumas. The offender needs help in seeing the origins of his problems. Part of his abusive habit pattern may have been in place since childhood. With

an understanding of his own victimization, he can reconcile himself with his past and grow beyond his developmentally arrested level of functioning.[15]

A treatment program needs to encompass reeducation, resocialization, and individual, marital, and family therapy supplemented by peer or self-help support groups. Improving parenting skills, increasing social skills, enhancing communication skills, assertiveness training, sex therapy, and stress management may also be important components of treatment.

If the offender experiences divorce as a result of his offense, he may need help with his sense of loss and fear. This can be done individually or in a group.

Characteristics of Treatment

Those who have worked extensively with offenders have noted a number of issues that seem to be common characteristics in regard to the treatment process. It is important to keep these cautions and qualities in mind while working with an incest offender:

1. You are dealing, often, with an unmotivated client. He is not usually self-referred. His cooperation and participation will often need to be mandated by some external authority, such as the court.

2. His sexual offense is not just a symptom; it is also a crime and needs intervention from both mental health and criminal justice levels.

3. The offender fears the social and legal consequences of disclosure and will tend to deny the offense or minimize his responsibility for his actions. He must not be allowed to deny his behavior, minimize the seriousness of his actions, or project responsibility elsewhere.

4. Don't keep secrets. The offender has operated from a position of power in regard to his victim and has maintained his control by demanding secrecy. Conventional therapy involves a contract of confidentiality. For any type of sexual offenders, this type of confidentiality reinforces the offender's position of power and control. Any and all suspected or known incidents of abuse must be reported to the proper authorities and all necessary steps taken to protect the victim(s). The offender

should be told in the beginning of treatment that all information can be divulged to any appropriate person or agency when deemed warranted by the counselor. The counselor's primary responsibility is for the protection and safety of the victim.

5. Incest is a sexual offense, but it is not predominantly motivated by sexual needs. It is the sexual expression of nonsexual needs. The offender needs help in uncovering the underlying nonsexual needs and issues prompting his incestuous behavior. He needs to know why sexuality has become the method of expression for these unresolved issues.

6. The offender's responsibility for the offense should not be minimized by viewing incest as solely the product of family dysfunction. Other family members may have played a contributing role in the development of the incestuous relationship, but the offender must be held accountable. Family therapy should be preceded by individual treatment, and should not be the only plan of action.

7. The offender tends to feel overwhelmed by the pressures and demands of life. He perceives himself as a helpless victim of social forces outside of his control. Therefore, treatment will need to contain very practical components which are aimed at teaching the offender how to cope more effectively with daily demands. This will include parenting, socialization, assertiveness, and conflict resolution training, as well as stress and anger management, communication skills, and other specific areas of instruction.[16]

Use of Groups in Treatment

Groups are widely recommended for treating sexual offenders. The group, comprised of other offenders, can confront denial and minimizing better than most therapists. Although painful, the offender learns to appreciate the candor of the rest of the group. He also learns that as he is able to become more honest, the group will give him more acceptance.

The group experience can give the offender a sense of belonging and inclusion that he has probably never before experienced. The acceptance, praise, and support of the group help immensely in the growth process.

The offender can see others growing and changing, which

gives him hope and encouragement for his own potential. He learns he is not the only one who has felt and acted this way.

A group experience forces the offender to deal with trust issues. He learns he can depend upon others to respond to certain of his needs, and he can see that he is able to give out to others. A reciprocal relationship based on equality and negotiation (rather than manipulation and power) can be learned in a group.

Groups are also very useful for victims and nonoffending spouses. Several organizations, such as Parents United and Parents Anonymous, have been formed to provide group support and help for victims and families of abuse.

Some groups for sex offenders are organized in a series of graded steps, much like Alcoholics Anonymous. In the early stages of treatment, it is recognized the offender has lost control of his behavior. Each promotion up the ladder represents his progress in establishing self-control and accepting responsibility for his actions. In the later stages of the process, the offender is asked to make restitution for his offenses by helping and serving others.[17]

Examples of these structured programs are Sexaholics Anonymous and Sexual Addicts Anonymous.[18]

Working with the Incestuous Family

At a certain point midway through the treatment process, it is appropriate and necessary to bring the treatment into a family focus. Prior to this time, the victim, nonoffending spouse, and offender will have been treated individually and/or in groups. The purpose of family therapy is to develop a functional and healthy family unit that is free of any incestuous bond. The primary goals for the treatment of the incestuous family are: 1. for the child and mother to regain a sense of control over their own lives; 2. for the mother and father to become conscious of and assume the expected parental roles, especially toward the victim child; 3. for the mother and father to resume a mature marital relationship where their sexual needs are mutually satisfied; and 4. for all family members to resume interdependent roles without the incestuous elements.

Treatment of the family is aimed at helping each person

move out of his or her isolated, trapped, hopeless patterns of living into a greater sense of freedom and ability to make sound choices. The following general objectives provide a foundation for tailoring the treatment objectives of a specific family.

1. To increase each member's belief in his or her ability to change from dysfunctional patterns to more productive ways of behaving.

2. To learn how to balance the needs of the abused child with the needs of the family.

3. To help the parents learn to manage their unmet dependency needs.

4. To encourage the parents and child to use people or activities as sources of support. The parents must learn how to turn to others for support when they feel overwhelmed or in need of specific help.

5. To help the family improve interactional patterns within and outside of the family.

6. To help the family improve self-esteem.

7. To encourage the family to decrease social and emotional isolation, and to increase interest in pursuing friendships, extended family, church involvements, or activities outside of the home.

8. To improve the family's communication skills so as to be more in touch with feelings and be better able to communicate in an open and direct fashion.

9. To help the family make emotional rules more explicit so as to be more flexible and responsive to the needs and protection of each member.

10. To work with the husband and wife to improve their relationship in order to lessen their fear of rejection or loss of one another.

11. To help the incest offender take full responsibility for the behavior and be able to verbalize this responsibility to the abused and to the other family members.

12. Where appropriate, to help the spouse of the offender take full responsibility for being an ineffective parent; to help that spouse refrain from projecting responsibility and blame onto the abused child or other people.

13. To inform the victim about whom to contact and what to do, should molestation occur again.

14. To teach family members to respect privacy and individuality within the family.

15. To help redistribute familial power so that one member is not in control of the rest of the family.

16. To help establish distinctions between generations. Adults need to act as adults. Children need to be seen as and need to be able to act as children.

17. To clarify family roles.

18. To help spouses find mutual emotional and sexual satisfaction together.

19. To teach family members to distinguish fantasy from reality.

20. To inform the parents of their need to provide sexual education and protection for children.

21. To help parents discuss openly their own upbringing and learn how they allowed sexual molestation to occur within their family.

22. To help Christian families to explore the concepts of confession, forgiveness, grace, and growth through pain and suffering. They need to know growth does not always come by eliminating all of life's problems but by learning how to apply God's principles to the problems.[19]

There are many details and techniques that would go into carrying out these objectives and goals. Space allows only a general outline of the kinds of topics that should be included in work with families. The experience and skill of the counselor will be important ingredients in bringing about restoration.

THE CHRISTIAN RESPONSE TO SEXUAL ABUSE

The response to any mental health issue is usually based on research and applied treatment or prevention. As Christians, we must focus on carefully researching the causes of sexual abuse and other forms of violence. The research must be thorough and comprehensive. Most of the research in abuse has been done only in the last fifteen years. For example, from its first issue, in 1939, until 1969, the *Journal of Marriage and the Family* did not print one article with the word *violence* in the title.[20] Articles on child abuse and related topics appeared in other medical and mental health literature beginning about 1962. The absence of systematic data regarding the religious component in abuse illustrates the need for concerned and committed Christians to do something about it. The whole person—intellectual, social, emotional, physical, and spiritual— must be included in any complete study of humankind.

While we need to investigate what causes abuse and how best to treat the victims and offenders, we must continue immediate efforts to stand by and help the victims in our midst. Whether on a personal or professional basis, every one of us will or has had an opportunity to minister to someone who has been victimized.

On a long-term basis, we can be involved in the modeling and teaching of concepts and application relative to the freedom we have under Christ. While not the only relevant concept for sexual offenders, it surely can speak to the insecurity behind the rigid, unyielding personality characteristic of many offenders.

In the New Testament, *freedom* comes from the word *eleuthros,* and means "unrestrained; to go at pleasure; exempt from obligation or liability; to be liberated."[21]

Freedom is the ability to act or think without compulsion or arbitrary restriction. This is a characteristic missing in the lives of sexual offenders. One aspect of our freedom is the escape from the death penalty for sin because of the death and resurrection of Jesus Christ. Our confession and belief in the redemptive work of Christ gives us eternal freedom (John 8:36; Rom. 3:24; 5:15–18).

Another aspect of freedom is the unrestrained opportunity to mature or come to completeness. Spiritual maturity is the practice of using our powers of perception to distinguish between good and evil (Heb. 5:14). This completeness of growth is needed in order for us not to be tossed about by deceitful teaching. We need maturity to have the proper discernment toward evil-inspired falsehoods (Eph. 4:14) and to have the knowledge of God's will (Col. 1:9).

Maturity involves giving up the old ways of thinking and developing the ways of behaving that are appropriate for a

Christian. It is the increasing ability to apply wisdom to every-day problems. The legalistic, authoritarian personality, often found in a sexual offender, needs instruction and discipleship from pastors, church leaders, family, friends, or counselors on how to give up a compulsive, rigid approach to the law. Such people also need words of encouragement and hope about the possibility of change. The insecurity residing in them can be touched by the knowledge that God does not require perfection before the law.

Christ calls the people to what they can *become,* not because of what they have *been.* Our maturity comes from that same hope—not because we have done such a good job of solving all of our problems, but because of how we can learn to do it better. The hope of improved ability to cope is part of the gift of freedom.

This liberty gives us the chance to take risks we otherwise might not try. The principle many people operate by is "Nothing ventured, nothing lost." If we don't take any chances, then we'll never risk losing anything. God's grace and knowledge can help release the rigid personality from the overwhelming burden of having to do everything right. We all have access to that freedom! As Mahatma Gandhi said, "Freedom is not worth having if it does not connote freedom to err."

Similarly, the poet John Keats once said, "Failure is in a sense the highway to success, inasmuch as every discovery of what is false leads us to seek earnestly after what is true; and each fresh experience points out some form of errors which we shall afterward avoid."

God doesn't require perfect vessels to carry out his purposes. In fact, I don't know of any biblical personages who didn't have weaknesses of some kind. And yet they were used of God. How can this be?

Look at David. His life was a strange mixture of good and evil. At one time it was filled with noble deeds, fine aspirations, and splendid accomplishments. Yet the life of David was stained with severe sin. Probably no biblical character displays such a wide range of moral and immoral behavior. The man who is mentioned as being after God's own heart (1 Sam. 13:14) is the same one who committed adultery with

Bathsheba and then arranged for her husband, Uriah the Hittite, to die in battle (2 Sam. 11). Yet Christ came to earth in human form as a direct descendant of David.

Samuel, the upright judge, was dedicated by his mother before his birth (1 Sam. 1:11) and then taken to be taught by the priest Eli. Just how effective a teacher could Eli be when Scripture says that "his sons made themselves contemptible and he failed to restrain them" (1 Sam. 3:13). He couldn't instruct and restrain his own sons, how could he do any good for Samuel? Because God called Samuel, he matured and ministered for the Lord in spite of Eli's failings as a father.

Samuel served the children of Israel well, but his own sons also turned against God, took bribes and perverted justice in their role as judges (1 Sam. 8:3–5). How can a man be so wise and upright, yet have children who seem so opposite?

Peter is a New Testament character with many successes and failures. He is called to follow Jesus, leaving behind his career as a fisherman to become a "fisher of men" (Matt. 4:19). Yet Peter is full of contradictions. He was presumptuous (Matt. 16:22; John 13:8; 18:10) and cowardly (Matt. 14:30; 26:69–72). He was self-sacrificing on some occasions (Mark 1:18), yet inclined to be self-seeking on others (Matt. 19:27). He demonstrated spiritual insight on some matters (John 6:68), but was slow to understand deeper truths at other times (Matt. 15:15, 16).

Peter made two great confessions of his faith in Christ (Matt. 16:16; John 6:69), but he also demonstrated a cowardly denial of that same Lord (Mark 14:67–71).

God doesn't need a perfect man or woman to accomplish his purposes, only a willing and honest heart. The sexual offending personality needs instruction on how to give up a self-imposed, dogmatic shield of protection and experience God's full measure of grace. As Christians with psychological and spiritual understanding, we can help the offender understand and apply God's grace. The result can give them true emotional freedom and release from the bondage of pretense.

PART III

ELDER ABUSE

CHAPTER TEN

ABUSE OF THE ELDERLY

AN ELDERLY COUPLE LIVED in an apartment with their twenty-two-year-old son. Born late in the marriage, he had physically abused them for years. During one incident he struck his mother in the back with a frying pan and clubbed his father with a stick. The father had a heart attack following the incident. The son was eventually placed in a mental hospital.

"Anyone who attacks his father or his mother must be put to death" (Exod. 21:15).

A sixty-eight-year-old widow with a heart condition and crippled with arthritis was physically and financially abused by her heroin-addicted son. An investigation revealed that the son stole money and sold the woman's property, including her color television and her stereo system. The son also ran up huge bills on the woman's credit cards. Caseworkers intervened and got the son to move out, but the widow refused to press charges.

"He who robs his father or mother and says, 'It's not wrong'—he is partner to him who destroys" (Prov. 28:24).

An eighty-five-year-old woman was allowed to lie covered with urine and feces for so long that bedsores developed and became infested with maggots. The granddaughter, apparently oblivious of her responsibility toward the old woman, frequently abandoned her charge, in one instance flying to Hawaii with a friend. The weapon used by the granddaughter to enforce her will was the threat of putting her grandmother in a nursing home. The old woman was terrified at the prospect.

"Do not cast me away when I am old; do not forsake me when my strength is gone" (Ps. 71:9).

INCIDENCE OF ELDER ABUSE

How well is our nation doing in regard to the commandment "Honor your father and your mother, so that you may live long in the land the LORD your God is giving you" (Exod. 20:12)? First, let's see how many older fathers and mothers are around to be honored.

According to the U.S. Census Bureau, in 1980 there were about 25.5 million Americans who were age sixty-five or over. That was an increase of nearly five million persons since 1970.[1]

Life expectancy is increasing, owing in part to the conquering of some of the communicable diseases of childhood, as well as to advances in solving problems of heart disease and cancer. People are living longer. One in nine persons in the U.S. is sixty-five years old or older. This is about 11 percent of the total population.[2]

It is projected that by the turn of the century, about one out of five citizens will be sixty or older. This translates to about thirty-one million older adults by the year 2000 and forty-five million by 2020. Our society is rapidly becoming one characterized by aged children caring for frail, elderly parents.

Unfortunately, things are not going very well for the elderly or the caregivers.

The House Select Committee on Aging submitted a report for the *Congressional Record* in May 1985. The committee concluded that about 4 percent of the nation's elderly may be victims of some sort of abuse, from moderate to severe. About 1.1 million older Americans may be victims of abuse every year. This would include one out of every twenty-five Americans.[3]

Other researchers have documented similar incidence figures. Pedrick–Cornell and Gelles, leaders in family violence research, suggest from five hundred thousand to 2.5 million cases of elder abuse each year.[4]

Lau and Kosberg estimated that one in ten elderly persons living with a family member are abused each year.[5]

While these figures are high, they may only be a fraction of the total problem. The published reports are based only on cases reported to social service agencies. Until recently only sixteen states had mandatory reporting laws. (Thirty-seven states had such laws by 1985.) Many professionals do not report cases of elder abuse, therefore, the estimates may be only a small portion of the total number of cases of some type of abuse.

The average person may find it hard to believe how widespread the problem really seems to be. It cuts across all classes of society. Abuse of the elderly occurs in small towns, large cities, suburbs, and in rural areas. It is a shameful and hidden problem. Although alien to the American ideal, it is a full-scale national problem. In fact, the frequency of elder abuse is only slightly less than child abuse. But elder abuse is far less likely to be reported than abuse of children.

The House Select Committee on Aging reported that while one out of three child abuse cases is reported, only one out of six cases of adult abuse ever come to the attention of authorities.[6]

The horrifying conclusion is that elder abuse is an everyday occurrence and another example of the breaking of the bond between parent and child. In this case, it is the adult child who breaks the bond. The 1960s was the age of awareness for child abuse. In the 1970s, domestic violence was dominated by spousal abuse. It appears that elder abuse is the dominant focus of the 1980s.

America may be the most powerful and advanced civilization in the world, yet thousands of elderly Americans are victims of chronic, continuing patterns of emotional and physical abuse and neglect. Until we can live up to the commandment to honor our fathers and mothers, we cannot make any real claims to being "advanced" in any moral or ethical sense.

The most commonly accepted categories and definitions of abuse include the following:

Physical abuse. Willful infliction of physical pain, mental anguish, or injuries such as bruises, welts, sprains, dislocations, abrasions, or lacerations; the use of disciplinary restraints; willful deprivation of services necessary to maintain physical or mental health; sexual abuse, restrictions on freedom of movement, unreasonable confinement, and murder.

Psychological abuse. Verbal assault, threat, taunting, condemnation, provocation of fear, and physical or emotional isolation; degradation or ridicule, insults, and demonstrated or spoken hostility.

Material abuse. The illegal or improper act or process of unauthorized use of the resources of an adult for monetary or personal benefit, profit, or gain; an act that deprives the aged person of the use of resources accumulated for basic needs in retirement; the theft or misuse of money or property—accomplished by force or through misrepresentation.

Medical abuse. Withholding of medications or required aids, such as false teeth, glasses, or hearing aids.[7]

Other types of abuse could occur under a general heading "violation of rights." This would be the breaching of rights guaranteed to all citizens by the Constitution, federal statutes, federal courts, and/or the states. Examples would include having one's mail opened and censored, being refused access to a telephone, or not being allowed visitors.

Self-neglect, which includes self-inflicted physical harm and the failure to take care of one's personal needs, usually stems from the elderly person's diminished physical or mental abilities and can be intensified by the attitudes and behavior of relatives or caretakers.

CHARACTERISTICS OF VICTIMS AND ABUSERS

The profile of the typical victim has come into focus through the research of the past ten years. Most often the abused victim is a woman of seventy-five or more years, with one or more physical or mental impairments. Women are more likely to be abused than men, in part because women tend to live longer than men. Also, men who lose their wives tend to remarry younger women who take care of them. Such men are then not dependent on their children for help.

The female victim is found at all socioeconomic levels, in both urban and rural settings. She is most often widowed or single, and is heavily dependent upon the family for her basic needs and for love and social interaction.

Most nursing care of the elderly occurs in the home. Of the noninstitutional elderly, 5 percent are homebound and about 85 percent have one or more chronic diseases that may result in physical care problems. More than half of the care given the disabled in the community is provided informally by a spouse, relatives, or friends.[8]

This suggests a major portion of the elderly have medical problems that routinely are being attended to by nonprofessional caretakers. This increases the chances for improper care, especially when the situation becomes chronic.

Data suggest that 84 percent of physical abuse is committed by relatives and that about 75 percent of the abused live with their abusers.[9]

Usually the abuser will be experiencing great stress. Alcoholism, drug addiction, marital problems, and long-term financial difficulties all seem to play a role in bringing a person to abuse his or her parents. Most abusers have histories of difficulty dealing with stress.

A son of the victim is the most likely abuser, and his form of abuse is usually physical. A daughter is the second most likely abuser, but she tends to resort to psychological assault or neglect.

Abusers can also include spouses, grandchildren, siblings, roomers, and landlords.

It is interesting to note that as a child the abuser, in many cases, was abused by the parents. Some researchers hypothesize that abuse is revenge for the abuser's own childhood experiences. Others suggest that violent behavior is a learned stress response inherited from one generation to another.

REASONS FOR ABUSE

Like other forms of family violence, there is no single explanation for why elders are abused. Any one factor, or a combination of factors, may be used to explain this form of violence.

Learned violence. One explanation is the learned use of violence. Children learn from observation and participation in the family that violence is an acceptable response to stress. Reinforced, perhaps, by violent approaches to problem-solving seen on television and in society in general, children grow up with a tendency to be violent.

The place of child abuse is very important here. According to one study done several years ago, one child in four hundred who was reared nonviolently later attacks his or her parents. One out of two children who was mistreated by his or her parents, however, later resorts to violence toward those same parents.[10]

Whether prompted by retaliation, revenge, pent-up anger finally being released, or a learned response to frustration, the final product is an adult child who has a strong tendency to abuse even his or her own father or mother. The pattern continues from one generation to the next.

Dependency. A second reason for abuse is the progressive and severe dependency which makes the elderly person vulnerable to abuse. There is something about human nature that rationalizes abuse or unkind treatment to a more unfortunate person. An adult who pushes around an invalid is responding to the same basic drives that incline a childhood bully to beat up on the little kids.

This cycle of violence can result in the learned helplessness condition described earlier in regard to spousal abuse. According to this idea, as they become increasingly dependent, elderly people come to feel that they have no control over their lives. They feel there is nothing they can do to change their situations. They may even come to believe they have brought the situation upon themselves. This helps keep them from reaching out for help, since they tell themselves nothing will change anyway.

Many elderly victims see the family home as the only alternative to a nursing home or other dreaded institution. They are afraid of being taken away from loved ones, even if abusive.

Filial crisis. Another hypothesis is that elder abuse is the failure of adult children to resolve the filial crisis. According to this idea, an important developmental task of adult children is to go beyond the stage of adolescent rebellion. Every teenager needs to work through the emancipation struggle with parents. Often the emotional struggles and conflicts that started in adolescence do not get resolved. Children just leave home, start their own families and visit on Thanksgiving and Christmas. Relationships are relatively calm as long as there are no major issues to solve between the adult children and their parents. But when adult children become caretakers for their parents, the old unresolved feelings and former defense patterns emerge, making the use of violence more probable.

Internal stress. The responsibility of caring for a dependent, elderly relative can lead to accumulative stress for the family. As a result of our mobile society, children tend to marry and move away from their parents. Instead of living close to parents and adjusting gradually to their aging, children tend to be insulated from the process. When one parent dies or becomes disabled, leaving the other alone and dependent, a sudden and added responsibility is dumped on the adult children. These children, with their own lives interrupted, often become confused and resentful.

The first step in potential abuse begins to take place. A hastily made decision to have the aging parent come and live in the adult child's home may later be regretted. The increasing disability of the parent may interfere with the status quo of the family. Financial and emotional resources may become drained. Children may have to share rooms, or the parents may lose privacy. This triggers a combination of guilt and resentment which can be expressed in abuse of the aged parent.

These adult children, sometimes called the "sandwich generation" because of their position between their elderly parents and their children, are exposed to a unique set of stressors. They are confronted with the loss of youth, the recognition of their own aging, and the impact of empty nests. All of this takes place on top of caring for two sets of dependents.

These middle-aged children want the freedom to live as adults without the burden of aged parents in the home. In an attempt to deal with the conflict, caretakers may overdose parents with drugs, tie them to beds, lock them up in closets, and threaten violence.

With increased pressure for two incomes, fewer daughters or daughters-in-law are free to be at home to care for the parents. This creates added work and fatigue. After the stroke of a mother, for example, an adult child knows the parent can't be left alone. But the child feels guilt, rage, frustration, and enormous fatigue after caring for her all night long and then having to go to work the next morning. This can make people frustrated, angry, and even violent.

As an example, a young woman beat her eighty-one-year-old father with a hammer and then chained him to a toilet for seven days. She told authorities, "I worked him over real good. Then I left him and rested. I watched television for a while."

She was angry and worn out and felt she did not have the emotional or physical resources to do anything but resort to physical abuse to get relief.

External stress. Another explanation is external stress. The earlier research on family violence recognized that external stress on the family was a major factor that contributed to violence. Studies have shown that elder abusers are likely to have alcohol or substance abuse problems, and that they experience some form of external stress, such as the loss of a job or a long-term medical problem. Other examples of external stress are troubles with a boss or coworkers, arrest or conviction for a crime, death of a close friend or family member, financial problems, pregnancy, in-law problems, and separation or divorce.

Any of these events, combined with a dependent parent, could bring about an overload of frustration.

Negative attitudes toward the elderly. Elder abuse may be reinforced by negative stereotypes toward elderly people and their place in society. Our society idolizes youth and fears the advance of age and the attendant dependency it brings. This negative image seems to have a correlation with the incidence of elder abuse in this country. In other parts of the world, where the traditional image of older people includes the respect due to an elder of the society, elder abuse is not a problem on the scale it has reached in America.

The distorted perceptions about the elderly may be a major force in the creation of situations conducive to abuse. These negative attitudes tend to dehumanize elderly persons and make it easier for abusers to victimize them without feeling remorse.

Perhaps the Old Testament injunction is prophetic in this area also: "Rise in the presence of the aged, show respect for the elderly and revere your God" (Lev. 19:32).

REPORTING

Victimized parents rarely report their abuse. Shame at being abused, fear of retaliation, and belief that they are the major cause (and therefore deserving) of the abuse, are some of the reasons elders have for not reporting. Sometimes victims of abuse do not have the physical ability to make a report, and some have been literally held prisoner and couldn't make a complaint if they wanted to.

All fifty of the states have mandatory reporting for child abuse. In 1980, only sixteen states had mandatory reporting laws for elder abuse. Between 1980 and 1985 that figure more than doubled, so that now thirty-seven states and the District of Columbia have some form of adult protective service laws. In other countries there are also variations in laws.

There is little consistency among these states as to who is required to report and what penalties will apply when there is failure to do so. In Connecticut, everyone is required to report, but in New Hampshire, only physicians are held responsible by the law.

Since there are no consistently developed services to handle the reports, the plight of the abused adult is still not good.

Cases abound where victims have come forward for assistance only to learn there is nothing available to help them out of their dilemma.

A major question is how to locate and identify the abused so intervention can take place in a timely and effective way. If the victim does not request help, there is a constitutional guarantee against the invasion of privacy. Child abuse laws are enforceable without regard to the opinion of the victims. Elders have the right, which children don't have, not to press charges against their abusers. This right must be protected. We don't want to remove one of the basic elements of free citizenship. However, we don't want to abandon our elders to the terror of abuse.

The only recourse is to educate both the potential victims and those who care for them. Abuse of the elderly is a situation where intervention is negotiated, not imposed. Elderly persons must be given some options that are acceptable and appropriate to their situations. A visiting nurse may strongly believe the elderly patient needs to be moved to a quality nursing home where needs would be properly met. If the older adult doesn't believe that is an appropriate thing to do, he or she has the right to say so. The best that can be done is to make sure the person has had an opportunity to exercise choice, without coercion, and with a clear understanding of alternatives.

Health care providers such as nurses and doctors are the front line observers for the detection of abuse. Much is being done by those professions to increase their skill in observing and validating suspected abuse.

Pastors have a unique opportunity also. The pastor is one who often has access to the elder adult through visitations. If the pastor has some bench marks to look for, any suspicious signs can be passed on to the proper authorities.

Because there is not a well-defined system for reporting and investigating in every state, the reader will need to take the time to find out the proper procedure for your particular locality. There may be a government commission on aging, or a report may go to the department of health and welfare.

The next section will describe some of the symptoms of

abuse that may be observed by visiting with elder adults and their caretakers. Some symptoms may need to be evaluated by medical personnel or with legal counsel. But a variety of indicators will be given so the pastor or other counselor has at least some general guidelines to go by.

SYMPTOMS AND SIGNS OF ELDER ABUSE

Abuse of the elderly seems more probable when the needs of the aged parent are great and the ability of the family to meet those needs is inadequate. This suggests the two main categories for observation: the needs and demands of the elder adult, and the resources of the family.

Severe abusers often have a history of violence, crime, or drug abuse. If you observe a family situation where the caretaker(s) have such a history, be aware of the potential for abuse and neglect.

It is a good idea, if concerned about a situation, to inquire with the child protective workers in your area. If there has been any report of abuse to children, then elder abuse should also be suspect. This can be approached both ways. If a case of child abuse is reported, ask if there are elderly parents in the home as well. If there are, be on the alert for potential elder abuse. If elder abuse is suspected, also be on the alert for child abuse possibilities.

A pastor or other counselor will have frequent opportunities to talk with members of families who consult them for a variety of reasons. As you talk with caretakers try to get an idea of their stress levels. Look for the caretaker who is burning out. If your impression of the caretaker suggests high levels of stress and minimal levels of coping ability, look further at the implications for abuse or neglect.

Doris Ferguson and Cornelia Beck have developed a rating scale that seems useful for identifying aged persons who are at risk for abuse. The assessment tool covers four areas that have the potential for contributing to elder abuse: health status of the aged; attitudes of the family and aged adult toward aging; living arrangements; and finances. H.A.L.F. is the acronym for those four factors. The thirty-seven items in the assessment tool are presented on pages 252–253.

Ferguson-Beck H.A.L.F.
Assessment Tool For Elder Abuse

The following set of observations can be applied to any living situation where an elder adult is being cared for by someone else. Look at each item and note only those that apply to the current situation. A rating scale of *almost always, some of the time,* and *never* can be added to each item. If a number of items results in positive responses, the question of abuse should be raised and appropriate action taken.

Health
1. Aged adult risk dynamics. The aged adult:
   a. is in poor health.
   b. is overly dependent on adult child.
   c. was extremely dependent on spouse who is now deceased.
   d. persists in advising, admonishing, and directing the adult child on whom he or she is dependent.
2. Aged adult abuse dynamics. The aged adult:
   a. has an unexplained or repeated injury.
   b. shows evidence of dehydration and/or malnutrition without obvious cause.
   c. has been given inappropriate food, drink, and/or drugs.
   d. shows evidence of overall poor care.
   e. is notably passive and withdrawn.
   f. has muscle contractures due to being restricted.
3. Adult child caregiver risk dynamics. The adult caregiver:
   a. was abused or battered as a child.
   b. has a poor self-image.
   c. has a limited capacity to express own needs.
   d. is an alcohol or drug abuser.
   e. is psychologically unprepared to meet dependency needs of parent.
   f. denies parent's illness.
4. Adult child caregiver abuse dynamics. The adult caregiver:
   a. shows evidence of loss of control or fear of losing control.
   b. presents contradictory history.

   c. projects cause of injury onto third party.

   d. has delayed unduly in bringing parent in for care; shows detachment.

   e. overreacts or underreacts to the seriousness of the situation.

   f. complains continually about irrelevant problems unrelated to injury.

   g. refuses consent for further diagnostic studies.

Attitudes Toward Aging

1. Aged adult views self negatively due to aging process.
2. Adult child views aged adult negatively due to aging process.
3. Adult child has negative attitude toward aging.
4. Adult child has unrealistic expectations of self or the aged adult.

Living Arrangements

1. Aged adult insists on maintaining old patterns of independent functioning that interfere with child's needs or endanger aged adult.
2. Aged adult allows adult child no privacy.
3. Adult child is socially isolated.
4. Adult child has no one to provide relief when uptight with the aged person.
5. Aged adult is socially isolated.
6. Aged adult has no one to provide relief when uptight with adult child.

Finances

1. Aged adult uses gifts of money to control others, particularly adult children.
2. Aged adult refuses to apply for financial aid.
3. Aged adult's savings have been exhausted.
4. Adult child is financially unprepared to meet dependency needs of aged adult.[11]

The chief concerns are elderly adults with accelerating care needs who reside in violent families, are associated with pathologic individuals, or whose caretakers are under a lot of stress. If you observe these conditions, intervention may be necessary.

PREVENTION

One of the ways to prevent elder abuse is to help the family determine whether or not they have the financial and emotional resources to care for their dependent parent. Is it really possible for another person—who is as physically dependent as a small child but who has the will and preferences of an adult—to live in the home?

The pastor may be in a position to help advise families about aging parents. Help families look at their resources and evaluate care alternatives that are both honoring to parents and in the best interests of the family. If you are not familiar with resources in this area, develop a working relationship with people in your locale who can act as a referral resource for you.

Someone from every church staff or congregation should be available to make home calls, especially if there is an elderly person with health problems. Such elders need attention from outside the home, even if there is no threat of abuse or neglect.

Of course, a fundamental prevention strategy is the teaching of nonviolent coping behaviors early in life. This has many implications which I will not develop here, but church teaching should give families the ability to combine their Christian faith with nonviolent conflict-resolution alternatives.

The church can also be active in teaching families about the aging process. Help dispel stereotypical attitudes about elderly adults. Involve families in intergenerational learning opportunities. Encourage them to extend support and friendship to older adults outside of their immediate family. Many families do not have grandparents living close by and could profit by "adopting" a grandparent for social and educational opportunities.

The church could also take the lead to initiate ministry to families that have older adults in the home. Families need help with respite care so they can get a break from the continual demands placed on them by their dependent parent.

Home-delivered meals, home nursing care, homemaker, home repair, home visitation, adult day care, transportation, counseling about physical and emotional needs of the elderly, legislation establishing mandatory reporting laws, and perhaps tax incentives for families who care for the elderly in their own homes—these are just a few of the programs or reforms that are needed.[12]

The family is the nucleus of civilization. Among the uncivilized African Hottentots, the son would ask permission of the tribe to end the life of his aged and feeble parents. The request would be granted, but then a going-away feast would be held for the fated parents. The whole tribe would attend and say good-bye before the aged ones were led away into the jungle and left to die.

In one respect, the savage Hottentots may have been a great deal more civilized than many modern American families. Let us do what we can to see to it that we do not despise our parents when they are old.

Our discussion of family violence comes to a close. The subject matter was not pleasant, but the painful reality of abused children and adults must be faced. The church community can be seen as a spiritual and emotional hospital for those who are hurting. Here is a tremendous opportunity to minister to those in our midst who hurt, whether they be victims or perpetrators. I pray each of you will now find yourself better informed to participate in the effort to end family violence and help those who have already been damaged. May God bless your efforts.

APPENDIX

RECOMMENDED RESOURCES

Written Materials

The following resources are drawn from the expanding number of materials being produced in the area of family violence and sexual abuse. Many of the listings can be used with victims, both child and adult, as well as abusers or offenders. Some of the references are aimed at the layperson as well as children and their parents. Also included is material useful in conducting seminars and workshops.

Adams, Caren, and Fay, Jennifer. *No More Secrets: Protecting Your Child from Sexual Assault.* San Luis Obispo, Calif.: Impact Publishers, 1981. An extension of the practical suggestions for parents first outlined in "He Told Me Not to Tell."

Backus, William, and Chapian, Marie. *Telling Yourself the Truth.* Minneapolis: Bethany House Publishers, 1982. Discussions of how thinking leads to behavior, from a Christian perspective.

Bassett, Cary. *My Very Own Special Body Book.* Redding: Hawthorne Press, 1981. Information about sexual abuse and incest, family roles and how to protect oneself. Illustrated, to be read to children.

Berry, Joy. *Alerting Kids to the Danger of Sexual Abuse.* Waco, Tex.: Word, 1984. Written for children, discusses types and causes of sexual abuse and how to ensure their own safety.

Burns, David. *Feeling Good: The New Mood Therapy.* New York: William Morrow, 1980. A secular book about self-talk and how to make changes that relate to depression and anger.

Byerly, Carolyn M. *The Mother's Book: How to Survive the Incest of Your Child,* Dubuque: Kendall/Hunt, 1985. A practical survival guide, with directory of services for each state.

Carl, Angela R. *Child Abuse! What You Can Do About It.* and related activity book, *Good Hugs and Bad Hugs. How Can You Tell?* Cincinnati: Standard Publishing, 1985. Very good material about child sexual abuse from Christian perspective.

Davis, Diane. *Something Is Wrong at My House.* Seattle: Parenting Press, 1985. Book about parents' fighting for children, grades one to six.

Edwards, Katherine. *A House Divided.* Grand Rapids: Zondervan, 1984. A former missionary tells her story of incest and the widespread effects of unreported abuse.

Fay, Jennifer. *"He Told Me Not to Tell":* A Parents' Guide for Talking to Your Child about Sexual Assault. King County Rape Relief, 305 South Forty-third, Renton, Wash. 98055. Helpful booklet for parents.

Fay, Jennifer, and Flerchinger, Billie Jo. *Top Secret: Sexual Assault Information for Teenagers Only.* King County Rape Relief, 305 South Forty-third, Renton, Wash. 98055. Booklet for teenagers.

Finkelhor, David. *Sexually Victimized Children.* New York: Free Press, 1979. Major researcher in child sexual abuse.

Fortune, Marie. *Sexual Violence: The Unmentionable Sin.* New York: The Pilgrim Press, 1983. A general book about sexual abuse written by a minister.

Fortune, Marie, and Hormann, Denise. *Family Violence: A Workshop Manual for Clergy and Other Service Providers.* Center for the Prevention of Sexual and Domestic Violence, 1914 North Thirty-fourth Street, Suite 105, Seattle, Wash. 98103. An excellent resource outlining content and procedures for one- or three-day workshops.

Forward, Susan, and Buck, Craig. *Betrayal of Innocence: Incest and Its Devastation.* East Rutherford, N.J.: Penguin, 1978. Discussion and illustrations of cases of incest.

Giarretto, H. *Integrated Treatment of Child Sexual Abuse: A Treatment and Training Manual.* Palo Alto: Science and Behavior Books, 1982. Detailed instruction manual of the best known program for treatment of victims and abusers.

Gil, Eliana. *Outgrowing the Pain: A Book for and about Adults Abused as Children.* San Francisco: Launch Press, 1983. A good secular book for victims.

Green, Holly Wagner. *Turning Fear to Hope.* Nashville: Thomas Nelson, 1984. A Christian perspective on spousal abuse. Includes topics such as submission, divorce, and forgiveness.

Grossman, Rachel, and Sutherland, Joan, ed. *Surviving Sexual Assault.* New York: Congdon & Weed, Inc., 1983. Practical guide to prevention and survival of sexual assault. Includes listing of state-by-state resources.

Hyde, Margaret. *Sexual Abuse: Let's Talk about It.* Philadelphia: The Westminster Press, 1984. Discussion of child sexual abuse in a general religious context.

————. *Cry Softly! The Story of Child Abuse.* Philadelphia: The Westminster Press, 1984. Study guide for ages twelve to fourteen.

Katz, William. *Protecting Your Children from Sexual Assault.* Little Ones Books, P.O. Box 725, Young America, Minn. 55399. A home Bible study including a parents' teaching guide and child's activity workbook prepared by members of the Christian Society for the Prevention of Cruelty to Children.

Kraizer, Sherryll. *The Safe Child Book:* A Commonsense Approach to Protecting Your Children from Abduction and Sexual Abuse. New York: Dell, 1985. Practical suggestions for parents.

Martin, Grant L. *Please Don't Hurt Me.* Wheaton, Ill.: Victor Books, 1987. Written to the victim or parents of victims. Covers child sexual abuse, spousal abuse and abuse of the elderly.

————. *Transformed by Thorns.* Wheaton, Ill.: Victor Books, 1985. Depression, anger, stress, worry, and anxiety can be stepping stones to growth. Useful for both adult victims and offenders.

Morris, Michelle. *If I Should Die Before I Wake.* Boston: Houghton Mifflin, 1982. Intensely realistic fictionalization of father–daughter incest told through eyes of the daughter.

Neidig, Peter H., and Friedman, Dale H. *Spouse Abuse. A Treatment Program for Couples.* Champaign, Ill.: Research Press, 1984. An outline of a program for the treatment of violent marriages.

Quinn, P. E. *Cry Out!* Nashville: Abingdon Press, 1984. Dramatic account of abuse and neglect written from child's point of view by the victim himself.

Ricks, Chip. *Carol's Story.* Wheaton, Ill.: Tyndale House, 1981. Personal account of suffering, guilt, and eventual spiritual freedom as a result of incest.

Sanford, Linda T. *The Silent Children: A Parents' Guide to the Prevention of Child Sexual Abuse.* Garden City, N.Y.: Anchor Press/Doubleday, 1980. Practical book for parents.

Select Committee on Aging. *Elder Abuse: A National Disgrace.* Washington, D.C.: U. S. Government Printing Office, 1985. The most recent national study on abuse of the elderly.

Smith, Nancy. *Winter Past.* Downers Grove, Ill.: InterVarsity Press, 1977. Story of repressed incest and victim's struggle with her faith.

Stowell, Jo, and Dietzel, Mary. *My Very Own Book About Me.* Lutheran Social Services of Washington, North 1226 Howard, Spokane, Wash. 99201, 1982. Workbook for children ages four to ten. Teaches prevention skills; can be used in therapy; both parents' guide and extensive therapists' guide available.

Strom, Kay Marshall. *In the Name of Submission.* Portland, Ore.: Multnomah Press, 1986. A Christian perspective for victims of wife battering.

Wachter, Oralee. *No More Secrets for Me.* Boston: Little, Brown, 1983. Positive and discreet stories about preventing sexual abuse for children, ages six to twelve.

Walker, Lenore E. *The Battered Woman Syndrome.* New York: Springer, 1984. A primary resource on the nature of spousal abuse.

Warrior, Betsy. *Battered Women's Directory.* Available from author at 46 Pleasant St., Cambridge, Mass. 02139. A comprehensive listing of shelters and services, both national and international, for battered women. Also includes guidelines for establishing services for abused women.

Williams, Joy. *Red Light, Green Light People.* Rape and Abuse Crisis Center, P.O. Box 1655, Fargo, N.D. 58107. Coloring book for children. Describes child molestation and good and bad touches.

Audiovisual Materials

This is only a partial listing of the increasing number of films, filmstrips, or videocassettes that are available on the entire range of topics within family violence. Several of the agencies listed in this resource section, such as the National Center on Child Abuse and Neglect, can provide current listings of audiovisual materials.

A Time for Caring: The School's Response to the Sexually Abused Child. (16mm/color/twenty-eight minutes). Lawren Productions, Inc., c/o G. F. Media, 333 North Flores St., Los Angeles, Calif. 90048. Focuses on indicators of sexual abuse and role of school personnel in helping the child.

Battered Women: Violence Behind Closed Doors. (16mm/color/ thirty minutes). MTI Teleprograms, Inc., 3710 Commercial Ave., Northbrook, Ill. 60062. Shows victims and abusers, as well as treatment programs.

Child Molestation: When to Say No. (16mm/color/thirteen minutes). Aims Instructional Media Service, Inc., 625 Justin Ave., Glendale, Calif. 91201. Four episodes illustrate different children in the least to most threatening of attempted sexual abuse encounters. Ages eight and up.

Child Sexual Abuse: The Untold Secret. (videocassette/color/thirty minutes). The University of Calgary, 2500 University Dr., N.W., Calgary, Alta., Canada T2N 1N4. Description of the many difficulties incest victims face. Rather monotonous overall quality but good for junior high, high school, or community education groups. Also appropriate for groups of incest victims.

Girls Beware. (16mm/color/twelve minutes). *Boys Beware.* (16mm/ color/fourteen minutes). DACOM Communications Media, Inc., 626 Justin Ave., Glendale, Calif. 91201. Suitable for adolescents. Examines subtle choices teenagers must make to protect themselves from sexual abuse. Film for girls explores incest.

Incest: The Hidden Crime. (16mm/color/sixteen minutes). The Media Guild, c/o Association Film, 7838 San Fernando Rd., Sun Valley, Calif. 91352. Good documentary produced by CBS News Magazine Series. Introduces the subject of incest, its prevalence and modern myths surrounding it. Includes practical suggestions for how family can prevent incest and sexual abuse.

Incest: The Victim Nobody Believes. (videocassette or 16mm/color/ twenty-one minutes). MTI Teleprograms, Inc., 3710 Commercial Ave., Northbrook, Ill. 60062. Allows audience to join conversation of three women, sexually abused as children. Good as impetus for discussion.

Interviewing the Child Abuse Victim. (16mm/color/twenty-five minutes). MTI Teleprograms, Inc., 3710 Commercial Ave., Northbrook, Ill. 60062. Filmed sequence of narrated interviews of abused and neglected children. Good training resource for all professionals.

No More Secrets. (16mm/color/thirteen minutes). ODN Productions, Inc., 74 Varick St., Suite 304, New York, N.Y. 10013. Tastefully prepared film on sexual abuse for grade school audience.

Shatter the Silence. (16mm/or videocassette/color/twenty-nine minutes). S-L Film Productions, P.O. Box 41108, Los Angeles, Calif. 90041. Dramatic portrayal of the adolescence and young adulthood of the incest victim. Feelings of typical incest victims accurately presented. Good for discussion.

Speak Up, Say No. (filmstrip/color/six minutes). Krause House, P.O. Box 880, Oregon City, Ore. 97045. Cartoon format, portraying Penelope Mouse and the problem of child sexual abuse. Ages three to six.

Violence in the Family. (four filmstrips/color/sound—cassettes, with teacher's guide). Human Relations Media, c/o Pleasantville Media, 175 Tompkins Ave., Pleasantville, N.Y., 10570. Explores incidence, causes, and characteristics of violence in American families.

Who Do You Tell? (16mm/color/11 minutes). MTI Teleprograms, Inc., 3710 Commercial Ave., Northbrook, Ill. 60062. Ages five to ten. How young viewer can use supportive adults when confused or threatened by a variety of dangers, including sexual abuse.

Organizations Devoted to Family Violence, Child Abuse, and Neglect

American Association for Protecting Children
9725 East Hampden Ave.
Denver, Colo. 80231
303-695-0811

Provides information on nature and extent of child abuse. Many books, reports, pamphlets, and other publications available. Provides national leadership through training, consultation, research, advocacy, and information dissemination.

Batterers Anonymous
P.O. Box 29
Redlands, Calif. 92373
714-383-3643

An organization for men who batter, based on the Alcoholics Anonymous model. Manual for starting BA group can be obtained.

Center for the Prevention of Sexual and Domestic Violence
1914 North Thirty-fourth St.
Suite 105
Seattle, Wash. 98103
206-634-1903

An interreligious educational ministry addressing sexual and domestic violence. Several publications available, including *Working Together*, a quarterly journal.

Center for Women Policy Studies
2000 P St., NW
Suite 508
Washington, D.C. 20036
202-872-1770

A feminist policy research center. Wide range of publications available, including *Response*, a quarterly journal dealing with the victimization of women and children and other topics. Also updated file of local resources throughout the country.

Childhelp, U.S.A.
6463 Independence Ave.
Woodland Hills, Calif. 91367
800-422-4453 toll-free number for obtaining local child protective services agencies.

C. Henry Kempe National Center for the Prevention and Treatment of Child Abuse and Neglect
1205 Oneida St.
Denver, Colo. 80220
303-321-3963

Provides training, technical assistance, and development of treatment programs for abused children. Rental of audiovisual materials available.

The Family Research Council of America
515 Second St., NE
Washington, D.C. 20002

Christian lobbying effort on behalf of the family. Newsletter available.

Formerly Abused Children Emerging in Society (FACES)
71 Haynes St.

Manchester, Conn. 06040
203-646-1222

Self-help support group for young adults.

National Center on Child Abuse and Neglect
Children's Bureau
U.S. Department of Health and Human Services
P.O. Box 1182
Washington, D.C. 22013
202-245-2856

Conducts research projects, and administers federal funds for child abuse prevention and treatment programs.

National Center on Child Abuse and Neglect Clearinghouse
P.O. Box 1182
Washington, D.C. 20013
301-251-5157

Dissemination resource for all types of books, pamphlets, reports, and instructional aids.

National Child Abuse Hot Line
800-422-4453

Information and referral.

National Clearinghouse on Domestic Violence
P.O. Box 2309
Rockville, Md. 20852

Numerous publications on domestic violence, most at no cost.

National Coalition Against Domestic Violence
1500 Massachusetts Ave., N.W.
Suite 35
Washington, D.C. 20005

Another clearinghouse for local resources.

National Committee for Prevention of Child Abuse
332 South Michigan Ave.
Suite 1250
Chicago, Ill. 60604
312-663-3520

Coordinating body for state chapters and other organizations devoted to the prevention of child abuse and neglect. Catalog of publications available upon request.

Parents Anonymous (P.A.)
22330 Hawthorne Blvd.
Suite 208
Torrance, Calif. 90505
800-421-0353

Self-help organization for parents under stress.

Parents United/Daughters and Sons United;
Adults Molested as Children United
P.O. Box 952
San Jose, Calif. 95108
408-280-5055

Self-help support groups and treatment program for sexual abuse; can refer to programs in local areas.

Seattle Institute for Child Advocacy, Committee for Children
172 Twentieth Ave.
Seattle, Wash. 98122
206-322-5050

Prevention of child abuse through school-based curriculum development, professional training, community education, and original research. Extensive educational materials available.

Sexaholics Anonymous
P. O. Box 300
Simi Valley, Calif. 93062

A fellowship of men and women who share their experience, strength, and hope. A program of recovery for those who want to stop their sexually self-destructive thinking and behavior.

Sexual Assault Center
Harborview Medical Center
325 Ninth Ave.
Seattle, Wash. 98104

Numerous bibliographies and summaries of material on incest, sexual assault of children and adults, sex offenders, and criminal justice system.

NOTES

Introduction

1. Jeannye Thornton, "Family Violence Emerges from the Shadows," *U.S. News & World Report,* January 23, 1984, 66.
2. American Association for Protecting Children, "Reports of Child Maltreatment Increase Again," *Protecting Children* (Spring 1985), 3.
3. William A. Stacey and Anson Shupe, *The Family Secret* (Boston: Beacon Press, 1983), 2–3.
4. Claire Pedrick–Cornell and Richard J. Gelles, "Elderly Abuse: The Status of Current Knowledge," *Family Relations* 31 (July 1982): 457–465.
5. Elizabeth Lau and Jordon Kosberg, "Abuse of the Elderly by Informal Care Providers: Practice and Research Issues." Paper presented at the 31st Annual Meeting of the Gerontological Society, Dallas, November 20, 1979.
6. Maxine Hoffman, *Pentecostal Evangel,* October 12, 1980, 12.
7. Marie Fortune, "The Church and Domestic Violence," *Theology, News, and Notes,* Fuller Theological Seminary, June 1982, 17.
8. Peggy Halsey, *Texas Methodist,* October 9, 1981.
9. Task Force on the Family, *Report of the Survey of Family Development Concerns of Pastors* (Wheaton, Ill.: National Association of Evangelicals, 1985), 1–5.

Chapter 1. The Frequency and History of Spousal Abuse

1. Office of Human Development Services, *Family Violence: Intervention Strategies* (Washington, D.C.: U.S. Department of Health and Human Services, May 1980), 4.
2. Lenore Walker, *The Battered Woman Syndrome* (New York: Springer, 1984), 156.
3. James and Phyllis Alsdurf, "Wife Abuse and the Church," *Evangelical Newsletter*, January 17, 1986, 4.
4. Sanford N. Katz, ed., *The Youngest Minority I: Lawyers in Defense of Children* (Chicago: American Bar Association, 1974), 33.
5. H. Norman Wright, *Communication: Key to Your Marriage* (Glendale, Calif.: Regal, 1974), 37.
6. Julia O'Faolain and Laura Martines, eds., *Not in God's Image* (New York: Harper & Row, 1973), 177.
7. Frances and Joseph Gies, *Women in the Middle Ages* (New York: Thomas T. Crowell Co., 1978), 46.
8. O'Faolain, *Not in God's Image*, 169.
9. G. G. Coulton, *Medieval Panorama: The English Scene from Conquest to Reformation* (New York: W.W. Norton and Co., 1938), 614.
10. Carroll Camden, *The Elizabethan Woman* (Houston: Elsevier Press, 1952), 148.
11. Marie Roy, ed., *Battered Women: A Psychosociological Study of Domestic Violence* (New York: Van Nostrand Reinhold, 1977), 14.
12. Carol Hymowitz and Michaele Weissman, *A History of Women in America* (New York: Bantam, 1978), 22–23.
13. Roy, *Battered Women*, 14.
14. Cited in R. E. and Russell Dobash, *Violence against Wives* (New York: The Free Press, 1979), 69.
15. William A. Stacey and Anson Shupe, *The Family Secret* (Boston: Beacon Press, 1983), 12.
16. Elizabeth Pleck, "Wife Beating in Nineteenth-Century America," *Victimology: An International Journal* 4, no. 1 (1979), 61.
17. Office of Human Development Services, *Family Violence*, 30–31.

Chapter 2. The Nature of Spousal Abuse

1. S. K. Steinmetz, *The Cycle of Violence: Assertive, Aggressive, and Abusive Family Interaction* (New York: Praeger, 1977), xvii.

S. K. Steinmetz, "The Battered Husband Syndrome," *Victimology* 2, nos. 3–4, (1977–78), 499–509.

2. M. A. Straus, R. J. Gelles, and S. K. Steinmetz, *Behind Closed Doors: Violence in the American Family* (Garden City, N.Y.: Anchor, 1980), 31–50.

Lenore Walker, *The Battered Woman Syndrome* (New York: Springer, 1984), 24–25.

Marie Roy, ed., *Battered Women* (New York: Van Nostrand Reinhold, 1977), 418–455.

3. Some of the following discussion was suggested by J. J. Ponzetti, R. M. Cate, and J. E. Koval, "Violence between Couples: Profiling the Male Abuser," *The Personnel and Guidance Journal*, December 1982, 222–24.

4. Walker, *The Battered Woman Syndrome*, 57–66.

William A. Stacey and Anson Shupe, *The Family Secret* (Boston: Beacon Press, 1983), 72–75.

5. Straus, Gelles, and Steinmetz, *Behind Closed Doors*, 109.

6. J. Balswick, "The Inexpressive Male: Functional Conflict and Role Theory as Contrasting Explanations," *Family Coordinator* 28 (1979): 331–336.

7. Walker, *The Battered Woman Syndrome*, 149.

8. A. L. Ganley and L. Harris, "Domestic Violence: Issues in Designing and Implementing Programs for Male Batterers." Paper presented at American Psychological Association meeting, Toronto, August 1978.

9. A. Rosenbaum and K. D. O'Leary, "Marital Violence: Characteristics of Abusive Couples," *Journal of Consulting and Clinical Psychology* 48 (February 1981): 63–71.

10. F. I. Nye, "Is Choice and Exchange Theory the Key?" *Journal of Marriage and the Family* 40 (1978): 219–33.

11. S. K. Steinmetz, "Violence Between Family Members," *Marriage and Family Review* 1 (1978): 1–16.

12. Rosenbaum and O'Leary, "Marital Violence," *Journal of Consulting and Clinical Psychology*, 63–71.

13. Kathleen H. Hofeller, *Battered Women, Shattered Lives* (Palo Alto: R & E Associates, 1983).

14. Walker, *The Battered Woman Syndrome*, 150.

15. D. C. Richardson and J. L. Campbell, "Alcohol and Wife Abuse: The Effect of Alcohol on Attributions of Blame for Wife Abuse," *Personality and Social Psychology Bulletin* 6 (1980): 51–56.

16. Straus, Gelles, and Steinmetz, *Behind Closed Doors*, 149–51.

17. Walker, *The Battered Woman Syndrome*, 15.

18. Ponzetti, Cate, and Koval, "Violence between Couples," *The Personnel and Guidance Journal*, 223.

19. Ostbloom, N., and Cruse, S., "A Model for Conceptualizing Child Abuse and Causation," *Social Casework* (1980), 164–172.

20. M. A. Straus, "Sexual Inequality, Cultural Norms, and Wife Beating," *Victimology* 1 (1976), 54–76.

21. Cited in S. B. Babbage, *The Mark of Cain* (Grand Rapids: William Eerdmans, 1966), 25.

22. E. Carpenter, "Traumatic Bonding and the Battered Wife," *Psychology Today* (June 1985), 18.

23. Ibid.

24. Ibid.

25. Marie M. Fortune and Denise Hormann, *Family Violence: A Workshop Manual for Clergy and Other Service Providers* (Seattle: Center for the Prevention of Sexual and Domestic Violence, 1980), 61.

26. Walker, *The Battered Woman Syndrome*, 95–96.

27. Ibid., 96.

28. Ibid.

29. Peter H. Neidig and Dale H. Friedman, *Spouse Abuse. A Treatment Program for Couples* (Champaign, Ill.: Research Press, 1984), 64.

Chapter 3. Crisis Counseling in Spousal Abuse

1. William A. Stacey and Anson Shupe, *The Family Secret* (Boston: Beacon Press, 1983), 105.

2. The following discussion draws many helpful ideas from sections in *Family Violence: Intervention Strategies* (Washington, D.C.: U.S. Department of Health and Human Services, 1980), 32–71.

3. Grant L. Martin, *Transformed by Thorns* (Wheaton, Ill.: Victor Books, 1985), 47.

4. Stacey and Shupe, *The Family Secret*, 122–127.

5. Lenore Walker, *The Battered Woman Syndrome* (New York: Springer, 1984), 119.

6. Stacey and Shupe, *The Family Secret*, 150–151.

7. Ibid., 150.

8. Ibid., 107.

9. Raymond I. Parnas, "The Police Response to the Domestic Disturbance," *Wisconsin Law Review* (Fall 1967), 914. Quoted in Stacey and Shupe, *The Family Secret*, 171.

10. Lynne Messina, "Spouse Abuse: Survey Shows Cases Widespread; 80 Percent Unreported," *Austin American-Statesman*, April 1979.

11. Stacey and Shupe, *The Family Secret*, 108.

12. Cited in *Newsletter* (New York: The American Jewish Committee, Institute of Human Relations, Summer 1983).

13. Vincent Bolli, "Arrest Deters Batterers," *Psychology Today*, August 1986, 8.

14. Christian Legal Society, P. O. Box 1492, Merrifield, Va. 22996, 703-560-7314.

Chapter 4. Treatment of Battered Women

1. Mary L. Roark and Stella Vlahos, "An Analysis of the Ego States of Battered Women," *Transactional Analysis Journal* July 13, no. 3 (1983),164–167.

2. Lenore E. Walker, *The Battered Woman Syndrome* (New York: Springer, 1984), 126.

3. Grant L. Martin, *Transformed by Thorns* (Wheaton, Ill.: Victor Books, 1985), 71–94.

4. James C. Dobson, *Love Must Be Tough* (Waco, Tex.: Word, 1983), 148–49.

5. Martin E. Seligman, *Helplessness: On Depression, Development, and Death* (San Francisco: W. H. Freeman, 1975).

6. Martin, *Transformed by Thorns*, 97.

Chapter 5. Treatment of Men Who Batter

1. Frances Purdy and Norm Nickle, "Practice Principles for Working with Groups of Men Who Batter," *Social Work with Groups* 4, nos. 3–4, (1981), 111–22.

2. Quoted in John W. Taylor, "Structured Conjoint Therapy for Spouse Abuse Cases," *Social Casework: The Journal of Contemporary Social Work*, January 1984, 13.

3. Purdy and Nickle, "Practice Principles."

4. William A. Stacey and Anson Shupe, *The Family Secret* (Boston: Beacon Press, 1983), 149–150.

Lenore Walker, *The Battered Woman Syndrome* (New York: Springer, 1984), 126.

5. J. Geller, "Reaching the Battered Husband," *Social Work with Groups*, 1 (1978),27–37.

6. Daniel J. Sonkin and Michael Durphy, *Learning to Live without Violence: A Handbook for Men* (San Francisco: Volcano Press, 1985).

Purdy and Nickle, "Practice Principles."

Jeffrey L. Edleson, "Working with Men Who Batter," *Social Work*, May–June 1984, 237–42.

Daniel G. Saunders, "Helping Husbands Who Batter," *Social Casework: The Journal of Contemporary Social Work*, June 1984, 347–353.

7. John W. Taylor, "Structured Conjoint Therapy," 11–18.

Peter H. Neidig and Dale H. Friedman, *Spouse Abuse. A Treatment Program for Couples* (Champaign, Ill.: Research Press, 1984).

8. Saunders, "Helping Husbands Who Batter," *Social Casework*, 352.

9. Neidig and Friedman, *Spouse Abuse*, 42–43.

10. Ibid., 114.

11. Purdy and Nickle, "Practice Principles."

12. Neidig and Friedman, *Spouse Abuse*.

Sonkin and Durphy, *Learning to Live without Violence*.

A. Ganley, *Participant's Manual for Working with Men Who Batter* (Washington D.C.: Center for Women Policy Studies, 1981).

Jeffrey L. Edleson, David M. Miller and Gene W. Stone, *Counseling Men Who Batter: Group Leader's Handbook* (Albany, N.Y.: Men's Coalition against Battering, 1983).

13. Edleson, "Working with Men Who Batter."

14. David D. Burns, *Feeling Good: The New Mood Therapy* (New York: William Morrow, 1980), 141–144.

15. Ibid., 144–77.

16. The instructions for relaxation response are adapted from C. M. Haney, and E. W. Boenisch, *StressMap: Finding Your Pressure Points* (San Luis Obispo, Calif.: Impact Publishers, 1982), 102–03.

17. Barbara Brown, *Stress and the Art of Biofeedback* (New York: Bantam Books, 1977), 85.

18. Sherod Miller, et. al., *Straight Talk: A New Way to Get Closer to Others by Saying What You Really Mean* (New York: New American Library, 1981), 102–03.

19. Neidig and Friedman, *Spouse Abuse*, 186.

20. Sonkin and Durphy, *Learning to Live Without Violence*, 76.

Chapter 6. Understanding Physical and Emotional Child Abuse

1. Straus, Gelles, and Steinmetz, *Behind Closed Doors,* 51–52.
2. Pamela D. Mayhall and Katherine E. Norgard, *Child Abuse and Neglect: Sharing Responsibility* (New York: John Wiley, 1983), 2–5.
3. Ibid., 18.
4. Gertrude Williams and John Money, eds., *Traumatic Abuse and Neglect of Children at Home* (Baltimore: Johns Hopkins Press, 1982), 16.
5. Ibid., 9.
6. Ibid., 14.
7. Mary Dunn, "500 Fetal Bodies Found," *The National Catholic Register,* February 21, 1982, 1.
8. American Association for Protecting Children, "Reports of Child Maltreatment Increase Again," *Protecting Children,* 2, no. 1 (Spring 1985), 3.
9. National Center on Child Abuse and Neglect, *Executive Summary: National Study of the Incidence and Severity of Child Abuse and Neglect* (Washington, D.C.: U.S. Department of Health and Human Services, December 1980).
10. Straus, Gelles, and Steinmetz, *Behind Closed Doors,* 62.
11. American Association for Protecting Children, "Reports of Child Maltreatment," *Protecting Children,* 3.
12. National Center on Child Abuse and Neglect, *Executive Summary.*
13. E. F. Lenoski, "Translating Injury Data into Preventive and Health Care Services," Unpublished paper, Division of Emergency Pediatrics, University of Southern California Medical Center, Los Angeles, 1973.
14. National Center on Child Abuse and Neglect, "Everything You Always Wanted to Know About Child Abuse and Neglect," *Clearinghouse on Child Abuse and Neglect Information* (Washington, D.C.: Department of Health and Human Services, n.d.).
15. Mayhall and Norgard, *Child Abuse and Neglect,* 103–105.
16. C. Henry Kempe and Ray E. Helfer, eds., *The Battered Child,* 3rd ed. (Chicago: University of Chicago Press, 1980), 347–365.
17. A. H. Green, "Self-Destructive Behavior in Battered Children," *American Journal of Psychiatry* 135 (1978), 579–82.
18. Blair and Rita Justice, *The Abusing Family* (New York: Human Sciences Press, 1976), 99.

19. R. S. Hunter and N. Kilstrom, "Breaking the Cycle in Abusive Families," *American Journal of Psychiatry* 136 (1979), 1320–22.

20. Quoted in Davis, *Help Me, I'm Hurt,* 10.

21. This material has been adapted from Crime Prevention Center, *Child Abuse Prevention Handbook,* rev. ed. (Sacramento: Office of the Attorney General, 1983), 7–10 and James R. Davis, *Help Me, I'm Hurt* (Dubuque: Kendall/Hunt, 1982), 7–11.

22. H. E. Marano, "The Bonding of Mothers and Their Babies," *Family Therapy Network Newsletter,* September 1981, 9–10.

23. Michael J. Martin and James Walters, "Familial Correlates of Selected Types of Child Abuse and Neglect," *Journal of Marriage and the Family,* May 1982, 267–76.

24. Mayhall and Norgard, *Child Abuse and Neglect,* 141–47.

25. National Center of Child Abuse and Neglect, "Everything You Always Wanted to Know," *Clearinghouse on Child Abuse.*

Chapter 7. Sexual Abuse of Children

1. Diana E. Russell, "The Incidence and Prevalence of Intrafamilial and Extrafamilial Abuse of Female Children," *Child Abuse and Neglect* 7, no. 2 (1983), 133–46.

2. H. Giarretto, *Integrated Treatment of Child Sexual Abuse: A Treatment and Training Manual* (Palo Alto: Science and Behavior Books, 1982).

3. Richard E. Butman, "Hidden Victims, the Facts about Incest," *HIS,* April 1983, 20–23.

4. Randy Frame, "Child Abuse: The Church's Best Kept Secret?" *Christianity Today,* February 15, 1985, 32–34.

5. Phyllis P. Hart and Mary Rotzien, "Survey of Pastors and Counselors on Incest." Paper read at Christian Association for Psychological Studies, Dallas, May 1984.

6. "Sexual Abuse: A Hidden Epidemic," *Newsweek,* May 14, 1984, 30–36.

7. Jennifer James, "Entrance into Juvenile Prostitution" (Seattle: University of Washington, August 1980); and "Entrance into Juvenile Male Prostitution" (Seattle: University of Washington, August 1982).

8. Ann W. Burgess, et. al., *Sexual Assault of Children and Adolescents* (Lexington, Mass.: Lexington Books, 1978), 123.

9. Katherine Brady, *Father's Days: A True Story of Incest* (New York: Seaview Books, 1979), 58–59.

10. W. M. Holder, ed., *Sexual Abuse of Children: Implications for Treatment* (Englewood, Colo.: American Humane Association, 1980), 85.

11. Astrid Heger, "Pediatrician Describes Examination for Abuse," *American Medical News*, March 22, 1985, 14.

12. Suzanne M. Sgroi, ed., *Handbook of Clinical Interventions in Child Sexual Abuse* (Lexington, Mass.: D.C. Heath & Co., 1982), 215–39.

13. Holder, *Sexual Abuse of Children*, 73.

14. Butman, "Hidden Victims," *HIS*, 22.

15. Marie M. Fortune and Denise Hormann, *Family Violence: A Workshop Manual for Clergy and Other Service Providers* (Seattle: Center for the Prevention of Sexual and Domestic Violence, 1980), 63.

16. Sgroi, *Handbook of Clinical Interventions*, 228.

17. Ibid., 215–18.

18. Ibid., 216.

19. Beverly James and Maria Nasjleti, *Treating Sexually Abused Children and Their Families* (Palo Alto: Consulting Psychologist Press, 1983), 25–27.

20. Ibid., 27–28.

21. Ibid., 28–29.

22. Ibid., 30–31.

23. Sgroi, *Handbook of Clinical Interventions*, 13–14.

24. Ibid., 10–12; 14–15.

25. Ibid., 15–17.

26. Ibid., 17–24.

27. Ibid., 24–27.

Chapter 8. Evaluation and Treatment of Sexually Abused Children

1. Suzanne M. Sgroi, ed., *Handbook of Clinical Interventions in Child Sexual Abuse* (Lexington, Mass.: D.C. Heath & Co., 1982), 269–308.

2. Ibid., 68.

3. Ibid., 71–72.

4. David Lloyd, "The Corroboration of Sexual Victimization of Children," *Child Sexual Abuse and the Law* (Washington, D.C.: National Legal Resource Center for Child Advocacy and Protection, 1981), 105. Fred Inbau and John E. Reid, *Criminal Interrogations and Confessions* (Baltimore: Williams and Wilkins, 1976), 111.

5. Marie M. Fortune, "Confidentiality and Mandatory Reporting: A Clergy Dilemma?" *Working Together* 6, no. 1 (Fall 1985), 5.

6. Ibid., 5.

7. Ibid.

8. This section draws from material found in Sgroi, *Handbook of Clinical Interventions*, 109–45.

Chapter 9. Treatment of the Sexual Offender

1. Marie M. Fortune, *Sexual Violence: The Unmentionable Sin* (New York: Pilgrim Press, 1983), 186.

2. Ibid., 187.

3. Suzanne M. Sgroi, ed., *Handbook of Clinical Interventions in Child Sexual Abuse* (Lexington, Mass.: D.C. Heath & Co., 1982), 225.

4. Ibid., 226.

5. Ibid., 227–28.

6. Ibid., 228.

7. Ibid., 229–30.

8. Ibid., 232–33.

9. Ibid.

10. Ibid., 237–38.

11. Ibid., 239.

12. Ibid., 233.

13. Ibid., 235.

14. Ibid.

15. Geral Blanchard, "Counseling the Sexual Addicted Incest Offender," *Protecting Children* 2, no. 3 (Fall 1985):10–11.

16. Sgroi, *Handbook of Clinical Interventions*, 236–37.

17. Judith L. Herman, *Father–Daughter Incest* (Cambridge, Mass.: Harvard University Press, 1981), 155.

18. Blanchard, "The Addictive Personality in Child Sexual Abuse," *Protecting Children*, 2, no. 1 (Spring 1985), 15–16.

19. Mayhall and Norgard, 337–339.

20. John E. O'Brian, "Violence in Divorce Prone Families," *Journal of Marriage and the Family* 33 (November 1971): 692–698.

21. Grant L. Martin, *Transformed by Thorns* (Wheaton, Ill.: Victor Books, 1985), 147.

Chapter 10. Abuse of the Elderly

1. Lee Pearson, "Elder Abuse: A Social Quandary," *Caring* 5, no. 1 (January 1986), 22–26.

2. Ibid., 23.

3. Select Committee on Aging, "Elder Abuse: A National Disgrace, Introduction and Executive Summary," *Caring*, 5, no. 1 (January 1986), 5–7.

4. Claire Pedrick–Cornell and Richard J. Gelles, "Elderly Abuse: The Status of Current Knowledge," *Family Relations* 31 (July 1982), 457–465.

5. Elizabeth Lau and Jordon Kosberg, "Abuse of the Elderly by Informal Care Providers: Practice and Research Issues." Paper presented at the 31st Annual Meeting of the Gerontological Society, Dallas, November 20, 1979.

6. Select Committee on Aging, "Elder Abuse."

7. M. R. Block and J. D. Sinnott, *The Battered Elder Syndrome: An Exploratory Study* (College Park, Md.: University of Maryland, 1979)

8. Pearson, "Elder Abuse," *Caring*, 23–26.

9. Suzanne Steinmetz, "Elder Abuse: One-Fifth of Our Population at Risk," *Caring*, 5, no. 1 (January 1986): 69–71.

10. Suzanne Steinmetz, "Battered Parents," *Society* 15, July–August 1978, 54–55.

11. Doris Ferguson and Cornelia Beck, "H.A.L.F.—A Tool to Assess Elder Abuse within the Family," *Geriatric Nursing*, September–October 1983, 301–305.

12. Nan H. and Jeffrey A. Giordano, "Elder Abuse: A Review of the Literature," *Social Work*, May–June 1984, 232–36.

INDEX

Grant L. Martin, Ph.D.

Grant L. Martin is a licensed psychologist and marriage and family therapist on the staff of the CRISTA Counseling Service in Seattle, Washington. A member of the American Psychological Association, he has published a number of articles in professional journals and is the author of *Please Don't Hurt Me, Transformed By Thorns,* and *Family Ministries in Your Church.*

Dr. Martin received the B.A. from Westmont College, the M.S. from the University of Idaho, and the Ph.D. in educational psychology from the University of Washington. Before entering private practice in 1974, he served three years as clinical professor at Western Washington University and three years as research coordinator at the Experimental Educational Unit at the Child Development and Mental Retardation Center in Seattle. He currently serves on the board of directors of the Christian Association for Psychological Studies.

He and his wife Jane reside in Seattle and are members of the North Seattle Alliance Church. They have two sons, Bryce and Lance.